EUROPE

EUROPE

Dream-Adventure-Reality

Greenwood Press

New York • Westport, Connecticut

Contents

*

PREFACE 9
Pierre Pflimlin

EUROPE: ONE CIVILISATION, ONE DESTINY,
ONE VOCATION 11
Hendrik Brugmans

DREAM
────────────────

EUROPE: THE ORIGINS AND ENDURANCE OF A DREAM 40
Jerzy Lukaszewski

THE INTER-WAR PERIOD, ZUSAMMENBRUCH AND AFTER 74
Leo Tindemans

THE GEOGRAPHICAL NOTION OF EUROPE
OVER THE CENTURIES 81
I. B. F. Kormoss

ADVENTURE
────────────────

THE COUNCIL OF EUROPE 96
Paul M. G. Levy

THE MARSHALL PLAN AND THE OEEC 105
Guy de Carmoy

THE SCHUMAN PLAN AND THE ECSC 110
François Fontaine

THE EDC, THE WEU, MESSINA, VAL DUCHESSE, ROME 118
Count Snoy et d'Oppuers

THE LAUNCHING OF THE
EUROPEAN ECONOMIC COMMUNITY 128
Hans von der Groeben

CRISIS AND CONFRONTATION 135
Pierre Gerbet

HOW THE COMMUNITY FACED THE NEW CHALLENGES 143
Emanuele Gazzo

REALITY

THE EUROPEAN MOVEMENT 156
Claus Schöndube

THE FABRIC OF EUROPE 167
Emile Noël

A BUDGET GEARED TO THE NEEDS OF
COMMUNITY POLICIES 175
Daniel Strasser

EUROPE, A PARLIAMENTARY DEMOCRACY 181
Hans Nord

THE FRONTLINE FORCES OF EUROPE 192
Roger Louet

CAPITAL, HEADQUARTERS, METROPOLIS... 201
Jean A. Pirlot

CITIZENS' EUROPE 207
Pietro Adonnino

EUROPE, THE HOPE OF THE THIRD WORLD? 211
Katharina Focke

EUROPE, AS SEEN BY THE REST OF THE WORLD 218
Robert Triffin

BRING IN THE EUROPEANS 222
Jacques-René Rabier

WHAT MAKES EUROPEANS TICK? 230
Jan Kerkhofs

EUROPE: AN OPPORTUNITY FOR WOMEN 234
Jean A. Pirlot

EUROPE AND ITS CHILDREN: THE PROSPECTS 236
Jan Dereymaeker

THE TREATIES OF ROME, 30 YEARS LATER 244
*How the actors and 'privileged witnesses' of the European construction
perceive the work achieved*

LANDMARKS IN THE EUROPEAN INTEGRATION PROCESS 259

THE SUCCESSIVE PRESIDENTS OF THE EUROPEAN PARLIAMENT
AND OF THE EUROPEAN EXECUTIVE 262

PREFACE

*

The European concept is as old as the history of our continent. Europe has gradually been forging its identity through the annals of Greco-Roman antiquity, Judaeo-Christian civilisation, the Renaissance, the Age of Enlightenment and the French Revolution. European man has existed since values, now universal, emerged on the 'extreme headland of Eurasia' that set freedom higher than submission, spirit over matter, human rights over absolutism. The European miracle has clearly taken place. Yet countless cruel, often absurd, wars mark the trail of these twenty centuries, calling into question the existence of human reason and of a shared sentiment among Europeans concerning a common destiny.

After two wars in this century, which sparked off in Europe and then ravaged almost the entire planet, leaving the people of Europe drained, ruined and demoralised, there was justification for seriously doubting that the European countries could win back their position in the world or even their freedom. The saving grace was provided by a generation of men, greatly influenced by what they had just lived through, who had enough courage and vision to learn the lessons of the past. When Robert Schuman, Jean Monnet, Konrad Adenauer, Alcide de Gasperi, Paul-Henri Spaak and others committed themselves to a totally new idea, that of the European Community, they provoked a revolution in international relations and swept away the reflexes inherited from the past. The concepts of domination and discrimination and the search for artificial balances between powers were replaced by the notions of equal rights and the delegation of sovereignty in the interest of common, efficient and democratic institutions. This radical turnaround in diplomatic practices inspired confidence in the 'construction of Europe', and made it into one of the most uplifting enterprises of our time.

The merit of the founding fathers of the European Coal and Steel Community and the Treaties of Rome was that they brought about a complete and tangible change in the type of relationship between member states, and that this was embodied in law and politically accepted by the national governments. The establishment of Community institutions, the development of joint policies and the funding of an autonomous budget has created a considerable Community heritage. It has allowed Europeans to experience an unprecedented rise in their standards of living, and to benefit from the advantages of a free economic, social and cultural area which now extends over twelve countries.

The review contained in this book, which marks the thirtieth anniversary of the signature of the Treaties of Rome, will lead to even wider understanding of the depth of the 'founders' dream' and its mobilising force. The European Community as it currently stands is far from the ambitions of the federalist project, as put forward in the enthusiasm of the The Hague Conference on May 10, 1948. But an irreversible trend began in those years when the West took stock of the dangers which were weighing upon democracy and the freedom of the European people, who had just been snatched from the jaws of a totalitarian regime, and were coming under the threat of another.

This trend must now find new impetus if Europe is to get back into synchronisation with history. The challenges of this century are waiting to be

answered. A major race has begun for the mastery of new technology. Our society is being destroyed by illnesses such as cancer and by unemployment. Economic and monetary disorder reign in a world divided by intolerable imbalances, which may engender dangerous conflicts. The military threat has doubled, and the more insidious threat of terrorism is upon us. Time is running out for Europe to take up these challenges, with the course of history running ever faster.

What is the current position? The EEC institutions have been slightly strengthened and the field of EEC action enlarged by the 'Single Act' adopted by the twelve member states of the Community at Luxembourg in December 1985. However, very little of this Act was inspired by the project for European Union, drawn up by the European Parliament. The move towards unification has received a new injection of energy, but its effectiveness is dulled by a resurgence of nationalism and the short- sightedness of national governments. I hope that this overview of thirty years of efforts, of successes and failures, authoritatively set down in the pages which follow, will make all officials more aware of the urgency of the tasks which lie before them, and will provide encouragement for all the advocates of a united Europe to carry on the fight.

PIERRE PFLIMLIN
Former President of the European Parliament

EUROPE:

ONE CIVILISATION, ONE DESTINY,

ONE VOCATION

✳

Hendrik Brugmans

COLLECTIVE MEMORY

Siegmund Freud taught that an adult's behaviour is often conditioned by events of his early childhood, even if these took place before he could consciously remember. For example, he may have been badly weaned. Or he may feel nostalgia for the warmth and protection of his mother's breast. He would possess no clear memory of this, but have 'complexes' which make him behave in a particular way, or, possibly, paralyse his behaviour.

What is true for the individual is arguably also true for entire societies. The collective subconscious has a name: history. So, when speaking of Europe, it is useful to look at its past. For example, how can the tragedy of Northern Ireland be explained without mentioning Oliver Cromwell, who has been dead for more than three centuries? How can Spain be understood without reference to the traces left by the Islamic victory during the Middle Ages? And Russia would be very different if it had not suffered from Mongol domination for a number of centuries.

It is therefore logical that a book on Europe and its future begins by looking at its past. The first need is to understand what is meant by the term 'Europe'. Is it perhaps no more than a word on the map, without any real significance? Or are we indisputably Europeans, from the North to the South, from the East to the West, as a result of our shared civilisation?

The people living on the European continent are often more aware of their differences than of their common links. But when they come face to face with another culture they feel that they are different from, say, a Chinaman or an Indian, an African or a Malay. Outside of Europe, we feel more 'European'. This is normal and perfectly legitimate. But this difference should not be misinterpreted.

When it is said that Europe is *different* from other civilisations, this does not mean that it is in any way 'superior' (or, as the case may be, 'inferior'). This is no place for a value judgement. It should simply be noted that we have a role to play in the world of tomorrow, a world which is becoming increasingly interdependent, and we can only accomplish it by exploiting our 'Europeanness' to the full.

'Europe' and its unification are words on many people's lips. But why just Europe? Why, since the current Community is 'economic', should the entire 'developed', industrial or post-industrial world not be integrated? Why not Europe plus the United States of America, Canada and Japan?

In fact, an organisation already exists which embraces all of these. It is called the 'Organisation for Economic Cooperation and Development' (OECD), and it carries out a great deal of valuable analysis and documentation. It warns its member states against dangerous economic trends, and gives some excellent

Europe is more than a geographical notion, which is anyway an increasingly relative concept (Peeters' projection).

advice (regardless of whether the country in question follows it or not). But the 'Community' is something quite different. It tries to integrate its partners, to unify a group of countries judged to have common interests. As Monnet put it: 'We are not trying to create a coalition, but to unify nations'. Of course, their separate identities are respected. And although the Community has, over the years, had its ups and downs, no-one is thinking of throwing in the sponge. As Charles Péguy put it, the most fertile ideas are not those which are fool-proof but those to which people return time and again.

Only a small minority is aware of the existence of the OECD, but everyone knows the EEC, with its headquarters in Brussels, its Court of Justice in Luxembourg and its Parliament in Strasbourg. People perhaps have little idea of its structure, its problems and its partial successes. But at least they know that it exists. Why should Europe not be perceived as a reality? The main objective of this book is to familiarise people with its evolution, its history in the making, its origins and activities.

EUROPE: ONE CIVILISATION, BUT MANY DIFFERENT CULTURES

If the man in the street is asked whether he is European, he may find the question surprising and reply 'Yes, what else would I be?'. To be 'European' is what Bergson called an 'immediate conscious fact'. The first chapter of this book analyses this European notion and attempts to demonstrate that it is a psychological, human and real fact. Europe is a civilisation among others, or it is nothing at all.

When the words 'civilisation' and 'culture' are used, what exactly is meant? Are they references to great literature, fine arts, science and music? Yes, to the extent that these are our common heritage. But the concept also includes social and political structures, and the ideas which govern our community life.

For example, all the European countries have experienced the phenomenon of socialism among the working classes, fired by the class war. The British Labour Party is, of course, different from the German Social-Democratic Party or from socialism in the Latin countries. But in all of Europe the proletariat

'We do not want to form a coalition of states, but a union of peoples'. (Robert Schuman, on the right, and his driving force, Jean Monnet).

have awakened to political consciousness at some point in time and waved the red flag with a greater or lesser degree of Marxist inspiration. Yet in the United States, which is close to our culture in many respects, this awakening never took place. A metal worker in Detroit has the same standard of living as his comrade in Essen or Boulogne-Billancourt. He has similar interests, since he would also like to work less and in better conditions for a higher wage. But it never occurred to him to found a socialist party. He has his trade union, which can organise long and troublesome strikes. But, historically, he has not wanted anything to do with the idea of 'socialism'. Why? A whole range of reasons lie behind this. Suffice to say that it is not an economic or technical phenomenon, but a fact of civilisation.

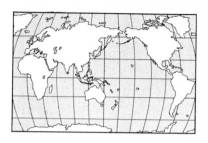

'Eurocentrism' has had its day (World map centred upon the Pacific Basin).

Belonging to Europe means belonging to a certain life-style and having certain aspirations, although with great differences from country to country and region to region. This is why attempts are being made to unify Europe. It is also why the greater part of the general public accept these attempts in good heart.

Yet cultural matters occupy a very small part of the EEC's attention, either in Brussels or in Strasbourg. Moreover, they are only spoken about when things are going badly. A communication from the Ministers stating that there is a great deal to be done in cultural affairs usually signifies that they have not managed to agree on questions considered to be more important, such as politics, economics or social affairs (as if culture were not part of the latter).

This silence is paradoxical, for when the failures of integration are analysed it becomes clear that the real obstacles are more often psychological, human, and therefore cultural, rather than material.

For example, when Denmark continually repeats that it only considers the Community as a free trade area, its arguments are, when it comes down to it, of a historical nature and therefore divorced from current reality. The Scandinavian countries feel more at ease among themselves than in a larger group which includes several Mediterranean countries. They are proud of their Welfare State system and of their lifestyle. They are overwhelmingly Protestant and are wary of Catholicism, of which they know little. Danish anti-federalism is a cultural characteristic.

Finally, on this point, it should be added that the 'founding fathers' of the EEC were not inspired by material motives. Schuman, Monnet, Alcide De Gasperi, Spaak, Adenauer and the like were not, when they created the European Coal and Steel Community (ECSC), aiming to improve management of the production and sale of these essential goods. The aim was to prevent polarisation which could culminate in the outbreak of another war. They wanted reconciliation between the New Germany and the countries with which Hitler had done battle. Their basic objective was to create a 'new' Europe, cleansed after the bloody war. The economy was only the means to an end. It pooled the interests of European nations. But this was only worthwhile to the extent that it constituted a step towards European federation.

WHERE DOES EUROPE'S DESTINY LIE?

The view of Europe as a civilisation has provided the basis and the justification for a union. But is not culture either global or national? Is there not a 'culture française' and a 'Deutsche Kultur'? Or are we all in the process of becoming citizens of the world?

The objection to a national definition is a dichotomy of true and false. It is

true that the nation states dominated Europe's history during the xixth and xxth centuries. It is also true, for example, that the British reason in a different way from the French. Traditionally, the former are more pragmatic, whereas the latter will seek a 'soul-inspiring formula'. It is one of the reasons why the process of European integration is so long and tortuous. It is fundamentally different from the formation of the American Federation in the 1780s. The ex-colonies on the east coast of the continent spoke more or less the same language, whereas the Europeans are much more attached to their particularities. A European who says 'I am Dutch' or 'Italian' is making a statement which goes much deeper than when an American says he is from Connecticut or Virginia.

In Europe, nationality is a concept so deep in people that it is impossible to uproot it. In any case, why should we want to destroy this sentiment of nationality? Diversity is, at the same time, our strength, our richness and our biggest problem. This is why even the most 'radical' federalists have never seriously considered trying to rid Europe of it. When nationalists accuse them of this, it is either because they do not know their facts, or because they are playing the demagogue. Whatever form Europe takes in the future, even if it is a federation, it will always be 'Europe of Nations'. To put it in a nutshell, it is not a question of becoming less patriotic, but of admitting that the solutions of contemporary problems are beyond the capacities of a state which has a population of less than 100 million. Even President Kennedy, at the head of the most powerful state in the world, said in a speech at 'Independence Hall' in Philadelphia that the historical era of independence should be replaced by the age of 'interdependence'.

Nation states are under no threat of dissolution. But they cannot live in a vacuum. To be able to survive in this day and age, they must join forces. But the Italians will remain Italian, the Flemish Flemish, the Germans German, and so on, all with their separate strengths and weaknesses. But no one nationality will be able to consider itself as God's gift to the earth; each may remain patriotic, but with a good pinch of self-critical salt.

However, this does not answer the question 'why Europe?' Why not, while we are at it, proceed immediately to a world civilisation? There are two answers, one contemporary, one historical.

To take the historical first, the great British historian Arnold Toynbee wanted to write the history of the entire world but came up against a dilemma: 'What is my understandable field of study?'. He concluded that before the xxth century there was no common destiny of the human race. It was impossible to describe in one breath the pre-Columbian, Tibetan, Chinese and Egyptian civilisations, since they did not go together. Some even seemed to have been ignorant of the very existence of the others. Consequently, they did not have a common heritage. Some did have tenous links with 'the world outside'. For example, in the Middle Ages a 'Silk Road' existed between China and Europe, passing through Turkestan. But it still could not be said that the two had a common historical experience.

But now the situation has greatly changed. For the first time in the history of the world, not only are the different continents kept in touch with each other by the media, but an event in South Africa has an immediate impact on policy in Washington, Peking and Moscow. Even the European states, despite their relatively small margin of manoeuvre, are obliged to react.

Consequently, a 'universal contemporary history' has come into being, but it has been imposed upon nations rather than created by them. This does not

mean that all the civilisations are in the process of amalgamating into a homogeneous magma where no-one will be able to recognise his own kin. The world may have a common destiny, but it certainly does not have a common culture!

CRISIS AND RESURRECTION

But because Toynbee concluded that humanity has never had a collective civilisation, nor even a collective destiny, does this mean to say that he is an ardent nationalist? Naturally enough, he does not deny the individual characteristics of each of the European peoples, nor the important role of nation states. But when he identifies the major cultural and social currents which have made us what we are (for better or for worse), he remarks that these have always been transnational. None of the important phenomena which have moulded our collective personality have ever been exclusively national.

Which phenomena are we talking about here? To name but two, the Middle Ages and Romanticism. If we do not look deep enough, we may think that both are dead and gone. But, in fact, both are alive and well in our European consciousness. Even an atheist takes an interest in the restoration of a Gothic church and, even if he does not go there to pray, he will go to admire an art and an architecture which he senses to be close to his heart. Similarly, romantic sensitiveness, far from being buried around 1848, is seen in many of our contemporaries.

And how can the term 'Middle Age' be applied to a non-European culture? Comparisons can of course be made, and feudalism has existed in other societies. But the reaction against feudalism in Europe, with the resultant explosion of communal liberties in market and craft towns, is indissociable from our perception of the feudal concept.

There has been, and still is, a monastic phenomenon in other cultures, particularly in Buddhism. But the Benedictine abbeys, which spread out from Portugal to Lithuania, gave us, according to the rule of Saint Benedict, a model of democratic autonomy which, much later, inspired municipal councils. This phenomenon is unique to Europe.

Saint Benedict, patron of Europe, writing his Rule (Extract from Zwiefalten Codex, 1138-1147, Württembergische Landesbibliothek, Stuttgart).

Romanticism was also a European phenomenon. A new mentality was suddenly born, which the Germans called 'Weltschmertz', the British 'spleen', the French 'mal du siècle' and the Italians 'malinconia moderna'. The signal was given by Goethe in 1774, with the publication of *Die Leiden des jungen Werthers* (The Sorrows of Young Werther). The hero of the novel committed suicide in the moonlight: it sparked off a wave of suicides right across Europe.

To take another, less sinister, aspect of Romanticism, writers in all the European nations began to write historical novels, although this style had never been seen before. It has still to exhaust its possibilities, as new authors follow in the footsteps of Walter Scott, Victor Hugo, Manzoni or Mickievicz. Similar reactions can also be traced in other ages and movements as varied as the Renaissance and Liberalism.

Three remarks should be made here. Firstly, the birth of a phenomenon is always linked to a region. Architecture and Roman art began in Catalonia, whereas their successor, Gothic art, first took shape in the Ile-de-France. The roots of the Renaissance are to be found in Italy, whereas the protestant Reformation started in an area which is now in the German Democratic Republic. This is one of the secrets of European vitality. If one region goes through a period of hibernation after some creativity, another can take up the

baton. Europe has creative diversity, and does not restrict a creation to its area of origin. Roman art swept all over Europe, as did the 'Italian' Renaissance.

Secondly, European civilisation has a thirst for renewal. The fact that Europe is currently going through a crisis should not, therefore, give too much cause for concern, since it has a tradition of crises and resurrections. Traditionalists have always argued that their values have declined. But the young have always invented new forms of thinking, art or action.

This does not mean to say that all crises are creative. Not all of the historical upheavals have been beneficial: some have caused human agony and despair.

Thirdly, it would be wrong to think that civilisations are necessarily doomed after a number of generations or centuries. Certainly, as Paul Valéry put it, 'we know today that our civilisations are mortal'. But not everything is deterministic. A civilisation can die young if it suffers an externally-applied shock, or from premature redundancy. Others, however, live to a ripe old age. Here again Toynbee proved to be correct when he developed his theory 'Challenge and Response'. A society, he said, can find itself faced with a life or death problem. It can respond badly. Or it can fail to respond at all; in which case, the verdict of history is severe – the death sentence. But it can also respond in a perceptive and daring manner. It will then receive a new lease of life. Europe, it could be argued, is currently facing the prime challenge of union. Will it gain new life from this challenge?

CULTURAL CROSS-FERTILISATION

How do civilisations arise and evolve? They do not live (or die) in a vacuum. They develop in specific surroundings determined by a number of factors, including:
- the geographical context,
- spiritual influences, almost always religious,
- shared experiences,
- openness or lack of openness to the outside world.

Each civilisation is intimately linked to a natural environment. The Inca empire was linked to high mountains, while Egypt, Herodotus felt, was a 'gift of the Nile.' It had to be seen in relation to the river and its narrow ribbons of fertile land either side which merge into the desert.

Geography gave to Europe three main features:
- the proximity of the sea, which is a 'permanent invitation to travel'. It is therefore not surprising that Europeans 'discovered' other continents;
- no extremes of landscape or climate which would have made a creative cultural life impossible. Warm sea currents have enabled the construction of towns in Finland and even within the Arctic Circle(1). Europe has no desert, savannah, tundra, prairies or pampas and the Alps and the Pyrenees have not proven to be insurmountable obstacles. Around the year 1000, Saint Bernard de Menthon was able to set up a monastery in the passage through the Alps which now bears his name (along with the famous mountain rescue dogs). This passage made possible the establishment of a commercial route between the Mediterranean and the North Sea;
- diversity of all sorts. Firstly, race. The Hungarians, and, in part, the Finns and the Bulgarians are descended from Asians who at one point gave up their nomadic life and were converted to Christianity. Europe's regions are also a source of diversity. Brittany is totally different from Normandy, Tuscany from Umbria, and the Brabant from Flanders. The peoples, the dialects and the

economic bases are all different(2). Europe does not have the immense plains or endless forests which fascinate us in the Soviet Union or Argentina. It has no jungle either. In Europe, everything seems to be 'man-sized'.

Europe's spiritual past is also marked with diversity. Although the surge of Arab culture in the VIIth and VIIIth centuries was inspired uniquely by Islam, Europe is the daughter of three spiritual sources: Rome, Athens and Jerusalem. There are grounds for adding a fourth: the Barbarians. The latter knew neither town, nor writing nor trade (three closely connected phenomena), but they produced an original culture which is clearly present in our life today. All our folklore is attributable to the Barbarians, from Easter eggs to weather cocks (Gallic, Celtic). Similarly, our fairy tales such as Tom Thumb and Little Red Riding Hood are not Roman, Greek or Jewish creations. The so-called 'primitive' tribes preserved a heightened sense of liberty, although the Romans stamped this out in other parts of Europe. The entire heritage of the three sources traditionally mentioned cannot be listed here. The following gives some general outlines:

Europe is above all a civilisation. Rome: Romulus and Remus.

— Rome was the king of the written law, an essential antidote to any arbitrary rule. The fundamental principles of the Roman system, which can only really be appreciated by someone who has lived under a totalitarian regime, were that: the accused must be considered innocent until proven guilty; a citizen should never be troubled twice for the same reason; where a case is not proven, a ruling should be in favour of the accused; no sentence can be passed prior to the existence of a law.

— 'Athens': the name is placed in inverted commas because the Greek heritage is so vast that no single town, no matter how prestigious, can be considered responsible for all of it. The Hellenic civilisation also covered the art of the islands, which is so surprisingly 'modern'. Greece was the sole inspiration for the great Byzantine civilisation, which we now dismiss so lightly, ('Byzantine attitudes'). Greek words which have passed into the European languages give some idea of cultural richness left by the Greeks: theatre, drama, scene, philosophy, metaphysics, ethics, epic poetry, lyrics, elegy, Olympic Games, democracy, tyranny, despotism, history, astronomy, analysis, synthesis, method (it is not by chance that most of our sciences end in 'logy'!), church, orthodoxy, heresy, dogma, bishop, deacon.

— Jerusalem was the twin home of Judaism and Christianity. In the case of Judaism the symbiosis of the European races with the people of the Bible introduced a tragic element of conflict, but also of inspiration, into our culture. Amsterdam is the most eloquent example of this. On the one hand, it was there that Rembrandt found his models and his Israelite friends. But it was there, too, that Nazi scientific barbarism stamped out an entire culture, an entire branch of humanity: the evil spread throughout Europe. As for Christianity, it both integrated the heritage of antiquity (for example, the Catholic Church is regulated by canon law directly descended from the Roman legal tradition) and inculcated moral values in the Europeans, which they use as a reference even if they do not adhere to them. If the Arab civilisation can be termed as 'Muslim', even if all Arabs do not believe in Allah, then Europe can be classified as 'Christian', even if, in the present day and age, churchgoers are in a minority.

How does Europe interact with the other civilisations of the globe? Both 'open' and 'closed' civilisations exist. Insular cultures have sometimes attained a very high degree of perfection. But without contact with the outside world, closed civilisations are usually devoid of any renewal process. Europe, on the other hand, is a prime example of a cultural community open to all influences. It is so open that, due to a lack of natural borders, it has frequently been invaded.

Throughout the Middle Ages, until the discovery of gun-powder, Europe was invaded by Asians. Occasionally, the assailants became integrated in European culture: the Hungarians are one example already mentioned. Sometimes, however, Europe was obliged to put up a fight. After the collapse of the Byzantine Empire, the Turks swarmed across the Balkans and the Danubian plain. They finally stopped at the gates of Vienna, where a 'European' army, with the Polish King Jan Sobieski at its head, pushed them back. The people of the region have a common memory of this shared experience to this very day. 'Turkish coffee' is a reminder of one of the more pleasant consequences of the invasion.

This conflict between the Christian and Muslim world (in which the French kings often sided with the latter) was sparked off by Christian aggression: the Crusades, a collective European experience if ever there was one. Of course, people no longer think of it with outright admiration, as they did in the not-too-distant past. We know, for example, that when Jerusalem was taken during the first Crusade, by Godfrey of Bouillon, an almighty massacre followed, in which, as one chronicler put it, 'our horses were swimming in blood up to their knees'. Our memories continue to be haunted by this adventure. In our modern-day language, a campaign against something (such as alcoholism or smoking) is often termed a 'crusade'. In Japan or India, this term would be meaningless. Common experience, either in defence or in expansion, therefore leaves an imprint.

Exploratory voyages are another example of this, and are again a bit like the curate's egg. Almost all the nations of our continent participated and this, at least, saved us from an excess of provincialism. As Kipling put it, 'And what should they know of England who only England know?'. This is true for the Iberian countries which gave their language to Central and Southern America. It is also true for the French, who handed theirs to Quebec. It applies to the Netherlands, whose literature is marked by its Indonesian colonies. It applies above all to Great Britain, which keeps links with its former world-wide colonies through the 'Commonwealth'. English became the most widely spoken language in the world after Chinese. The 'English speaking world' had no problems surviving the first modern anticolonial war: that of the United States.

Europe has certainly left its mark on the world. But it has also been marked by it. Initially considered as prey and the victim of invasions, it became expansionist itself when its chance came round. It has profited from its contacts with the world outside, even when these have been violent. It owes a great deal to Central Asia, from certain cavalry techniques to the use of the stirrups and the practice of gelding a certain proportion of stallions.

But a major source of inspiration for our culture has been Islam, as known in the Holy Land and in particular Spain, which for almost eight centuries was part Muslim. It is not by chance that a number of European languages, and in

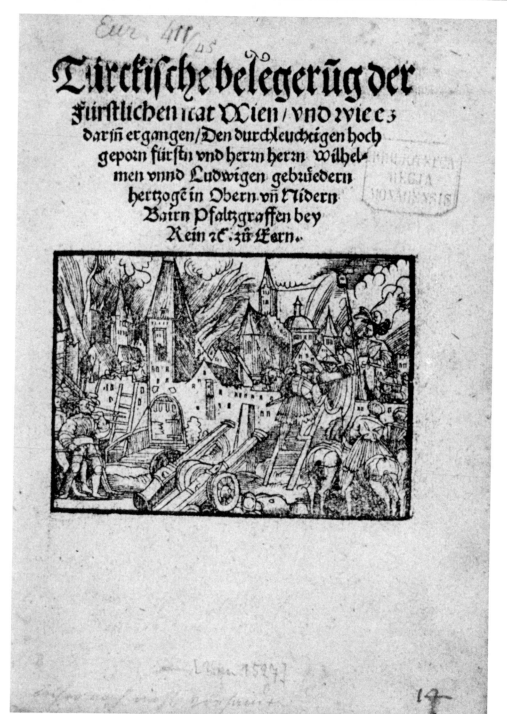

Türckische belegerüg der
fürstlichen stat Wien / vnd wie es
darin ergangen / Den durchleuchtigen hoch
geporn fürstn vnd herrn herrn Wilhel-
men vnnd Ludwigen gebrüedern
hertzogē in Obern vn Nidern
Bairn Pfaltzgraffen bey
Rein ıc. zū Eern.

The Europeans often only unite under external pressure: the Turks before the gates of Vienna (1529 manuscript).

particular Spanish, have kept Arab words. Examples include names of goods, such as cotton and alcohol; names of sciences, such as algebra and chemistry; maritime words, such as admiral; and other words such as mattress and alcove.

Moorish Andalusia was, in many respects, a more civilised society than anything in today's world. It produced the best doctors of the Middle Ages, the best 'Morocco leather' goods, the best weaponry (the most reliable swords were produced in Damascus, but also in Toledo). In the less tangible field of the intellect, the Jews were the 'carriers of intellectual germs'. Saint Thomas Aquinas did not assimilate Aristotle directly from Greece, but through Spain...

The Europeans discover the entire world: monument to explorers in Lisbon.

and the Jews had something to do with this.

Finally, colonialism has transformed our daily life, our cooking habits and our vegetation. If the words tobacco, bananas and tomatoes have a Spanish ring about them, it is because Spain brought these products back from its colonies to Europe. Tea and coffee are commodities which have even created meeting places. It is not by chance that in Vienna, which formed the buttress of the Turkish world, cafes have become a centre for literature, commercial and political discussion.

If there has ever been a civilisation open to all influences, to the assimilation of products from the outside world, it must be Europe. The remarks of the great historian Fernand Braudel, quoting Lucien Febvre, provide a fitting end to this section. He imagined the surprise of Herodotus if he were to find himself on the banks of the Mediterranean in the twentieth century.

The Mediterranean is a very old crossroads. Men, beasts of burden, cars, merchandise, ships, ideas, religions, lifestyles have all converged on this area, enriching its history for millenia now. Even what are thought to be Mediterranean plants – olives, grapevines and wheat – originated far from the sea, although they came to the area very early in its history. If Herodotus, the 'father' of history, who lived in the vth century BC, could come back among the tourists of today, what a surprise would be awaiting him! Lucien Febvre imagined him repeating his voyage in the Eastern Mediterranean:

'How astonishing! These golden fruits, these dark green bushes, orange trees, lemon trees, mandarin trees, he does not remember seeing them during his lifetime. Good gracious! These are Far Eastern species, brought by the Arabs. These strange plants casting unusual shadows, which are prickly, exotic flowers, strange names, cactus, agave, aloe, prickly pears, he never saw them

during his lifetime! Good gracious! They are American species. Those big trees with pale leaves have a Greek name, eucalyptus, but he had never seen anything like it. Good gracious! They had been brought by the Australians. And the cypress, brought by the Persians, he had never seen either...'.

Lucien Febvre then described the strangeness of our modern meals, which have nothing in common with the food of yesteryear. What is true for the Mediterranean is true for the rest of Europe. Openness, an ability to assimilate all that the world can offer, from near or far, without breaking the extraordinary thread of continuity running through its history: truly Europe has a continous but changing identity.

The splendours of Europe

I have sometimes felt that Europe should be compared with a musical movement of *tema con variazioni*. The variations are, of course, clear. But when one tries to comprehend the in-depth meaning of these phenomena, it becomes clear that our national and regional differences are variations which can only be understood by examining the common 'themes'. English Romanticism is naturally different from Polish Romanticism, which is closer to the German or the Italian variety. But we all belong to the same historical family, which has never known closed national frontiers.

One problem remains which it would be dishonest not to tackle. Has the vortex of contemporary life destroyed this sense of culture, and therefore the historical continuity, in Europeans' minds? There are powerful arguments for this case. Although, for example, in France, the generation of Charles de Gaulle held education in literature in the highest esteem, the same is not true today. It is said that France needs all the engineers and technicians that it can get if it is to hold its own among modern nations. In Germany, too, where once so much 'Altphilologen' were attached to scholarliness, the number of pupils who study Latin and Greek is falling off rapidly.

Nowadays, the humanities – a specifically European subject – are given short shrift almost everywhere. A scholar of the humanities is considered rather snobbish and stuffy. This is contrasted with modern democratic trends, based upon the computer, information technology and the space adventure. Our infants play happily with sophisticated machines and feel quite at ease with them, just like Japanese children.

It is true that Europe needs this. But is equally true that if a culture without moral standards or regard for literature or art steps into the shoes of the culture which made Europe what it is today, the result will be a soulless society no longer fired by humanitarian ideals.

Any human action worthy of the name is inspired by something very deep down inside and very individual. It is attributable to our ideals, to a sense of renewal and revival. It is not enough to master technology, which changes at increasing speed. We must also put it to the service of an end objective. Hitler understood this, and, on the basis of his value system, achieved sensational 'progress'. The first jet plane belonged to the 'Luftwaffe', and the V1 and the V2 were first-rate weapons. The motorways built under Italian fascism are another example of technological progress linked to an end objective.

What I am trying to say is that those who claim that technology is 'neutral', and can replace without risk of adverse consequences an aging humanistic culture, are making a serious and basic mistake. Technology is an instrument

which can be profoundly abused or which, on the contrary, can be used as a release from drudgery.

It is absurd to be against technology. But to worship it is criminal. Its potential benefits depend on the attitude of technology users.

Where does Europe stand in this controversy? Perhaps the answer is to be found in an act of faith, and in a number of concrete facts. In a letter written by Denis de Rougemont in 1949 to the European Parliamentarians in Strasbourg, in the framework of the Council of Europe, he referred to European inventions, but not uniquely mechanical or material ones: 'Without going back as far as the flood, or even to the Ancients, which is something America did not experience, or the Renaissance, which Russia did not experience, what have we Europeans invented in the space of one hundred years? To list a few things at random: Marxism and psycho-analysis, sociology and historical synthesis, the general theory of relativity and nuclear physics, the radio and the cinema, penicillin, radar, rationalisation of industrial processes, metal constructions, pupil-involvement, teaching methods, trade-unionism, cooperatives and all of modern art, from painting to music, literature, poetry, drama and sculpture. Almost all the leading lights in these fields are Europeans, and rare are those who have not learnt their trade from our masters, in our schools, on the pavements of the cafés in Paris, or from our books. In fact, the entire modern world can be said to be a European creation. For the benefit or the disadvantage of the rest of the world'. (Neuchatel/Paris, Ides et Calendes, 1950).

The author did exaggerate slightly. An American, Taylor, invented rationalisation of industrial processes. But a French trade-unionist, Hyacinthe Dubreuil, replied to Taylor's positivism, adding workers' humanism to rationalisation.

The list drawn up by Rougemont is an inspiration for the future. Although it is true that the list of Nobel Prize-winners has, since the beginning of the century, contained more non-European names in the exact sciences, this may be a symptom of our current loss of momentum. This may have resulted from our compartmentalisation, our national provincialism.

EUROPE WITHOUT FRONTIERS

Let us stop for an instant, and ask fundamental questions: What do we mean by Europe? Where does it begin, and where does it end? After centuries of colonial experience, has it become 'without frontiers'? Does it go beyond the Atlantic?

Let us begin with America, both Anglo-Saxon and Latin. Both came from the European fold. Compassion should be felt for the Red Indians, and the fate they have net. American colonisation was built on massacres and slavery, with Europe deporting tens of millions of Africans to the American continent.

But alongside these horrors, certain facts need highlighting. Firstly, it is highly surprising that entire empires, such as the Aztecs, the Toltecs, the Mayas and the Incas, were conquered so quickly. Entire civilisations have been wiped out, apparently without trace, although the Europeans (the Spanish in this instance) only numbered a few hundred against many millions. What was the reason for this dramatic collapse?

Firearms and the cavalry used by the Europeans are not reason enough. They may have surprised the natives, but was the element of surprise enduring? The facts do not seem to indicate so. Cortès suffered military defeats which could have proved final. During the 'noche triste', in the town which was to become

Mexico Ciudad, he lost a large proportion of his troops and had to retreat in great haste. In the same way as British tanks were not the sole reason for the Allied victory in 1916, the muskets of the colonising forces do not explain everything.

Another possible explanation exists. In Aztec mythology there was a king god who had been obliged to leave the country and who, it was rumoured, would make a glorious return one day surrounded by men with olive complexions and black beards. Perhaps, it was thought, the colonising forces were the god's entourage! This was why a very warm welcome was given, to which the Western barbarians, cynical and rapacious, responded in the most brutal manner.

But this explanation, which may be valid for Central America, cannot be applied to the Andes, India or Indonesia, where resistance was also weak.

And Japan adopted a somewhat different attitude to colonisation. They observed the Europeans, and studied the new technology which they brought. They then selected and adapted techniques which they found useful. They took on experts to teach them unknown sciences. A Dutchman was responsible for the first 'Flora Japonica'. But after they had squeezed the lemon dry, they eliminated what was not useful. Christians, who represented a large section of the population, were persecuted. The Japanese were quite content to import canons, but not religion.

In the era of expansionist colonialism, each country was 'colonisable' to a greater or lesser extent. Certain nations reacted strongly, others timidly. This does not excuse the cruelty of the Westerners, but it explains their astonishing success in regions of the world which were totally unknown to them. Moreover, in a world dominated, or directed, by technology, the colonies received something in return, so that the experience was not entirely negative. Certain tropical illnesses were cured, roads were built, electric power stations rose, industrial management methods were introduced, and all this knowledge has proved to be indispensable to the countries which have now become independent. It is natural that at first they should have had difficulties in exploiting this knowledge. They do not have centuries of scientific and technical research behind them, as Europe does. For them, the modern world is the product of sudden and brutal European importation. History did not give them the time to adapt to the requirements of a complex and rapidly changing society. This is also true of politics. Democracy did not install itself in Europe in a flash, as Athena was born fully armed from the head of Zeus. A number of generations were required.

All these modern ideas have been introduced outside of Europe at the same time. The Europeans have a role to play, since they set the machine in motion. Not as new kinds of colonisers, nor as guardians, but as partners on a cooperative and equal footing. Europe would act in a much more enlightened manner overseas if it were not so hellbent upon immediate gains.

In any event, one thing is certain: European presence is now more evident overseas than during colonial times. More Europeans live overseas today. They have not all gone there for humanitarian reasons, but their departure would create serious problems and leave past difficulties unresolved. Similarly, European industry and universities now play host to a large number of workers and students from the 'South'. This has both fortunate and unfortunate consequences: the revival of racism is one of the most worrying of the latter. However, it is totally utopian and destructive to imagine that the Third World will one day ever be 'rid' of Europe, and vice-versa.

Finally, it is telling that a number of developing countries prefer to do business with Europe than with America. Europe should therefore not become introspective, and it has no reason to be so. The historical significance of the Conventions of Yaoundé and Lomé must be placed in this perspective.

EUROPE LEAVES ITS MARK

Europe has left its mark on all the world's continents. But this is particularly true for North and Latin America. What has become of them? Have they remained 'European'? Or have they been transformed into new civilisations, with roots in new geographical and human surroundings? Is America still European?

The answer is different for the two parts of America. Canada and the United States have expanded to such an extent and have met with such different problems that they have indeed become culturally autonomous. In much the same way, Japan has become totally separated from China, which is nevertheless its 'mother civilisation'. On the other hand, the Hispano-Portuguese venture has not been so successful, and Latin America has remained much closer to its Iberian origins. A visitor to Chicago will be struck by a sense of being in a non-European world, but an observer in Buenos Aires feels much more at home.

This situation has been illustrated in poetry. Take, for example, the work of the Nicaraguan poet, Rubèn Dario. His work is of great literary stature, but seems to be run through with questions: Who am I? Am I Latin American? A Nicaraguan patriot? Or, perhaps, a Spaniard living outside of Europe? Or perhaps a descendant of the Mayas, whose disappearance remains a mystery?

This eternal questioning of one's identity can also be seen in the work of Eugenio Paz, a Mexican. His language was certainly imported from Spain, in the XVIth century, along with the Christianity which imbues every aspect of people's lifes, touching even the atheists and the agnostics. But beyond this conquest, how can the ancient Indian culture be incorporated? Rubèn Dario has always had problems chosing his identity. Is he Latin American? Spanish in exile? On a voyage? In his subconscious, the European contribution is alive and well. There had been no brutal break. In contrast, if the work of a North American poet, such as Walt Whitman, is studied, no trace is found of the sentimental attachment to the 'Old World'. Not only did the United States break away in a heroic war, but they no longer expected anything from run-down old Europe. 'Pioneers, oh pioneers!' – Whitman draws on the names of all the States and regions, which unite, create and continually re-create a civilisation filled with energy, vitality, courage, success and perpetual adventure. Europe is far away, and has nothing left to offer: it should be left to its decreptitude. No Latin American would ever make such a remark.

As always, the explanation is to be found in history. Let this be a warning to those who want to remove history from the schools, thus depriving children of knowledge of their roots and, consequently, of their future.

At the end of the XVIIIth century, the British Empire lost its great North American colony. One generation later, from the Rio Grande to the Strait of Magellan, a similar liberation took place. But although Washington's attempt flourished, the same cannot be said for the South. There, federalism, which was the ideal of the 'Libertador' Simon Bolivar, failed, and rivalries between states prevented evolution. Moreover, the social structures introduced and

The Boston Tea Party (1773): the British empire was soon to experience the amputation of its great North-American colony.

perpetuated by an aging Spain also acted as a factor of both stability and immobility. The age-long prestige attached to the sword resulted in the calcification of military 'castes', which, rather than defend their country, spent their times in the barracks and the clubs, interfering in the country's internal policy. In the United States, this was never the case. The army, which had to intervene in a long series of bloody conflicts, never became a political influence. Eisenhower took care to don civilian clothing before standing as President. General MacArthur received a rapturous welcome in New York on his return from the Philippines and from Korea, yet he failed in his attempts to be elected President.

North America was therefore characterised very early on by a great deal of dynamism and a highly puritanical society. Catholic Latin America, on the other hand, quickly learned to procrastinate reform. But when did North America break away from Europe? The generation of the War of Independence was, to a certain extent, still made up of emigrant Europeans. European visitors to the house of Benjamin Franklin in Philadelphia or to that of Jefferson in Monticello felt 'at home'. Independence did not signify a cultural break. Political America was to be born later. When, then, did Americans begin to feel 'American'?

If a date has to be put to this event, only one is possible: 1803. Napoleon, who was mulling over the idea of invading England, needed money for his Boulogne Camp. In the end, he turned his forces on Austria, won the Battle of Austerlitz, and fed his ambition on this military victory. But where did he get the money from? From America! The Emperor carried out the most far-reaching act of his career in selling Louisiana to America!

From this date United States history changed course. The thirteen ex-colonies situated on the western shore of the Atlantic, which until then had been mesmerised by Europe, broke free from their trance. They discovered that together they formed a powerful continent, since so-called 'Louisiana' extended from the Gulf of Mexico to Canada. A vast area to be discovered and to be farmed. A heady challenge! The immense adventure of the trek to the Far West began. The objective: the Frontier!

John F. Kennedy was later able to win a presidential election by calling his compatriots to join in a new adventure, the 'New Frontier'. Every American felt ready to respond to this call. Yet few Europeans fully understood. America had spoken to the Americans. It had found the language of its non-European history and its future.

EASTERN EUROPE:

HAS ANYTHING CHANGED?

Border problems exist in Europe. Where does Europe 'end'? At the Urals? At the 'satellite' countries of the USSR? At the USSR itself? The answers to these questions have to be sought in history.

Firstly, it should be said that the people of Central Eastern Europe have never doubted that they belong to our civilisation. Their literature forms part of the European 'whole', as does their architecture. The Gniecno Cathedral is 100% Gothic. Czech baroque, along with that of Portugal, is one of the jewels of this school. And if Kundera is not European, who is?

It is clear that the current 'Iron Curtain' is not an historical necessity. It represents the demarcation line that the Soviet Army could not cross, after 1945, without risking a nuclear war, for which Moscow was, in the post-war period, not ready. Moreover, it not only cuts Europe in two, but also an old nation, Germany. History would have to be greatly falsified to say that Goethe, in going from his native town of Frankfurt to Weimar (where he spent some particularly fruitful years), passed to the East!

There are undoubtedly differences between maritime Europe and Danubian and Balkan Europe, and between Baltic Europe and Europe of the North Sea. But it has already been argued that these variations are Europe's forte.

The question must be seen from a totally different angle in the case of Russia. But whether it is European or not is something only the Russians can decide. And it may not even be helpful to adopt a purely geographical definition of Europe and argue that in the east the Urals mark the point where it ends. The Urals are only a chain of mountains and a river filled with fish, which do not even separate one Soviet Republic from another. It is true that at one point a stone is to be found marked 'Europe' on one side and 'Asia' on the other. However, we should not let this mislead us. Boris Pasternak describes his childhood disappointment at crossing this false 'frontier' and finding that nothing had changed. And, indeed, how could it have changed, for this had been the same country since at least the xvth century, when the Cossacks began to colonise Siberia, with the foundation of Novosibirsk. The Russians themselves do not like the expression 'to the Urals', which seems to them to indicate that 'Asia should be given to the Asiatics', or, in other words, Siberia to the Chinese.

Aside from this cartographic tradition, which artificially defines Europe, a political observation needs to be made. Western Europe is not currently dealing with the Russian people, but with a coherent Euro-Asian power, the Union of Soviet Socialist Republics, which extends from Poland to the China Sea. Vladivostok is every bit as Soviet as Leningrad. If the USSR was invited to join a European Federation, the equilibrium of this 'monstrum' would be found around Irkutsk. An organisation of small and medium-sized countries cannot be integrated with an empire which extends over tens of thousands of kilometres. It is possible to imagine that Moscow might want to 'swallow up' its various Western neighbours, with their heavy industries and, in particular,

their sea ports. Europe needs peaceful and, if possible, friendly relations with the Soviet empire. Europe must open its frontiers to Soviet goods and to Soviet ideas... on the condition that Moscow makes a similar move. Good neighbourly relations are the best guarantee that the weakest will not be absorbed by the strongest.

After the Second World War, the Soviet Union annexed the three Baltic republics, and imposed 'russification' upon them. Will this integration be permanent? Again, this is not for Western Europe to decide, but for the Lithuanian, Latvian and Estonian peoples to say once they have regained their freedom of speech. A Ukrainian separatist movement continues to exist. Ukrainian emigrants claim that the Ukraine would also break with Russia if it got back its freedom. But how can we know this? For the time being Western Europe's role can only be to observe, with impartiality, the evolution of the situation.

However, the central question still has to be answered: is there a Russian civilisation which is different from our own, or is it just a variation on the common theme?

Russians have always been intrigued by this question. Their 'glorious century', the XIXth, saw a previously unequalled explosion of spiritual vitality, which was dominated by the debate between 'Westerners' and 'Slavophiles', in which the latter have gained the most ground. Dostoevsky, in his famous speech on Pushkin, left no doubt about this. According to him, Russia had too great a future ahead of it to let itself join the decadent and faithless European club (which he knew well). It is hardly for us to decide whether he was right or wrong. It should not be forgotten that the 'first' European Russia, that of Kiev, collapsed to the Mongols, who then dominated it for centuries.

Neither a sudden wave of warmth from one of the sides, nor a feeling of superiority will settle this open 'Russian question'. Contacts are difficult given the fractured nature of our relations with the current regime. We can only hope that more openness will be shown in the future... on both sides.

And of course, the problem is that Russia is one thing, the Soviet Union another and the 'satellite' countries a third. The latter are controlled by Moscow's heavy hand. Although they clearly feel their culture to be 'European', they have been marked by the post-war years. If they won back their independence, would they be able to integrate in their current state into our 'Community'? They could, if they so decided, form a Community of their own, based on what they wanted to retain from their recent history. Between the two Communities, confederation links could be established. This would perhaps be the best solution for all concerned... including the Soviet Union.

At any rate, firm movement towards integration in the West remains a condition *sine qua non* for protection against the law of the strongest. Union will provide the only path to our ultimate goal: a peaceful world which keeps its individual richness and, within this world, a re-united Europe...with perhaps Vienna as its capital!

EUROPE: AN EXTRA DIMENSION

If the efforts of our Community have not been very spectacular, and if the nationalist backlash has occasionally resulted in paralysis, one reason is that integration has too rarely been placed in its historical and global context.

For the first time in human history, all the people of the planet have a shared historical experience. They are subject to a common destiny, for better or for

worse. But, for the time being, no common vision unites them. President Kennedy caused a one-second revolution in people's consciousness on all continents, when he called them 'Fellow-citizens of the world'. The US cry was perhaps not followed up by long-term action, and this is reason for re-launching Kennedy's theme and giving it tangible content. No European country could do this single-handed. United, Europe could be capable of it. But what message can it launch?

The first current concern of the world's people is the preservation of peace. Up until now, the 'balance of terror' has been the main solution proposed. It reassures few people. An alternative may only be found gradually through limited, short-range reforms. However, their significance will lie in the direction they take.

Yet to suggest a vision of the future is to be accused of 'utopianism'. This is the customary reaction of those who wish to maintain the status quo. They have first to be asked: can it be believed that the current state of affairs will protect us from a catastrophe? Second: is it not true that any historical impetus arises from ideas marrying pragmatism with utopianism, and which, while derided at the outset, eventually become reality?

If our requirement is preservation of peace, nothing effective will be done without the establishment of a global political power, responsible for certain matters which have taken on global significance. At a time when some of our weapons of destruction are being banned, with even military powers agreeing on the need for this, the ideal of a universal legal system which would become the real driving force and underpinning of pacifism is no longer an illusion. No nation, no ideological system would, in principle, be able to refuse a joint authority with 'limited competence but real powers', which would guarantee that a nuclear war would never take place.

European integration has at least shown us one thing. Practical cooperation has proven to be workable between former enemies. Immediately after the 1939-1945 carnage, this possibility seemed inconceivable. But now this active reconciliation, which is in the tangible interest of all, seems the most natural thing in the world.

Intellectually and politically, Europe, as it moves towards integration, has a major global role to play. The United Nations is only a discussion platform, and not a world High Authority. The compartmentalisation between its 150 member states makes it impossible to implement a coherent policy, even when the goodwill is there. It is not capable of settling the interminable disarmament question. Time is being wasted which could be used to find a solution. But without real power, no policy is possible.

At present, things being what they are, who is in a position to propose a system of universal law which alone can guarantee peace? Surely not either of the superpowers, with their vetoes and aspirations of world domination. On the other hand, the tiny states do not have the necessary authority. And Europe...? Perhaps, if it proves able to set a precedent of fifty years of peace on its own territory, it will then be qualified to engineer 'world peace', with ideas for a solid infrastructure at world level.

Three comments need to be made. First, a Europe which wears itself out fighting over the price of milk or the financial contribution of one of its members, and which, until the new Single Act is implemented, will not even be a 'Common Market', will not have the necessary prestige to undertake such an important initiative. If Europe is to re-gain its authority on the world scene, it must first assert itself on home ground.

'We have to build a kind of United States of Europe' (Winston Churchill, 1946, bust at the Council of Europe in Strasbourg).

Second, a politically united Europe would be an example for others to imitate and a model which could inspire other macro-regions, such as the Arab world, Black Africa, South Asia and Latin America. Attempts at integration are already underway, and a federalist push in Western Europe would be interpreted as a signal of hope throughout the world.

Finally, if the world has an urgent need to be reorganised...and not only by multinationals which have, at least, understood the needs of our time...one of the essential conditions will be a radical reduction in the number of member states in any world organisation. A dozen or so regional federations could carry out fruitful dialogue.

EUROPE UNDER THE GAZE
OF THE WORLD

European integration must be directed towards a future universal framework. Europe must become a centre of initiative, pointing the way ahead. This role is diametrically opposed to the one which Europe is currently playing. It is losing momentum, and is being directed from Washington according to the latter's

The unification of Europe is dependent upon Franco-German reconciliation: Aristide Briand and Gustav Stresemann...

security needs. It is seemingly becoming less and less capable of providing a 'great design' of the future.

While it is true that the EEC must take on real power if it is to have any impact, its internal image is also vital. It is by it that non-EEC nations will judge us. This can be illustrated by a number of examples.

The Third World is already here in Europe, in the form of the millions of Turkish, North African, Indian, Jamaican or Surinamese fellow citizens, workers from Black Africa or other poor countries. Consequently, the EEC's credibility is placed at risk if, while drawing up the best possible development projects, for example under the Lomé Convention, it allows its immigrant workers to live in poor housing and to work in difficult, badly paid and dangerous occupations.

A second example is provided by the EEC's so-called 'Regional' Policy. The Community has a Fund (which, it is true, only gets a very small amount of financing) to help regions lagging behind the others, often because a heavy 'twilight industry' has previously provided the main source of income. As these regions realise that they can turn directly to the EEC for help, their importance increases. In Belgium and Spain, two countries where decentralisation is politically sanctified, this trend is gathering momentum. Others will follow, even within states which hitherto have been centralist. What can be concluded? That the European Community is opening the way to a new political concept, going beyond traditional state control. This evolution, if it continues, is bound to leave its mark on the world outside.

A further example comes from a bit further back in time. Shortly after the war, a team of nuclear physicists succeeded in founding and running the European Centre for Nuclear Research (CERN) near Geneva. The success of this venture has been astounding, probably because the governments which funded it have never insisted on getting a 'juste retour' (a fair return on their contribution). They left the scientists to get on with their work, without quibbling over nationality, which allowed the Centre to select the best. Its exploitation for short-term national interests has been avoided. This is one area where the 'brain-drain' to the United States has been plugged.

The CERN is now visited by Soviet and American colleagues, who seek

inspiration from the European work. Other examples of scientific cooperation, such as 'ARIANE' and 'GIOTTO', strengthen Europe's position in the world.

To stress the point again, our main preoccupations have lost their national character. They all require at least regular transfrontier consultation and frequently transnational institutions prove necessary.

When the ecologists declare their distaste for 'Europe', but remark that acid rain gives them nightmares, it has to be said that acid rain has the nasty habit of crossing frontiers! Carried along by wind currents, it causes destruction in neighbouring countries. As a result, for ecological action to be effective it must be European. Although pollution of the Seine only affects France, that of the Rhine has proved dramatically to be a matter of concern for five nations. The problem cannot be tackled within national frontiers. It can only be solved on the basis of a European Ecological Charter – provided that this is not only written, signed and ratified, but that its application is effectively verified.

In some cases, all that is needed is regular contacts between officials. In others, more 'federal' solutions will prove to be indispensable. Demonstrations in the street for peace, safety or well-being, as if an individual national government could provide all of these, have become archaic gestures.

To sum up, if Europe is to turn the spotlight of the world upon itself, European society must rouse itself and demonstrate that it is capable of forgetting old-fashioned national concerns and of unifying.

THE NEED FOR INTEGRATION

However one analyses the problems of contemporary society, one thing is clear: the nation state is no longer an adequate political instrument for achieving the changes necessary for the twenty-first century.

Wide debate of appropriate solutions is necessary. The Club of Rome, in its book 'Limits of Growth', gave voice to generally shared concerns. It called into

Konrad Adenauer and Charles de Gaulle in Reims Cathedral in 1962.

question the philosophy known as 'Progress'. It placed question marks where earlier generations had placed enthusiastic exclamation marks. 'Science' had been the solution to all the world's ills. It was both the means and the objective. Everything which it made possible was considered as beneficial, and its execution necessary. It is no exaggeration to say that today, and not only because of the nuclear bomb, this optimism is no longer shared.

Europe has its fair share of experts and researchers, but less confidence is placed in them than in the past. Medicine makes spectacular progress, yet a billion human beings die without medical care. A 'green revolution' has allowed Europe to reap bounteous harvests, but the spectre of hunger haunts the Third World. Our machinery becomes increasingly sophisticated, but vast numbers of people are unemployed in the industrialised or 'post-industrialised' countries.

These observations are not new. Solutions are needed, but none has been suggested up until now. Moreover, any solutions will have to be applicable not just to a region or to a nation, but to entire continents, occasionally to the entire world. It must therefore be emphasised once again that the traditional nation state no longer meets the needs of our century and will be even less fitted to those of the XXIst.

This is a personal conclusion. But it was also one reached by President François Mitterrand, despite his long insistence on the need for France to preserve its independence. In the long preface to his publication *Reflexions sur la Politique extérieure de la France* (Reflections on French Foreign Policy, Paris, Fayard 1986, pp 13/14), he stressed that the vast number of links between the old nations limit national margins of manoeuvre: 'Since the beginning of the century, France has renounced national sovereignty on countless occasions. The objectives of agricultural policy are decided in Brussels, international cases which affect our interests are brought in The Hague, internal EEC conflicts settled in Luxembourg. Our trade is governed by the regulations of the GATT, the EMS intervenes in the management of our currency, the EEC in the setting of fishing zones and pollution standards for our cars, and we adhere to all sorts of

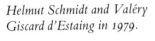

Helmut Schmidt and Valéry Giscard d'Estaing in 1979.

*François Mitterand
and Helmut Kohl in 1984.*

conventions without a backward glance'.

Mitterrand provided concrete proof of the need for transnational solutions. But until now they have been fragmented, sporadic, without overall vision or organisation. I personally am convinced that only a federalist approach is capable of bringing about the necessary synthesis. It frees us from the burden of nationalism weighing on our ideas and our actions, because it rejects the false principle that political power is indivisible.

Sovereignty? No-one is entirely sovereign in this day and age, but everyone has a share of the power. A District Council has powers, but is a sub-division of the central authority. A Regional Council, such as the Tenessee Valley Authority during the Great Recession, must take all the initiatives of which it is capable. The nation will conserve a sufficiently large part of its independence for its identity to be maintained. Well-organised continents or sub-continents have a role to play in areas where the nature of the problem makes them the best placed to solve it. Finally, some of the most worrying questions of today, such as peace and the use of the oceans, can only be resolved in an intercontinental or world context.

Within this global concept, two warnings must be issued. First, it would be a great error to tend to delegate decisions further up the ladder, since a government's democracy is best assured by its closeness to the people. Secondly, a fervent attachment to national policies must be stamped out, for

they have lost their effectiveness and, consequently, their pragmatic nature.

Decentralisation, where appropriate, and unification of Europe are currently the two main aims of federalists. Although their simultaneous achievement would be the best, the European priority would seem to be the most urgent.

REGIONS MUST PLAY A WIDER ROLE

Decentralisation-integration. It is significant that the prerogatives of the old form of nation state are currently contested by both these trends.

Two political revolutions are taking place. At the same time as the EEC has set up a Monetary System within which the Ecu is becoming a generally accepted currency, the regions are awakening and calling vigorously, even aggressively, for real powers. The EEC has finally decided to set up a real common market, made up of twelve countries without internal customs barriers. Yet at the other end of the scale, regionalism is strong in Belgium, Spain and in parts of Britain.

Is this a contradiction? Can Europe be united through devolution? Devolution does not signify that the club of nation states will be joined by an independent Catalonia, Scotland, Basque country, Flanders or Wallonia. But in some instances, a government 'closer to the people' is desirable. Ethnic and linguistic groups want their share of autonomy. Will this just add to the complications? Anyone who is afraid of complications in a complicated world should consider changing planet or at least denounce democracy, which will always require long drawn-out discussion and complex decisions.

Therefore, from two sides, the traditional principle of the centralist, sovereign state is under attack. Not by ideologies run wild, but by the evolution of society. Resistance to hegemony, to the despotism of majorities, to cultural assimilation has been a permanent feature of European history. Philippe II learned this to his cost, as did Louis XIV, Napoleon and Hitler after him. Europe has always asserted its diversity.

Some of the regions were states in the past and were wrongly drawn into 'national' uniformity. Some regions find themselves with a foot in two separate countries, such as Catalonia, the Basque country, North and South Tyrol and Macedonia, which is tugged between the Bulgarians and the Yugoslavs. In Eastern Central Europe in particular, the right of peoples to have control over their own territory was trampled underfoot, because it was tied up in a very complex ethnic mosaic. Here again, federalism is necessary, for it is unrealistic to give them all their own ethnically homogenous and indivisible state. But it is necessary both to organise large economic areas within which smooth material expansion is viable, and to allow a sub-region, or even a village speaking a separate language, an education system which meets its requirements.

Europe's regions have different requirements for a number of reasons. One just mentioned is linguistic which, quite rightly, gives rise to the call for cultural autonomy and television and radio programmes in the minority language. But economic regionalism also exists, which often coincides with linguistic divisions.

Experience has shown that in countries where the capital is all-embracing, the outlying regions have often suffered economically. An eloquent example of this was provided by François Gravier, in his work 'Paris et le Désert français' (Paris and the French Desert). People are now beginning to react against this state of affairs. A European union of maritime and outlying regions has been

set up, on the initiative of Brittany. The Regional Committee of the European Parliament regularly consults it. It is significant that those in favour of decentralisation are also in favour of European federal democracy. They look for a solution to their local problems in the continental framework. They use the EEC system and are well acquainted with Brussels and Strasbourg.

In conclusion, the late Denis de Rougemont was right when he said that the construction of Europe would continue to be difficult if national governments were expected to do everything. He thought that regional autonomy could give a fresh impetus to European union.

THE LAST BREATH OF THE FEUDAL SYSTEMS

When European union is finally seriously undertaken, it will not resolve all Europe's problems. But it will allow them to be tackled in the most suitable framework. Union alone will provide the shock necessary to erode old habits and persistent obstacles.

After the post-war Liberation of Europe, some groups strove for the renewal of the European nations. In all of them, including the defeated powers, grass-roots movements (more often than not growing out of the Resistance), proposed programmes of national renewal. These failed everywhere. For a short time, they were the centre of public attention. Then everything fell back into the national rut. The advocates of the programmes therefore realised that a new renewal framework was necessary, which would be uniquely European.

A lot of water has since passed under the bridge. Integration is no longer a distant utopia. But at the same time, national resistance has hardened, and the former West German Chancellor, Helmut Schmidt, felt worried enough by the oil crisis to say that in ten years time, less of a common market would exist. Schmidt's provocative prediction appeared in a book full of statistics, 'Die Europäische Desintegration' (European Disintegration), by Franz Urlesberger, a lucid observer and a convinced European.

This nationalist reaction has led to an ebb in European trends. Though they are devoid of any hope for the future, there is no doubt that reactionary trends remain in European society. But what, in fact, is meant here by 'nationalism'? First and foremost, nationalism should not be confused with the attachment which every normal human being feels for his 'country'. This sentiment is much stronger today than in the past. Clear proof of it has been given by Black Americans, trying to trace back their roots to their African ancestors. A similar phenomenon is to be seen in European regions. Why?

In a world which is in the process of unifying, there is a desire to know one's origins, one's identity. One sign of this is to be found in the recent proliferation of works on King Arthur and the vestiges of the Celtic civilisation. The *Journal de Bord de Saint Brendan* (Saint Brendan's Log) has been republished, and a country is revered if it keeps alive 'traditional belief in the supernatural, the extraordinary and fairies'. At the same time, on the shores of the Mediterranean, the poetry of the troubadours and the faith of the Cathars have come back into fashion.

Some of these trends contain more humanism and more hope for the future than others. They do not all have the same value. But, in any event, they are totally dissociated from administrative nationalism, which endlessly places barriers in the path of European construction. A Spaniard who re-reads with enthusiasm the poem of *El Cid* or a Fleming who enjoys remarking that the

Roman de Reynard is better in Dutch than in French are not necessarily nationalist. Everyone has this kind of preference, and is naturally proud of his own heritage.

Destructive nationalism is quite different. First of all, it clings to a state (which, in itself, is not at all sentimental or cultural). It then exalts *the* nation and places it above all the others, which is highly destructive.

This type of nationalism is fairly recent. And it is international. Experts who have studied it, such as Eugen Lemberg and Hans Kohn, believe that it found its origins in the French Revolution and in Romanticism. Almost all our national anthems date from this time. People attached to this sort of nationalism attribute all sorts of qualities to the nation, which is considered as the most pure, the most noble of all. Love of the Fatherland becomes sacred, since the national collectivity is placed above everything, as if it were an ecclesiastical brotherhood. The nation proclaims itself to be the incarnation of right and wrong, of supreme law. God is supposed to watch over all the soldiers coming under its flag, and those who die in battle are 'martyrs'. As the vocabulary shows, this kind of nationalism is a sort of pseudo-religion. In other words, it offers to countries which have lost their religion a substitute metaphysical link.

Christian churches, which have recovered the universal dimension, are beginning to denounce this blasphemy. Nationalism among the working class is no longer a source of solidarity. Its manifestation is now seen in football stadiums in a violent manner.

But although romantic nationalism has lost its original capacity to draw men together into action, its administrative talents have flourished.

We live in an age where states have grown in importance. The Welfare State was created under social democracy. It is mainly the creation of the Left, and the same parties responsible for its creation are today those most reluctant about relinquishing national sovereignty. It is therefore logical that the general public, protected by *its* state, fears the creation of a Federation 'dominated by foreigners' in which it has no faith. On the other hand, another faction of the Left-Wing has not forgotten that Federalism represents transnational solidarity: but when negotiating in the EEC arena, they have their reasons for not giving in to the European temptation. For fear of seeing their power reduced, they introduce increasingly complex regulations into their customs systems. Why? Because an economic 'disease' in the neighbouring country might so easily infect them also. Nationalism inspires instinctive wariness of what lies across the border.

CONTROLLING OUR DESTINY

The time has come to round off this introduction. I offer a number of propositions:
– The contemporary world functions increasingly on a global scale, particularly in areas such as the economy, education, diplomacy and defence.
– However, 'politics' remain, in the eyes of the general public, principally or entirely national; nevertheless, people are beginning to understand that national governments no longer have sufficient margin of manoeuvre to re-build our society.
– A situation in which contemporary material facts are neither absorbed and processed by public psychology nor by suitable or adequate institutions is disastrous for democracy. National political parties are burning themselves out making electoral promises which they are no longer capable of carrying out; as

a result, people have lost confidence in 'politics', and consequently in democracy.

- This being the case, the competence and incompetence of national states must be examined, and a transfer of sovereignty carried out without sentimentality, since efficiency demands such a move.

- The world is presently involved in a series of problems which cannot be solved by traditional nations, but whose consequences will affect, sometimes seriously, entire populations; real powers should be given to bodies operating at the source of the problem.

- This necessitates a federalist-type regime, where power will no longer belong uniquely to national governments, but will be divided out according to pragmatic requirements, ranging from district autonomy through regionalism and a united Europe to a world legal order; each would have its place, in an equilibrium which would have to be revised on a regular basis.

- Man's behaviour is, to a large extent, conditioned by national education or, at any rate, by the concentration of history on the nation. However, more modern concepts of the past tend to show that in reality the major civilisations, of which Europe is an example, are plurinational and pluriregional.

- Our (European) civilisation is perhaps not superior to the others, but it is the most global: it was responsible for cartographic skills, and has influenced the other continents, often by a population transfer.

- In the present day and age, Europe, which was so creative in the past, seems to be in decline and in danger; its position in the world makes it highly vulnerable, and its national compartmentalisation deprives it of military, economic and intellectual opportunities.

- Europe is uncomfortably sandwiched between the two 'superpowers', although it has a larger population and a greater economic potential than both of them; in the event of an international crisis it would no longer be able to have control over its fate, but risks becoming the theatre for someone else's war.

- Though the problem of peace remains fundamental for Europe, it cannot influence evolution from its present state of weakness and disunion; Europe cannot influence the decision of the Soviet Union to direct its SS-20s on European targets, or that of the United States to turn its missiles against the Soviets – it can only look on and grumble.

- Peace will not be the child of sterile negotiations on disarmament: it will arise from the creation of a universal legal order. Europe, which has no expansionist ambitions, should be well placed to take daring initiatives in this direction. But people will laugh in Europeans' faces if they call for a world federation while they are still incapable of uniting themselves.

- Similarly, in the Third World, Europe has cards to play. Contrary to expectations, it has not broken links with the 'South' that are a legacy of its colonial past. In fact it is more at ease there than are the Americans. However, Europe's reputation suffers from the way in which it continues to treat its immigrant workers.

- On the other hand, every time that Europeans unite their forces they obtain startling results, better than those which the two superpowers boast about.

- An evolution of the European Community towards a pragmatic type of federalism is both possible and essential: national egoism has obstructed progress in negotiations in the EEC's Council of Ministers; moreover, these negotiations cannot be controlled or modified by either national parliaments or the European Parliament.

– A move towards increased efficiency and EEC democracy will be a difficult process, but there is no certainty that an alternative exists.

If it so desires, Europe can become, as Emmanuel Mounier put it, a 'pivotal region'. It can present the model of a society which is both traditional and focussed on the future. It can give the people of the world hope and set them an example. It can lead them towards a peaceful and reconciled world. It can demonstrate that even conflict and tension can be used as stepping stones towards something good, and that unity will only last if founded upon diversity. The dream of what Europe *could* do is without end.

But it must first respond to the challenge which is before it now: that of loosening hegemony and promoting freedom in solidarity with one and all.

SELECTED BIBLIOGRAPHY

1. Salvador de Madariaga, *Portrait de l'Europe* (Portrait of Europe), Paris, Calmann-Lévy, 1952, p. 14: 'The heel of Italy is at a latitude slightly further north than Philadelphia, but whereas in Philadelphia rivers are frozen in winter, no one in Otranto has seen ice anywhere but in a glass of vermouth.'
2. Fernand Braudel, *L'Identité française* (French Identity), Paris, Arthaud-Flammarion, 1986, p. 42: 'Sometimes a quarter of an hour's drive can change everything, rather like an interval in a theatre. This is true for all of Europe.'

Dream

EUROPE:

THE ORIGINS AND ENDURANCE

OF A DREAM

✳

Jerzy Lukaszewski

THE ROOTS

The outlines of a civilisation. Across the millennia, the pursuit of dreams, or utopia, in the richest sense of these terms, has guided Europeans and has given meaning to their thoughts and actions. Very early on, the concept of unity was associated with the unceasing search for freedom and justice. Generation after generation, men and institutions strove to break down the barriers between peoples and to unite them in a sense of common destiny, in common structures and principles.

The endurance of the European dream has culminated in the attempts in the xxth century to build European union. This dream was present in the culture of the Old World even at the time of its greatest division, when nationalism surged and the nation state was all. The past and the future are like the tributaries and the mainstream of a river. The former continuously feeds and influences the latter. History is a living reality which must be understood if the future is to be predicted and shaped.

Moreover, is not the basic identity of people bound up in the way in which they understand and assume history? Is not civic spirit, both national and European, inspired by history, by the memory of tribulations and glory experienced together? Are the major ideologies of the xixth and xxth centuries anything other than a manner of interpreting history? Is not historical culture an essential and indispensable part of culture itself? It is therefore a good thing that this book reserves a place for an overview of all that has been imagined and achieved in the past in the name of European unity. However, in scrutinising such a vast subject, the dangers involved in summarising and generalisation should not be forgotten.

Europe is not being considered here as a geographical entity, but as a spiritual entity, a human accomplishment. The European continent is a changing and artificial concept. Its boundaries have been fixed at different places in different centuries. On the other hand, European civilisation – or, in other words, a set of generally shared values, social and political institutions, intellectual and material accomplishments, lifestyles and attitudes – is clearly identifiable among the other major civilisations of the world. Of course, care must be taken not to paint too rosy a picture. European civilisation is tainted with crimes, depravation, greed, egotism and arrogance. But it would be wrong and absurd to place the emphasis only on these defects. European civilisation developed a sense of self-criticism very early on, and learned to question and contest accepted ideas and authorities. It soon became a synonym for unequalled curiosity and intellectual creativity. It developed a taste for research, taking risks, surpassing itself, boldness and sacrifice. Europe and the concept of

universalism are inseparable. Greeks, Romans and Christians thought and legislated not for a nation, but for all of humanity. The European civilisation gave birth to the ideal of freedom and brotherhood of men.

The term and notion of Europe find their origin in Greek mythology. They have taken on various forms, but have always kept their core of significance for the interdependency or mutual inspiration of civilisations. According to legend, Europa, the outstandingly beautiful daughter of Agenor, King of Tyre, was abducted by the god Zeus (transformed into a bull for the occasion) and taken to Crete to become queen and to found a dynasty. The kingdom of Tyre being in Asia, the latter is therefore seen as the ancestor of European civilisation and the womb of different religions and cultures.

The Greeks applied the name Europe not only to their territory, but also to the lands situated to the north and west of it. When speaking of this part of the world, their geographers mentioned its extraordinary richness and variety, the harmony of land and sea, plains and mountains, forests and fields. They emphasised the clemency of the climate, which fostered the development of man and of his creative faculties. Their judgement has since been corroborated. As the Swiss historian, Gonzague de Reynold, put it: 'Europe finds its roots in a finer and more delicately tuned structure and has a more personal and firmer character than Africa or Asia.... Physically, Europe is the only articulate continent, and appears more as the creation of intelligence than of nature. Europe is the continent which tends to move beyond its boundaries... It was created to be the globe. Its lines of force extend beyond Asia to stretch towards infinity above the ocean. The other continents are heavy and immobile. Even on the map, Europe seems to move'.

Europe to a large extent owes its vast cultural diversity to its natural diversity. In no other part of the world is there such a richness of forms and expressions of human life in such a small area.

Greece. The forerunner of European civilisation, both in its diversity and unity, is to be found in the Hellenic world. To quote Paul Valéry: 'We owe to Greece the very feature which perhaps distinguishes us the most profoundly from the rest of humanity. We owe it spiritual discipline, the extraordinary example of perfection in all areas. We owe it a way of thinking which refers things to man, to a whole man...'.

Europe inherited philosophy from the Hellenic civilisation. Would European thought have been able to reach such heights without the initial push from Socrates, Plato, Aristotle and Epicurus? The sciences were also inherited from the Greeks. In all the European languages, the various scientific disciplines have Greek names. Hellenic civilisation also gave Europe the complete range of arts, along with the taste for harmony and beauty. Centuries ago, the Greeks provided rational interpretations for the creations of nature and man.

Ancient Greece created the form of social and political life which later became a characteristic of European civilisation, namely the *polis* (city). This was the breeding ground for the types of governments which appear throughout European history: aristocracy, tyranny and democracy. Slavery was a part of the Greek *polis*, and the numbers of slaves increased with the growth and diversification of the economy. They were essentially composed of prisoners of war and their descendants. But the freemen of the *polis* were numerous, sometimes in a majority, and were truly free, unlike their counterparts under the Oriental monarchies. They practised the arts, sciences and politics. They filled the *agora* and went to the theatre to see plays which are still put on today.

These dramas show man as a unique and irreplaceable universe, complex and fragile, man faced with his often tragic destiny, man with the deepest corners of his soul, with his hunger for justice and love, with his urges and his dreams, his despair, his follies and his crimes.

The hearth of culture and the art of living, Greece became the stronghold and the symbol of freedom when the Persian empire made an impressive military effort to subjugate it. On September 13, 490 B.C., a Greek army of freemen soldiers commanded by Miltiades defeated a Persian army with forces several times superior. Ten years later, on almost the same day, the Athenian fleet destroyed that of the King of Persia at Salamis in one of the most famous naval battles of all times. The advance of despotism was stopped. The West had beaten the East. The legend of the indestructible force of freedom became a permanent part of the European spiritual patrimony.

Greece was the very antithesis of immobility and introversion: rather, it focussed on expansion, adventure and discovery. Starting out from the microcosm of the *poleis* (cities) and the ports around the Aegean Sea, the Greeks went on to explore and colonise the shores of the Black Sea, Sicily, southern Italy and southern Gaul, where they founded towns which, by their economic and cultural development, equalled those in old Greece.

The Hellenic world was undeniably a single civilisation, but it was divided politically. Rivalry and wars between the *poleis* created fertile ground for unification imposed from the outside. Brought together by force by the Kings of Macedonia, the Greeks fought hard to conquer the East. Age-old monarchies fell under their attack. Led by Alexander the Great, the Greeks became masters of Asia Minor, Persia, Mesopotamia and Egypt. They dominated immense populations and territories by stamping them with their political and intellectual culture. 'Hellenistic' civilisation was thus born. Antioch, Alexandria and other Asian and African towns became as much, if not more so, the beacons of this civilisation as Athens, Thebes or Syracuse. But interpenetration did not only take place in one direction: the Greeks were profoundly influenced by the Eastern civilisations.

The vast political edifice of Alexander plunged into chaos and division after his death. In the IInd century B.C. Greece fell under the domination of the Romans, who presented themselves as the defenders of Hellenism against the hegemony of Macedonia.

Rome. To quote Paul Valéry once again: 'Wherever the Roman Empire ruled and wherever its power made itself felt... wherever the majesty of its institutions and its laws, wherever the apparatus and the dignity of its magistery were recognised... there is something European'.

The age during which a small city in Italy built up a vast state, unequalled in its achievements and its splendour, has always fascinated people. From the Vth century B.C. onwards, the Romans extended their rule over the rest of the peninsula, and then to southern Europe, the Middle East and North Africa. Once they had conquered Gaul and the British Isles, they spilled out of the Mediterranean region and brought into their sphere of influence and culture a large part of the Celtic peoples.

The Empire was essentially created by military conquest. The Roman legions were merciless in the face of stubborn resistance. The fates of Carthage or of Jerusalem bear witness to this. But the Romans had no intention of wiping out the subjugated nations, or their religions, laws and traditions. Unless the circumstances required the use of extreme means, they respected the

local institutions and propitiated unity and diversity. Rome did not destroy the various different social and cultural systems in its power sphere, but superimposed itself upon them.

The Roman heritage forms an essential part of the European patrimony. Stimulated by Hellenic influences, philosophy, the arts, literature and the sciences flourished under the Roman Empire and handed down impressive and refined works. However, there are other reasons why Rome should be considered as one of the main springs of European civilisation and as a catalyst of its unity. Roman law is one of the foundations of Europe. It shaped its social, political and economic institutions. It protected man from arbitrary rule. Applied from Asia Minor to the Iberian peninsula and from Gaul to Libya, it was a key element of cohesion of the Empire.

After the passage of Rome from a political system which the Greeks defined as aristocracy to a monarchical system, the Emperor never placed himself above the law and always presented his decisions as an interpretation or application of the law. Moreover, even in the imperial period, the state continued officially to be called a Republic and the institutions which existed formerly, such as the Senate, were maintained.

The concepts, terms and emblems of the Roman political, administrative and legal system are still in force throughout Europe today, associated in collective memory with greatness and perfection. Rome built temples, amphitheatres, thermal baths, roads, bridges and aqueducts, many of which still dot our countryside and give some idea of its methods, needs and aspirations.

Rome weaved a fabric of interdependence and affinity over vast areas of southern and western Europe, the Middle East and North Africa, whose populations did not need to be coerced into maintaining it. The Empire became the framework of a fertile social and cultural osmosis. Synonymous with the *pax romana,* it guaranteed safe existence, trade and material and spiritual progress. It generalised a type of human existence characterised by a sociability rarely seen in history. It operated on the basis of values born in this small Latin city which became the capital of the world, values which have been passed down as 'Roman virtues': courage, strictness, service, sacrifice, patriotism....

Trajan's column, symbol of Roman genius.

Although some peoples initially bore Roman domination as a yoke, as time passed they felt proud to be part of the Empire and the title of Roman citizen became coveted in all the provinces. This citizenship, which was initially granted on a selective basis, was given to all free men by the Emperor Caracalla in 212 A.D. This crowned the astonishing unification work which subsequent generations looked back upon with nostalgia. In people's imagination it became a golden era and something to be aimed at once again.

Christianity. The social mobility favoured by the *pax romana* allowed the Eastern religions to gain a foothold in the very centre of this Empire and in its Western provinces. These religions were brought to the west by merchants, employees of the Empire returning to their homeland, legion soldiers, slaves brought by force and, of course, by preachers. A number of centres of Judaism were established in several of the large Italian, Spanish and African towns. But it was Christianity, which had the same origins as Judaism, which radically transformed the religious nature of the Empire. The idea of a single God, common to the two religions, appealed to a section of the educated classes, familiar with the philosophical traditions of Rome and Greece and looking for moral renewal. However, Christianity found its followers mainly among the

Constantine the Great galloping on horseback after his victory over Maxentius in 312: Christianity is definitively grafted on to the Roman Empire.

slaves, the poor, the persecuted, among those who suffered from the harshness of the Roman order, or those who were revolted by its social injustices and its perversions.

The rapid spread of the new religion, the fervour of its followers, their categorical refusal to have anything to do with the state religion, their complete rejection of the existing society, led to inevitable conflict with the Roman authorities. But the courage of the Christians in face of their cruel persecution only increased the attractiveness of their religion. In 313, the Emperor Constantine authorised its free practice. Ten years later, he himself was converted. In 391, Christianity was proclaimed the Empire's official religion. It was hoped that it would lead the state out of a deep crisis which was increasingly threatening its unity.

Christianity was fundamentally universalist. It addressed itself to all men, regardless of their race, culture or social position. Moreover, it preached that they were brothers and all equal children of God. To the principle of respect for man, expressed by Greek philosophy and drama and by Roman law, Christianity added the idea that man was created in the image of God, that he was free to take his own decisions and that he was alone responsible for his own salvation.

The gradual interpenetration of the new religion and of the Roman order is one of the most crucial historical phenomena, and one of the most complex and the most interesting to study. Christianity was born in the fight against this order. But in the end, it helped the latter to survive. Roman ideas and structures had such a weight of tradition and efficiency that they imposed themselves upon Christianity as an inescapable reference framework.

The osmosis gradually resulted in the descendants of the great Roman families entering into the service of the Church. The territorial and hierarchical structures of the Church were largely modelled upon those of Rome. The osmosis was further consolidated by the adoption of Latin, the main language of the Empire, as the language of the Church. But its most striking symbol was the installation in Rome of the successor to Saint Peter, the first of all bishops, responsible to God alone. Thus the town which, from the time of the Emperor Diocletian, ceased to be the capital of a vast state, kept its vocation as the capital of the world. The memory of the universal Empire has thereby been preserved within the Church, and it is the Church which has tried over the centuries to re-constitute the Empire as a prop for its spiritual mission and as the best guarantee of peace between men and between states.

When, in the vth century, borders were smashed by the 'Barbarians', the Burgundians, the Suevi, the Vandals, the Visigoths, the Ostrogoths... who flooded into Italy, Gaul and Spain and the other regions of the Empire, the Church remained in place and set to their christianisation. In doing so, it transmitted to the 'Barbarians' the heritage of Rome. Thus, despite the destruction and miseries caused by the invasions, there was no abrupt break between the old and the new worlds. The invaders widely adopted the lifestyle of the conquered countries. They mixed with the local populations. They began to speak Latin or its derived languages and assimilated the nostalgia of the universal Empire.

The 'Barbarian' states created on the ashes of the Western Empire, which finally gave way in 476, found inspiration in the Roman order and tended to reconstruct it. An example is provided by the remarkable political work of the Ostrogoth chief, Theodoric, who became King of Italy (493-526).

Christianity added a key element to the Greek and Roman heritage. It

became one of the determinant factors in the unity of the civilisation which, since the Renaissance, has been known as European. Paul Valéry sums up this process well: 'Wherever the names of Caesar, Gaius, Trajan and Virgil, of Moses and Saint Paul, of Aristotle, Plato and Euclid have simultaneous significance and authority, there is Europe. Every race and every land which has been successively Romanised, Christianised and subjugated to Greek intellectual discipline is absolutely European'.

THE AGE OF RECONSTRUCTION

Transition. Between the Vth and the VIIIth century, the threat of a total break with the past hung over the territories of the former Roman Empire. Economic, social, political and cultural decline threatened an irreversible return to barbarism. An urban exodus left towns in ruins. A subsistence economy, based on primitive agriculture, took the place of a trading economy and a division of labour. Apart from a few isolated centres, education and artistic and scientific activities fell by the wayside. Standards of behaviour became very rough and disreputable. Insecurity, wars, pillage and destruction reigned for several generations.

In the VIIth and VIIIth centuries, a wave of Islam swept the Middle East, North Africa, the Iberian peninsula and southern Gaul. At the battle of Poitiers (732), a Christian army broke the back of the Arab invasion and stopped its progress. The Iberian countries returned to Christianity a few centuries later, but the eastern and southern banks of the Mediterranean, including the cradle of Christianity, plus the biggest and most famous towns of Antiquity and the ancient granaries of the Empire, were lost to Islam for ever. The Mediterranean, which was previously the *mare nostrum*, the internal lake of the Empire, became a border zone between two sharply different and hostile worlds.

Moreover, a deep split appeared within Christianity. A certain division had already been seen in Rome's heyday. Latin had always been the predominant language to the west of the Adriatic and Greek to the east. The division of the Empire, which became definitive in 395, accentuated this duality. The West was later to be invaded, fragmented and brutally changed, leading to general regression, whereas the East succeeded in safeguarding continuity, urban life and a fairly high level of economic and cultural development. On this backcloth, fundamental theological, philosophical and liturgical differences appeared between the Church of Rome and the Church of Constantinople. Rome jealously guarded its universalism, or its 'catholicism', to use a Greek word, and its independence from all political powers, whereas Constantinople allowed itself to be controlled by an imperial authority, thus exposing to view the Oriental influences to which the Hellenic world had been submitted since the time of Alexander the Great. The final break between Roman and Greek Christianity came in 1054. Each issued excommunications, and the split between the two Churches took on the form of a conflict between two civilisations. The Roman Church lost ground to Islam, whereas the Greek, or 'orthodox' Church, made considerable advances. Taking advantage of a period of prosperity and power for the Byzantine Empire, the Orthodox Church brought Christianity to Bulgaria and Serbia in the IXth century and to the Kievan Russian state at the end of the Xth.

Charlemagne. During this period of crisis and contraction, the Roman Church remained, despite everything, the backbone of the West. It supported Western

The back of the Arab invasion of Europe is broken: the battle of Poitiers in 732 (Miniature; Froissart Chronicles in 1472, Musée Condé, Chantilly).

civilisation through its hierarchical organisational network, its deep rooting in history and its dedication to the cause. It educated the governing classes and improved moral standards. It was led often by remarkable personalities, such as Pope Gregory I (596-604), a descendant of a family of Roman senators. It was above all in the Church, the papal court, the monasteries and the schools founded alongside the cathedrals that the dream survived of a universal empire which would put an end to the chaos, guarantee security and well-being to mankind and support the Church in its soul-saving mission. The coincidence of this dream with the ambitions of a great prince eventually resulted in the rebirth of the unification dream.

Charles, later called Charlemagne, became King of the Francs in 771. Using his intelligence, his tenacity and his skills as a warrior, he built up an important state, comprising not only Gaul but large parts of Italy and Germania. He realised that to consolidate and extend his kingdom he needed to attain historical legitimacy, an ideal and the benediction of the Church. The latter was happy to give it and, on December 25, 800, Charlemagne was crowned Emperor in Rome by Pope Leo III.

The centre of gravity of the restored Roman Empire was no longer to be found in Italy, but to the north, on the Meuse and the Rhine. The political capital was at Aquae Grani (modern Aachen). With the exception of the British Isles, the Empire comprised all the Roman Christian countries between the Germanic and Slav pagans in the East, Byzantium in the South East and Islamic Spain in the South.

The administrative structures of the new Empire corresponded largely to the districts of the Church and of the former Roman Empire. Charlemagne brought about a key stage in Europe's evolution, and his legislative work had lasting consequences. He created conditions for the revival of education and cultural activities. His Empire brought down the curtain on a period of regression and chaos, which had begun with the Barbarian invasions. It provided history with an example of the separation of spiritual and temporal powers, where each helped the other but kept its independence and specific areas of competence. (This example was very important for the institutional, social and intellectual development of the West, different from that of the Byzantine monarchy). It bore witness to the indestructible force of the unification dream, inherited from Rome and safeguarded by Christianity.

The Empire of Charlemagne was, however, subject to centrifugal forces, which eventually resulted in its downfall. The subsistence economy, which was still widespread in the IXth and Xth centuries, meant that productive activities were fragmented and intellectual horizons limited. The undeniable cultural revival between the VIIIth and IXth centuries was not strong enough to result in general acceptance of a great political ideal, or to moderate primary ambitions and instincts. The Charlemagne Empire officially survived until 924. But in reality, well before this date it was divided into territorial entities, governed by the descendants of the Emperor or by other princes. Some of these entities were the forerunners of modern-day states.

The disintegration of the Empire marked a new period of confusion and danger. Cultural and educational activities were again pushed into the background. The papacy lost the stability and the support which had been offered to it for a number of years by the Carolingian dynasty. It gave way to conflicts between the leading Roman families and lost a great deal of its authority. Survival of the West was put under severe threat by devastating and bloody invasions. In the first half of the IXth century the Normans launched their

The last invasion of England: at the battle of Hastings in 1066 William the Norman defeats King Harold (Bayeux Tapestry, Musée de l'Evêché, Bayeux).

fearsome raids to the north, and the Arabs conquered Sicily and ravaged southern Italy. At the beginning of the xth century, the Hungarians, coming from Asia, fanned fire and shed blood in several regions of Germania.

The summit. However, the post-Carolingian crisis was only a temporary black period. After a frightening population drop, following the Barbarian invasions, and long periods of stagnation, the West experienced strong population growth. Between 950 and 1150, the number of inhabitants increased by an estimated 50%, and subsequently grew at an even faster rate. A much more diversified economy gradually replaced the subsistence economy, helped by quantitative and qualitative progress in production methods and the development of navigation, trade and monetary circulation. Towns began to fill again, in Italy, France, Flanders and Germany, and gradually resumed their traditional functions. These changes provided the impetus for the flourishing of Europe in the xii[th] and xiii[th] centuries. However, no one spoke of Europe but rather of Christianity, which served as a unifying force between men and nations, from Naples to London and from Cracow to Paris. It determined the specific nature of Western civilisation up against the Islamic and Byzantine worlds. At the end of the ix[th] century, a chronicler, no doubt familiar with classical texts and concepts, still called the Charlemagne Empire *Europa vel regnum Caroli*. But this

expression then disappeared from the vocabulary, and did not make a comeback until the xv^th century, at the time of the Renaissance.

Roman Christianity, truncated by Islamic conquests and then by the separation of the Eastern Church, expanded rapidly in the xth and xi^th centuries. Bohemia, Poland, Hungary, Denmark, Norway and Sweden were evangelised by Rome and entered its sphere of influence. Thanks to their conversion, these countries outgrew primitive social and political structures, built important and lasting states, and integrated themselves into a rich and ancient culture.

Spiritual renewal and deepening went hand in hand with this expansion. These were to a large extent due to the extraordinary development of monastic life and in particular of the Benedictine order inspired by the Cluny Abbey in Burgundy. It was in these monasteries that the widescale reform of which Pope Gregory vii was an eloquent advocate took shape. The Gregorian reform aimed to cure society of its ills, beginning by uprooting the failings which had enfeebled the clergy and the episcopate: corruption, a low intellectual and moral level and, in particular, dependency on temporal power which incessantly intervened in ecclesiastical nominations. The Benedictines were later joined in their efforts by the Cistercians, the Dominicans and the Franciscans.... The movement was fundamentally European. A dense network of abbeys and convents obeying the same rules expanded over the Western countries and offered them a framework, a support and a common style.

This groundswell brought rapid results. At the end of the xi^th century and the beginning of the xii^th, the Roman Church presented itself in a new light. It was spiritually and intellectually strengthened. Its influence was enhanced by a new generation of priests, bishops and monks, full of dedication and inspiring respect and trust. Great pilgrimages from one end of Europe to the other were a demonstration of this strength of faith and of Western unity.

Faith and unity were expressed in a particularly forceful way by the great enterprise of the Crusades. It was at the Clermont Council in 1095 that Pope Urban ii, former prior at Cluny and a leading advocate of the Gregorian reform, developed the idea of liberating the Holy sites of Christianity and attaching them to the West. The idea was greeted with enthusiasm and was rapidly translated into action. In 1099 the Christians seized Jerusalem, but they did not hold on to it for long. In 1187 the town was re-conquered by the Muslims. The Western implant in the middle of the Islamic world was rejected and later Christian efforts failed to reverse this. The epic of the Crusades extended over almost two centuries. The work of men, they provided a demonstration of heroism and glory, greed and infamy, all tangled together as in a Shakespearian drama. They gave a clear picture of the character of European society in the last centuries of the Middle Ages.

This society was like a brightly coloured mosaic, composed of a wide ethnic and cultural diversity and of a multitude of kingdoms, fiefs and city states which provided the backcloth for many tensions and conflicts. But the people who made up this diversity shared certain essential values, felt that they belonged to the same world and were ready to act together at crucial moments. Identification with a kingdom, a culture or an ethnic group and loyalty to a prince or some other territorial authority ran parallel with faithfulness to the Church and to that part of feudal society known as 'order' or 'estate' stretching beyond the boundaries of the territorial entities over the entire realm of Roman Christianity. The clergy formed a truly European stratum, and recognised the authority of the pope before all other. The knighthood of all the

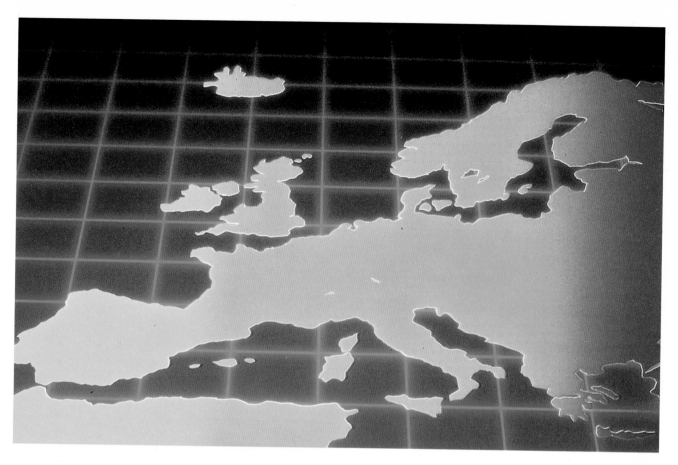

Europe

The major challenges are planetary now.

'We, the elected representatives of the people, are Europe'
(The European Parliament in session in Strasbourg, January 1987).

'We, the representatives of the states, are Europe'.
(Group photo of the Luxembourg European Council with Grand-Duke Jean and
Grand-Duchess Joséphine-Charlotte., December 2, 1985, after having
approved the European Act).

Tapestry by Jean Lurçat in the 'Salon Bleu' in Strasbourg: 'The hilt of his sword was emblazoned with the insignia of mankind'.

The abduction of Europa, daughter of Agenor
(Pompei Fresco, Museo nazionale, Naples).

*The nation state has dominated our history in recent centuries
(frieze of monument to the French Revolution, Paris).*

The main elements of geographical diversity in Europe: the sea.
The Mediterranean (above) and the North Sea...

countries shared a feeling of brotherhood, due to the fact that they led the same lifestyle and had the same ideals and code of honour. It was therefore not surprising that men came from all over Europe to free the Holy Land. Town leagues paid no heed to the boundaries of kingdoms or fiefs, and they occasionally stretched over vast parts of Europe. European society of the last centuries of the Middle Ages was not therefore a mechanical and loose juxtapositioning of ill-assorted elements; rather it was a solid pyramid of superimposed blocks, or 'orders', which together formed the feudal system and which survived, at least in theory, to the French Revolution. It was made up of the clergy which strove to save souls, the nobility which defended the Christians and the third estate which produced the riches.

The papal authority, which had drawn the entire West into the gigantic enterprise of the Crusades, was also in a position to impose internal peace. The 'truce of God' was due to the efforts of Popes Urban II, Calixtus II and Alexander III, and it was generally accepted and observed by the princes, knights and cities.

The vitality which characterised the West in the XIth, XIIth and XIIIth centuries was not limited to demographical, social and economic spheres. The Gregorian reform resulted in a significant number of new schools and centres of intellectual activity. In the main cities, the number of masters and pupils in cathedral and abbey schools increased to the extent that the educated community became a separate stratum in the population. The concerns, interests, tastes and lifestyle of this community, which jealously guarded its independence, prompted them to form a guild alongside the craftsmen and merchants. This guild became known as *universitas*, which underlines both the range of disciplines which were studied and its openness to all men regardless of their origin and culture. The popes and the kings gradually provided the guilds with charters which defined their structure, their internal regulations and their autonomy.

As early as the XIIIth and XIVth centuries, the most famous universities of Europe were born: Bologna, Paris, Salamanca, Naples, Oxford, Heidelberg, Vienna, Prague, Cracow.... They were normally composed of four faculties: arts, theology, law and medicine. Universities, like the monastical orders, the knights or the city leagues, were a European phenomenon which spread horizontally across all of the West and ironed out differences between the nascent monarchical states. The point of honour for each of them was to bring together masters and students from all over the West. The pupils were organised in 'nations' according to their country of origin and in everyday life used their mother tongue. But they more often than not formed a fraternal community and studied in a Latin of increasingly high quality as the authors of Antiquity were rediscovered.

The Romanic style was an artistic and spiritual expression of this Europe bubbling with economic and cultural activity, with the Gregorian reform, the first universities and the Crusades. The cathedrals, baptistries, castles and townhouses, built in Romanic style from Asturias to Poland, from Apulia to Flanders, gave an idea not only of the wherewithal and the inspiration which ran through this age, but also of the deep unity of the West.

The Empire was reconstituted in 962. In the same year, Otto, of the Saxon dynasty, King of Germania, conqueror of the Hungarians and ruler of Northern Italy, was crowned Emperor by Pope John XII. The Church had kept up its nostalgia for the Empire for centuries. It still expected that the Empire would support its work and saw it as a guarantee of peace between Christians.

The great European adventure of the Crusades: the siege of Jerusalem in 1099 (Illumination on manuscript of Jacob van Maerlant, 1332, Groningen University Library).

But the revived Empire was far from resembling that of Ancient Rome or that of Charlemagne. Apart from Otto III (983-1002), son of a Byzantine princess, who was a truly universalist ruler, the Emperors served first and foremost their dynastic interests. Since the Empire was essentially composed of German lands, it gradually became identified with the latter. Already in the XIIth century the name *imperium Teutonicorum* was occasionally substituted for *imperium Romanorum*.

Moreover, a violent conflict broke out between the Empire and the Church. Theoreticians and advocates of the Gregorian reform, and first and foremost Pope Gregory VII himself, believed that there should be no temporal influence on nominations to ecclesiastical posts. However, Emperors, and in particular Henry IV, felt that advantages could be gained by choosing, or 'investing', bishops themselves.

The Investiture Quarrel between Henry IV and Gregory VII, symbolised by the Canossa episode (1077), opened a long period of tension and conflict between the spiritual and temporal powers. The Empire was the first to suffer from this development. Its authority was contested in Italy by the powerful Guelph party, and its sway was openly rejected by France in the West and by Poland in the East. Its German pillars were shaken by the action of the Holy See. Little by little, and in particular after the Great Interregnum (1250-1273), the Empire was reduced to the status of a mere state among others. Only its name conjured up a glorious past and contributed to the preservation of the dream of Western political unity.

Its decline was viewed with regret and concern by some of the greatest minds of the period, such as Dante Alighieri. The illustrious poet was worried about peace and convinced that it would be broken if there was no supreme monarch above the kings. He did not want the kings and the diversity they represented to be wiped out. But the universal monarchy, i.e. the Empire, should, he felt, accomplish, along with the Holy See, *ordinatio ad unum* – the harmonisation of differences in the name of the common interest. This was the idea running through Dante's *De Monarchia*, a passionate call for unity.

The West divided

Crisis. The Papacy did not seem at first to be affected by the conflict with the Empire. It reached the summit of its power and influence in the XIIIth century. Innocent III (1198-1216) tried to implement the idea, developed by a number of authors of his time, that the Holy See was the supreme authority, not only in the spiritual community of the Church, but also in the temporal community, the *respublica christiana*, an organisation within which the Emperor was above all kings and princes but below the Pope who was only answerable to God. All temporal power should come from the supreme authority of Rome and should reflect it, in the same way as the moon reflects back the light which it receives from the sun.

Certain historians interpreted this plan as a foretoken of a theocratic power and a threat to man's freedom. They therefore considered that the conflict between the Papacy and the Empire, which weakened the two rival forces, paved the way towards freedom and European pluralism. This idea merits attention. However, it cannot be denied that the decline of the papal authority, which began in the XIVth century, corresponded to a long period of fragmentation, tensions and bloody conflicts in Europe.

However, it was not the weakened Empire which plunged the Papacy into

In Canossa, in 1077, during the investiture controversy, the excommunicated Emperor Henry IV begs the forgiveness of Pope Gregory VII and kneels before his wife, Matilda, ally of the Pope (Latin manuscript, Vatican library).

the most serious crisis of its history, but rather France, which humiliated it and obliged it in 1309 to transfer its seat from Rome to Avignon. The decision taken by Gregory XI in 1377 to put an end to the 'Avignon captivity' and to return to Rome opened up a very deep split in the Church, during which two or even three rival popes argued over the pontifical throne.

The Kingdom of France was, at the beginning of the XIVth century, the most powerful state in the West. It had a population of around eighteen million inhabitants. Its very powerful monarch strove to implement the theory, drawn up by his legal advisers, according to which the 'king is emperor in his kingdom', and was entirely independent from any spiritual or temporal authority. This theory heralded the state becoming an end in itself, having no moral or political obligations beyond its boundaries, and using all means to promote its own particular interests.

France was not the only dynastic state to claim equality with the Empire and complete independence. England, with a population of barely four million, threw less weight than France, but the development of its political and military organisation made it, in the XIVth century, one of the key actors in European history. In the Iberian peninsula, powerful Christian kingdoms emerged from the incessant struggle against the Islamic presence. Aragon extended its power over the Balearic Islands, Sicily, Sardinia and Naples. Castile, in the first half of

the XIIIth century, wrested from the Muslims their two most important bastions in Spain, Cordoba and Seville. The union of these two kingdoms, sealed in 1469 with the marriage of their crowned heads, Ferdinand and Isabella, resulted in the creation of a large monarchy which exercised a great influence on the evolution of Europe and the world.

The year 1492 marked the end of the last Islamic kingdom in Spain, that of Granada, and the discovery of America. The exploits of Columbus, like those of Vasco de Gama and other navigators in the service of the King of Portugal, opened up an age in which vast European empires were built overseas, maritime trade was rapidly developed, and great riches and power amassed. The Atlantic shores of Europe became more important than the Mediterranean. The dynastic states began to build up fleets and colonies, and turned their attention away from Europe. In an extroverted Europe, internal divisions became more plain. The race for the riches in the 'Indies' exacerbated the conflicts between states until they became almost permanent.

In the East, Poland, following the example of France and rejecting that of Bohemia, had refused to recognise the imperial authority as early as the XIth century, but played the card of its allegiance to the Papacy. It overcame its feudal fragmentation and consolidated its forces and structures under Casimir the Great (1333-1370). Thanks to its union with Lithuania, it succeeded in building a very large state and reached its own peak in the XVth and XVIth centuries, under the Jagellonian dynasty.

Everywhere else, whether it was Hungary or Burgundy, states embarked upon a policy of independence and expansion at the expense of their neighbours. This policy provoked devastating and bloody wars, such as the One Hundred Years War between England and France, the war between England and Scotland, that between Venice and Genoa or that between the powerful state of the Teutonic Order and the Polish-Lithuanian monarchy. These wars, along with unfavourable climatic changes and the plague which, between the middle of the XIVth century and the end of the XVth, struck Europe on average every eight years, resulted in a frightening demographic regression. The population of France was cut by half in one century. England, Italy and Spain suffered comparable losses. Poverty and despair gave rise to tension and social unrest. Literature and painting of this period convey pessimism and fear of the future.

Apart from the rise of dynastic states, a powerful cultural phenomenon grew up, known under the name of the 'Renaissance', which repudiated the ancient authorities incarnating the unity of the West. The origins of the Renaissance are complex. The decadence of the Roman Church no doubt accelerated its advent. The arrival in Italy of Greek scholars and artists, leaving Byzantium which was under threat by the Turks, and bringing with them their knowledge of pre-Christian Hellenic culture, was certainly a factor in its development. The rediscovery of the pre-Christian world in all its splendour became the revelation of the XVth century. Italy, followed by other Western countries, was swept by a craze for pagan art and philosophy. Secularization and humanism shook off the precepts and the prohibitions of Christianity and placed man, following the example of Ancient Greece, at the centre of its concerns.

The phenomenon took on a European dimension but, paradoxically, was detrimental to the unity of the West. The new ideas opposed the structures and values which dominated in the Middle Ages, henceforth considered as a Barbarian epoch. The idea of a Christian West with the Holy See at its head and of a universal Empire with the task of protecting and supporting the latter

Christopher Columbus discovers America in 1492.

IMAGO · ERASMI · ROTERODA
MI · AB · ALBERTO · DVRERO · AD
VIVAM · EFFIGIEM · DELINIATA ·

ΤΗΝ · ΚΡΕΙΤΤΩ · ΤΑ · ΣΥΓΓΡΑΜ
ΜΑΤΑ · ΔΙΞΕΙ

· MDXXVI ·

Erasmus, European humanist 'par excellence' (Engraving by Albrecht Dürer, 1526).

appeared to many as outmoded. Kings and princes, often won over to new ideas, seemed to incarnate both reality and the future, as opposed to the dreams of the past.

Europe split. The Renaissance and humanism sowed the seeds of dispute within the Church itself. The Reformation, or protestantism, was one of the outcomes of this wave of cultural, social and political change which flooded the West in the xvth century. It accentuated the divisions in Western society. Firstly, it rejected the authority of Rome and, implicitly, the unity of the Christian world. Liberation from such a distant centre of control seemed to be a prerequisite for revival. Secondly, there was not one Reformation, but several, symbolised by Wycliff, Huss, Luther, Münzer, Zwingli, Calvin.... These very profound movements were often tied to the historical and cultural features of

one country, and were inapplicable to another. Occasionally they were the expression of not only spiritual, moral and intellectual aspirations, but also of social or ethnic tensions. The powerful Hussite movement, which shook central Europe in the xv[th], xvi[th] and xvii[th] centuries, remained an essentially Czech phenomenon. Moreover, the different Reformation movements fought not only against the Roman Papacy, but also amongst themselves. For example, there was a very violent conflict between Lutheranism and Anabaptism in Germany.

The proselytism of the Reformation, and its desire to pass on its ideas to as large a number of Christians as possible, prompted it to abandon Latin and adopt local languages. Latin was associated with Rome, considered to be a synonym for corruption and decadence, if not for the Antichrist. In 1521, Martin Luther began to translate the Bible into German. His example was widely followed not only by the Protestants but also by the Catholics who had no other choice than to employ the methods of their adversaries. There can be no doubt that the development of vernacular languages was given a decisive push by the Reformation, even if the beginnings of this process dated back to an earlier period. The regression of Latin, which for centuries had been the language of the Church, the arts, the sciences and politics all over Europe, implied a serious setback for the unity of the West.

The overturning of the old values and their replacement by the new met the explicit or vague aspirations of the middle class. The discoveries, the development of navigation, trade and credit, the invention of the magnetic compass, of printing and gunpowder, profited this world as much as it put the old 'orders' at a disadvantage. Cities played a key role in the economic recovery at the end of the xv[th] century, after a long period of slump. They grew in size (Naples – 150,000 inhabitants, Venice – 100,000 inhabitants, Paris – 200,000 inhabitants) and in wealth. The most active and cultivated elements of society were concentrated in the towns. Yet reality was smothered by a system inherited from the Middle Ages, which gave privileges to the Catholic clergy, whose audience was shrinking, and to the landed nobles, whose role declined with the invention of gunpowder and changes in the technical and social organisation of defence. It is therefore not surprising that humanism and the Reformation were welcomed with hope and open arms by the middle classes. These forces eroded away the old order, which was judged to be sluggish and unjust. On the other hand, unlike the Catholic Church, they brought back into favour commercial and financial activities and attached ethical value to material success.

The Reformation and the cities proved themselves to be welcome allies for kings and princes who had hoped to be able to cut the knot of dependency with the Papacy and the Empire and wanted to consolidate their power against the latent opposition of the clergy and the nobles, whose aspirations did not stop at the borders of the dynastic state and whose loyalties still went to the ancient, universalist powers. An alliance therefore grew up between the prince, the local variety of Reformation and the middle classes against the Catholic Church and the landed gentry. Protection of the Protestant Church and securing of its allegiance, development of the local language and gradual elimination of Latin seemed to offer an effective course of action to replace 'horizontal' ties with single 'vertical' loyalty to the sovereign. In the majority of countries won over to Protestantism, state churches developed very rapidly. The sovereign thus held in his hands supreme political and spiritual authority. The application of the French idea that the king must be 'emperor in his kingdom' was now complemented by the idea that the King should be Pope in his Kingdom.

Absolute monarchy progressed rapidly and the sense of common interest and common destiny of the West declined.

The action of states and sovereigns was upheld by a new political thought – of which Machiavelli was the undisputed master – which analysed the mechanics of power and refused any reference to moral considerations or general finality. Jean Bodin (1529-1596) wrote: 'The greatness of a prince, to put it bluntly, is nothing else than the ruin or diminishment of his neighbours; and his strength is nothing else than the weakness of others'.

The impossible step backwards. Because of the changes in Europe and the influence of centrifugal forces, the attempt by Charles V to inject new life into the Holy Roman Empire – *sacrum romanum imperium* – and to reassemble around him the Christian West ended in failure. King of Spain from 1516 and Emperor from 1519, Charles V was master of an impressive political domain, of which Burgundy, the Netherlands, Northern Italy and Naples were part. His power and riches were increased by his immense American colonies. He strove to give internal cohesion to this political realm in the name of the Catholic religion and to unite Christianity in the fight against the Turks. However, in order to destroy the Emperor's plans, the King of France, Francis I, concluded an alliance with the Sultan Suleyman the Magnificent, and gave active support to the Protestant princes of Germany.

Worn down by his enemies, Charles V resigned himself to the consequences of his failure. Since the restoration of the religious unity of his states had proven to be impossible, he accepted in 1555 the Peace of Augsburg which officially recognised the Lutheran churches. Each prince obtained the right to choose his religion and to impose it upon his subjects. The principle of *cuius regio eius religio* (the religion is determined by he who reigns) thus triumphed. The following year, before abdicating, Charles V divided up his states, with those of Central Europe going to his brother Ferdinand and Spain with the Netherlands and the American colonies to his son Philip, consequently consecrating the political division of Europe.

The imperial dignity went to Ferdinand. The Hapsburgs acquired it for the first time in 1273, after the Great Interregnum, and held it from 1400 to 1806, apart from the brief period 1742-1745. But this rank was only token. The imperial crown, definitively elective since the Golden Bull promulgated by Charles of Luxemburg in 1358, became an object of trading and represented less and less real power. The Elector princes and the other German princes founded states which were practically independent and conducted a dynastic policy which was scarcely different from that of the Kings of France, England or Spain. The Hapsburgs therefore took it upon themselves to consolidate and extend their hereditary states in Central and South-Eastern Europe. They were consequently more often identified with Austria than with the Empire. Austria was a reality whereas the Empire had become an abstract relic of the past.

The Church struggled throughout the XVth, XVIth and XVIIth centuries to preserve the unity of the West against the Turkish threat and to stop the advance of the Reformation. It caught up with the times, and introduced the word 'Europe' into its vocabulary. But it interpreted this word as a synonym of Christianity. This was the meaning always given to it by Pope Pius II (1458-1464), noted not only for his tireless activity to restore the authority of the Church but also for his loyalty to the idea of an Empire allied to the Holy See. In 1445, well before his election to the pontifical throne, Enea Silvio Piccolomini developed and defended this idea in his work *De Ortu et Auctoritate*

Romani Imperii (The Rise and the Power of the Roman Empire).

The Turkish threat, which for more than two centuries was a catalyst for initiatives promoting European unity, became very real in the xvth century. The Turks had taken over from the Arabs as the ruling race in the Muslim world, and had built up a vast empire including Anatolia, Armenia, Mesopotamia, Syria, the Hejaz – with the holy towns of Islam – Egypt and the best part of North Africa. Steeped in Islamic messianism and in the long warrior tradition of a people who previously had been nomads, they established their first bridgeheads in Europe in 1354. They conquered Bulgaria in 1371 and Serbia in 1389, reducing these kingdoms to Turkish provinces and encircling what remained of Byzantium. It was clear that after the fall of the Byzantine barrier the Muslim tidal wave would surge towards the West.

Popes and their emissaries redoubled their efforts to prevent this disaster. The skilful diplomacy of Cardinal Cesarini brought the establishment of an alliance between Ladislas the Jagellonian, King of Poland and of Hungary, and the republics of Genoa and Venice. In 1443 the armies of Ladislas advanced into the Balkans and won a victory at Nish. They then advanced in the direction of Constantinople, hoping for active help from the Genoese and Venetian fleets. This help did not come and the Polish and Hungarian armies were wiped out by the Turks in the Battle of Varna, on November 10, 1444. The young King Ladislas and Cardinal Cesarini perished alongside the cream of Christian knights. Constantinople could no longer hope for help. On May 29, 1453 it was stormed by the Turks who made it the capital of their empire a few years later. The last living monument of an age-old great and sublime civilisation disappeared under the weight of the Islamic avalanche.

From this time on, in accordance with the logic of their political, religious and military tenets, the Turks waged war against Western Christianity. Apart from a number of truces, the fighting lasted several centuries. On August 26, 1526, Louis the Jagellonian, King of Hungary and of Bohemia, died along with his army in the bloody battle of Mohacs. With the exception of some narrow fringes in the north and the west, held by the House of Hapsburg, and the principality of Transylvania in the east, Hungary became a simple Turkish province. Vienna and Cracow were now under the direct threat of the Ottoman Empire.

The Turks did not suffer their first defeat until 1571. In this year, the fleets of a number of Christian states, brought together by tireless papal diplomacy, won a great victory over the Sultan's fleet. The naval battle of Lepanto destroyed the myth that the Turks were invincible. But more than a century of political and military efforts were required before the Islam wave began to subside. It was only in 1683 that a large Christian army, headed by the King of Poland, John Sobieski, inflicted a decisive defeat on the Turks before the walls of Vienna, and opened an age of gradual re-conquest of South-West Europe. The alliance between Poland and the Empire, the basis of this change in fortunes, was concluded under the patronage of Pope Innocent XI. The centuries of war against the Turks certainly increased the sense of a common destiny in a number of European countries, particularly the Catholic ones, but did not result in any permanent political structure.

Apart from rallying the West against the Turkish threat, Rome was always attempting to restore the religious, moral and, in the long term, political unity of the Christian countries. Profoundly weakened and shaken by the Reformation and secularization, the Catholic Church had gradually recaptured some of its vitality and dynamism. From 1540, it had a formidable weapon in the shape

of the Society of Jesus. This new order, well adapted to the spirit and the challenges of the age, took root everywhere in Europe. Its objective was to win the Old World back to Catholicism. In 1563 the Council of Trent resulted, after eighteen years of work, in a strengthening of the structures and doctrine of the Church to cope with the intellectual revolution of the Renaissance. The great plan for the spiritual reconquest of the West was called the Counter-Reformation. Some historians also call it the Catholic Reformation. It stopped the decline of Catholic Christianity and stimulated powerful forces within the Church. The explosion of baroque art, the artistic expression of the Counter-Reformation, added a glorious and permanent feature to the cultural patrimony of Europe.

However, the confrontation between the Reformation and the Counter-Reformation did not lead to decisive success for either side or to the religious unification of Europe. Thanks to the tireless activity of the Jesuits, the Counter-Reformation pushed back Protestantism in France, Poland, Hungary and Bohemia and preserved these countries for Catholicism. But it proved incapable of winning back the majority of the German countries and of Switzerland, the northern Netherlands, England, Scotland and the Scandinavian countries. The terrible wars of the xvi^{th} and xvii^{th} centuries, and in particular the Thirty Years War, in which religious and dynastic interests were closely intertwined, left a large part of Europe in ruins and decimated the population, but did not eradicate the fundamental religious division. The Peace of Westphalia, in 1648, consecrated this division. It reaffirmed the principle of *cuius regio eius religio*, which removed dynastical states from any allegiance to an outside higher authority, thus leaving the way free for the consolidation of absolutism within national boundaries.

In the countries which had not chosen the Reformation, the princes tried to exercise an influence on the Catholic Church. French Gallicanism became the model for this trend. Moreover, the role of the assemblies which limited the monarchical power was becoming increasingly restricted in the majority of European states. Here again, France set the example. The Estates General were only called to a meeting three times in the xvi^{th} century, once in the xvii^{th} and once, for the last time, in the xviii^{th}. A new doctrine, mercantilism, attempted to reinforce the power of the princes by the use of economic means. Colbert became a great master of this policy. Many writers justified and glorified absolutism and presented their sovereign as a kind of God on earth, whether out of conviction or servility. Alongside the ancient monarchies, whose roots were to be found in the Middle Ages, new states appeared, such as the Republic of United Provinces in the northern Netherlands, where the religious factor played a very important role in shaping a sense of national identity.

The policy objective pursued by each government was to accentuate the independence and particular character of every state. It could not fail to influence the cultural and social substrata within national boundaries. It reinforced the role of religious, ethnic and economic factors which, since the Reformation, had tended to favour internal unity and differentiation vis-à-vis the outside world. Divisions and conflicts were no longer a part of dynastic policy but of the collective psychology. The people of a state were gradually transformed into a single society within which dynastic loyalty doubled with a feeling of distinct existence and destiny. The formation of modern nations had thus begun.

In the xvii^{th} and xviii^{th} centuries, the survival of the states in a divided Europe depended on the maintenance of a balance of power. It was in the name

of this balance that Catholic France allied itself with Protestant monarchies and even with Muslim Turkey in order to counter the power of the Emperors of the Hapsburg dynasty. Later, England formed coalitions in the name of the same principle. Certain historians assert that at this time, despite continual wars, there was a feeling in Europe of belonging to the same civilisation, and that the warring parties considered themselves as partners in a game, the rules of which were respected by both sides. They further maintained that the object was to weaken the other partner but not to annihilate him. Perhaps this assertion had a grain of truth in it. But the fate of Poland in the XVIIIth century gives some idea of its limits.

However, the division of Europe did not kill the dream of unity. It was present in the numerous references to the past and plans for the future. Some of these plans were very ambitious, aiming for profound unity, as at the peak of the Middle Ages and at the time of the Crusades. Others were more realistic and, accepting the reality of sovereign states, aimed essentially at restoring peace, trust and cooperation by the development of international law.

As early as the XVth century, George Podiebrad, elective King of Bohemia, linked to the Hussite movement, drew up a plan for union between his country and France and Venice. He intended that the union be open to other states, in particular to Poland and Hungary. His project was very elaborate, and included an assembly, a court of justice, an army and a joint treasury. Designed as a rampart against the Turks, it coincided with the objectives of Pope Pius II. But it differed from the latter in that it excluded from the union both the Emperor and the Pope, and was in fact as much anti-Catholic as anti-Turk. Plans for a *respublica christiana*, predominantly Protestant, were later penned by Lutherans such as Melanchton and Peucer and by the Huguenot François de la Noue.

The Catholics were not left behind in this cry for unity. At the beginning of the XVIIth century, the Italian Dominican Tommaso Campanella, author of a famous and strange utopia, *Civitas Solis* (The Polity of the Sun), denounced the Reformation, claiming that it was responsible for the division of Europe. He called for the reconstitution of a single Christianity and a single universal Empire. At the same time, the eminent Spanish Jesuit and jurist, Francisco Suarez, developed in his treatise the idea of an international public law to guarantee peace and closer relations between states. He declared: 'There is not a single state which has enough resources to be able to survive without support, association or mutual relations, for its well-being and for utilitarian ends, out of necessity and for moral reasons, as proven by experience itself. There must therefore be laws which direct and govern states in this sort of community...'. This idea was taken up and developed by the famous Dutch jurist and diplomat Grotius (Hugo de Groot), who called upon states to create a 'Society of Nations'. It is noteworthy that in his masterly work *De Iure Belli et Pacis* (On the daw of War and Peace), published in 1625, Grotius always called Christianity what other scholars of his time were already calling Europe.

Maximilien de Béthune, Duc de Sully (1559-1641), a Protestant, minister and friend of King Henry IV, went much further. In his old age, he drew up a project for a European federation, which he called a 'very Christian Republic'. Like past and future projects, this 'great design' was inspired by a desire for peace. Sully felt that his Republic needed a strong common denominator and that this denominator should be the Christian faith, whether Catholic or Protestant. If the Turks were converted to Christianity, the doors of the Republic should be opened to them. But Sully did not plan on letting in Muscovite Russia and did not consider Orthodoxy as an equivalent of

Melanchton, companion and principal collaborator of Luther (Painting by Lucas Cranach, Uffizi, Florence).

Catholicism or Protestantism. A wide gulf separated the West and Russia which, since the fall of Byzantium, considered itself the 'third Rome' and the refuge for the true Christian religion.

In order to be viable the Republic had to be internally balanced. In other words, conditions should be such that there could be no hegemony. Sully saw his Republic as made up of fifteen states, some of which already existed and others which should be created: the Holy See, the Empire, England, Bohemia, Denmark, Spain, France, Hungary, Poland, Sweden, Venice, a republic of Belgium, a big Helvetian republic, an Italic republic and a Lombard Kingdom. Two of these states would have a special defence role: Hungary as a rampart against the Turks and Poland as a bastion against the Muscovites and the Tartars. The Republic would be placed under the authority of a very Christian Council, made up of representatives of the member states, nominated every three years, and meeting each year in a different town. The Republic would have an army, whose task would be not only to ensure external defence, but also to enforce the decisions of the Council in the member states.

Gottfried Wilhelm von Leibniz, one of the most brilliant and ecumenical thinkers of all times, did not hesitate, despite his Lutheran faith, to proclaim his admiration for Europe of the Middle Ages and to call for a return to the spiritual and temporal unity of all Christians. He wrote in 1676: 'In this Kingdom of Christ which now had Christ himself as Head and Sovereign, it was accepted by all that two supreme magistrates, the Pope and the Emperor, should exercise power on His behalf, the former spiritual power, the latter temporal. And it was clearly in the interest of all Christians to be united under a common authority, so that they could together safeguard peace and at the same time deter the enemies of the faith.... The correct thing to do is to invest the Emperor with power over a large part of Europe and with a sort of supreme sovereignty corresponding to that of the Church...'

In 1693, William Penn, an Englishman who had spent part of his life on the other side of the Atlantic where he founded and governed the colony of Pennsylvania, wrote his *Essay towards the present and the future Peace of Europe*. In this work he defended a project for European union rather like that of Sully: 'Now if the sovereign princes of Europe... agree to meet by their stated deputies in a general diet, estates or parliament, and there establish rules of justice for sovereign princes to observe one to another... Europe would quietly obtain the so much desired and needed peace to her harassed inhabitants...' This same theme was tackled in 1712, in a work entitled *Mémoires pour rendre la paix perpétuelle en Europe* (Essay on How to Bring Permanent Peace to Europe), by Charles-Irénée Castel de Saint-Pierre, a French ecclesiastic and diplomat. He conceived a project for a confederation, the 'European Society', which would be governed by a Senate made up of representatives of the member states. Like Sully, the Abbé de Saint-Pierre wanted the European Society to be an example of internal balance. However, he admitted that the Emperor should have special status. Although he proposed that no sovereign member of the Society possess more than one state, the Emperor was to be exempted from this rule.

Using as a base the ideas of the Abbé de Saint-Pierre, Stanislas Leszczynski, the scholarly King of Poland and Duke of Lorraine, wrote in 1748 his *Mémorial de l'affermissement de la paix générale* (Essay on How to Strengthen General Peace), in which he criticised the unchecked sovereignty of states – a source of ambitions, fears, jealousy and conflict – and gave his ideas on a Union of European Republics. A Republic was for him a state in which the supreme

power was restricted by an effective parliamentary institution, along the lines of the Kingdom of England or that of Poland. Clearly, even in divided Europe, many voices called for unity in the name of peace and progress. The dream was still alive.

EUROPE IN SIGHT?

New hopes. At the beginning of the XVIIIth century, the word Europe gradually supplanted that of Christianity. Secularization developed rapidly, the Counter-Reformation having run out of steam. Scientific, philosophical and historical thought developed by leaps and bounds.

The Old World went through a new period of expansion. Wars were less bloody; progress was made in agriculture and medicine, resulting in population growth at a rate not seen since the XIIIth century. The number of inhabitants of Europe rose from 118 million at the beginning of the century to 187 million at the end. The population of towns was increasing at a more rapid rate than the total population, and it was in the towns that the 'take-off' of the West was being prepared. In the space of a few decades economic and social changes took place which led up to the industrial revolution, first in England and then on the continent.

The progress in productivity, trade, navigation and banking was to the advantage first and foremost of the middle class, which became more numerous, richer and better educated. The main consumers of culture, they saw their aspirations and complaints systematised, justified and amplified by innumerable authors. Critical thought was stimulated by Cartesian philosophy and by progress in the exact and human sciences.

This phenomenon was European. A passion for mathematics, physics, chemistry, medicine, astronomy and natural history developed in all the European countries. At the same time, new historical, economic, political and social thought made headway. Philosophers, men who worked to push back the shadows of the past and forge a path to Enlightenment, joined forces in freemasonic lodges whose network spread over the entire Western world.

Like Greek philosophy, Roman law or the Christian message, the new way of thinking was deeply universalist. It seemed to indicate that Europe would be united in the name of Reason. The liberal doctrine of Adam Smith (1723-1790) emphasised the advantages of an international division of labour and called for the abolition of customs barriers. New historical syntheses appeared, which interpreted the past on the scale of a common civilisation rather than of a single country. Their authors demonstrated a clear sense of European patriotism, like the Italian Giovanni Batista Vico (1668-1744), whose theory of the evolution of societies has fascinated many historians. The same can be said for the Englishman Edward Gibbon (1737-1794), author of *The Decline and Fall of the Roman Empire*, who declared: '...A philosopher is allowed to extend his views and to consider entire Europe as a republic of which the inhabitants have all reached more or less the same degree of culture and perfection'. Montesquieu (1689-1755) contested the political philosophy inherited from Machiavelli and clearly revealed his attachment to Europe: 'A prince thinks that he will be made greater by the ruin of a neighbouring state. On the contrary. Things are such in Europe that all states are dependent on one another.... Europe is a state made up of several provinces'. Montesquieu also gave an admirable lesson in European and universalist spirit: 'If I knew that something which was useful to me would harm my family, I would put it out of my mind. If I knew that

something which was useful to my family would not be to my country, I would try to forget it. If I knew that something useful to my country would harm Europe and the human race, I would consider it a crime'.

Ball fan of the Nations of Europe (Cabinet des Estampes, Bibliothèque Nationale, 1733, Paris).

Jean-Jacques Rousseau (1712-1778) took up the scheme of the Abbé de Saint-Pierre, and made a very concise and to-the-point summary of it. Although he did not share all of the views of the ecclesiastical scholar, he was nevertheless very enthusiastic about his project: 'Never has a greater, more beautiful or more useful project occupied the human spirit than that of a permanent and universal peace between all the people of Europe; never has an author more merited public attention than he who proposes the means for implementation of this project...'.

Voltaire (1694-1778), a key figure of the Age of Enlightenment, considered Europe, excluding Muscovite Russia, 'as a kind of large republic divided into several states, some of which are monarchies, others mixed, some aristocratic, some popular: but they all correspond one with the other, they all have the same religious base, although divided into a number of sects, they all have the same principles of public law and of politics, unknown in other parts of the world'. Hundreds of miles from Ferney, where Voltaire lived, the great German historian August Ludwig Schlözer (1735-1809), professor at Göttingen, spoke of Europe in much the same terms. He stressed the deep unity of European civilisation and underlined the contrast between the institutions which protected man against arbitrary rule in the West and those which perpetuated despotism and slavery in other regions of the world.

The intellectual revolution of the Age of Enlightenment and the economic and social changes which accompanied it could not fail to provoke a movement in favour of political change. Calls were made for the abolition of absolute monarchies and of feudalism, for the elimination of all sorts of barriers set up by the state in economic, social and cultural life and for the introduction of guarantees of individual freedom.... In all the countries of the West, the most

enlightened and the most dynamic sectors of the population formed 'patriotic' parties or associations. The meaning of 'patriotic' was, at least until the French Revolution, that defined by Lord Bolingbroke (1658-1751) in his *Letter on the Spirit of Patriotism*, namely more attachment to freedom and to the ideals of the Enlightenment than attachment to one's native land.

Patriotism and Philosophy joined forces in the rejection of religion, and of Catholicism in particular, and of the values of the Middle Ages. Edward Gibbon considered the Middle Ages as the 'triumph of barbarism and religion'. In 1788 Christoph Martin Wieland (1733-1813), one of the most eminent personalities of the Enlightenment in Germany, noted: 'In the biggest and most beautiful part of Europe, the most noble forces of Humanity are still suffocated under the weight of what remains of the barbarian society, of the uncertainty and the errors of a savage and dark millenium'. Rejecting the past, the Patriots called for a social and political order conceived and guided by Reason. Links were established between patriotic groups in the different countries, which formed a sort of European fraternity.

The exhausted, sterile, corrupt and cynical *ancien régime* moved into a very stormy period in the last quarter of the XVIIIth century. Its first defeats took place in North America. The proclamation of independence of the United States, on July 4, 1776, the vote of the Declaration of Rights by the continental Congress of Philadelphia, and the complete failure of the military operations launched by England against the rebels represented a resounding victory for the ideals of the Enlightenment. The European Patriots considered the events in America as their first victory and as a harbinger of a break with the *ancien régime* in their own countries. In a letter to La Fayette, George Washington supported this conviction: 'I see the human race united like a big family by the ties of fraternity. We have sown the seed of freedom and union which will germinate little by little all over the earth. One day, a United States of Europe will be formed on the model of the United States of America.'

The Patriots on both sides of the Atlantic were not wrong. The revolutionary wave had barely subsided in America when it inundated Europe. It shook Ireland and caused a great tension in England. In 1782, it swept away the patrician regime in Geneva and in 1786 chased out the *Stathouder* of the United Provinces. In 1788 it submerged Poland, leading to a radical reform of the social and political structures and resulting in intervention from neighbouring monarchical powers set on stamping out the 'Jacobins of Warsaw'. In 1789 it arrived in Belgium. Shock waves were felt all over the rest of Europe: in Germany, the Hapsburg Empire, Italy and Spain...

The French Revolution was the culmination of this vast process. All Europeans were immensely impressed by the triumph of the elected representatives of the people over the monarchical power in the biggest Western country, by the abolition of the society of 'orders', the introduction of civil equality and the Declaration of Human Rights. The revolutionary power in Paris felt that it had a European mission and believed that it could claim the support of all free men. On May 15, 1790, Robespierre declared to the *Assemblée nationale*: 'It is in the interest of all nations to protect the French nation, since it is from France that freedom and happiness are bound to spread all over the world.' What did the word 'nation', whose meaning changed over the centuries, denote to Robespierre? He understood it as being a social body which has its own existence independently of the monarchical state, within which it has been maturing for centuries. (The nation and the state had already been dissociated by J.-J. Rousseau in his essay *Considérations sur le*

Gouvernement de Pologne, Reflections on the Government of Poland – written in 1772 – predicting that the Polish state would disappear, but announcing prophetically that the Polish nation would survive). The word also meant a social body assembled around the ideals of the Revolution and largely open to anyone who wished to join it.

The French nation, which swept away the absolute monarchy and religious superstition and raised the banner of freedom, equality and brotherhood,

appeared to many Europeans as the incarnation of generosity and hope. In Germany young poets, philosophers and academics – future leaders of Romanticism and of the national movement – such as Arndt, Fichte, Gentz, Görres, Schilling, Schiller, the brothers Schlegel, showed boundless enthusiasm for France or even declared themselves French. The revolutionary powers in Paris were delighted by this show of allegiance. Given the celebrity of Schiller, French citizenship was granted to him by a special act of the Convention.

In order to reply to the expectations of the Patriots, to bring the revolutionary message to the four corners of Europe and to smoke the supporters of the old regime out of their hiding holes, the Convention declared itself ready, by a decree of November 19, 1792, to 'grant fraternity and help to all nations which want to recover their freedom'. The French armies flooded Europe and, thanks to their help, 'sister republics' were proclaimed: Batavian, Helvetian, Cisalpine, Cispadane, Ligurian, Roman, Parthenopean... This evolution fulfilled the hopes of the old Emmanuel Kant which he expressed in his famous work, *Zum ewigen Frieden* (Towards Permanent Peace): '... if, by good luck, a powerful and enlightened nation formed itself into a republic (which must by nature tend towards permanent peace), there would thus be a centre of federal alliance with which other states could join, in order to ensure their freedom, in accordance with the idea of international law, and gradually extend this alliance by other associations of this type'.

Following the example of their French older sister, the new republics abolished serfdom, the privileges of the nobility and the clergy, provincial autonomy and internal customs. They introduced civil equality, freedom of work, unity of the national market and state centralism. Their governments were made up of patriotic groups which were impatient to erase the past and to put into practice the theories of the Enlightenment. The enthusiasm of the social and intellectual renewal and of the fraternity of nations seemed to be the safest guarantee of Europe's unity. But this turned out to be an illusion. French influence and presence in the different countries quickly became onerous and was increasingly felt as the yoke of foreign hegemony, particularly when control of the French Republic passed into the hands of a single man.

When, in 1804, the First Consul Napoleon Bonaparte took the title of Emperor, he voiced his ambition not only to rule France but the entire West. He stated clearly in a letter of January 7, 1806: 'I have not succeeded Louis XVI, but Charlemagne...'. However, there was no room in Europe for two Empires, one issued from the Revolution, based on the Civil Code and backed by the middle classes, and the other incarnating an age-old tradition, the society of 'orders' and faithfulness to the Catholic Church. Conflict was inevitable. The Battle of Austerlitz settled the affair. Francis von Hapsburg, who suffered a crushing military defeat, was forced to give up, on April 6, 1806, the splendid title of Roman Emperor and accept the rather banal one of Emperor of Austria.

Paris became the capital of a European system resting upon a new legitimacy. But the components of this system were reduced to the role of pawns in the dynastical policy of Bonaparte. Certain of the sister republics were incorporated into France. Others were transformed into monarchies, the thrones of which were given to members of Napoleon's family or to his protégés. The immense area controlled by France, which stretched from Madrid to Warsaw and from Naples to Hamburg, included a plethora of satellite states around the hegemonic power. Austria and Prussia, without

The main elements of geographical diversity in Europe: the moor.
France (above) and Scotland...

...The islands: Ibiza. The rivers: the Rhine.

The mountains: the Brenner.

Is perhaps Eastern Europe less European than the West (Buda Castle, Budapest).

Europe is above all a civilisation: Athens, the Acropolis.

*Jerusalem, centre of the 'European' world from 1099 to 1187. On the right:
Charlemagne teaching his son Pepin (Miniature from the archives of Modena
cathedral). Following page: Europeans, builders of cathedrals (Miniature, 1460,
Österreichische Nationalbibliothek, Vienna).*

being simple vassals of Paris, had no choice but to align their foreign policy and, to a certain extent, their domestic policy with those of France. Europe, with the exception of Great Britain and Russia, was politically united.

However, this system suffered from serious defects. It was based on the supremacy of a single state, on arbitrary rule and on coercion. The institutions, copies of French models, often did not correspond to the traditions, culture and aspirations of the various nations. French generals and emissaries had the last say, and decided in accordance with the interests of the hegemonic power. Economic exploitation, conscription, the continual passage of troops, and the brutal repression of any insubordination all culminated to exasperate the nations which had welcomed the French as brothers and liberators. In southern Italy, Spain and the Tyrol, the French presence came up against stubborn resistance, not from the princes, the nobles and the priests but from ordinary people whose beliefs, dignity and property had been violated. Faced with increasing hostility, the French became introverted and regarded others with suspicion. Twenty years after the taking of the Bastille, the Europe of brother nations and sister republics dreamed of by the Patriots was nothing more than a shattered illusion.

Europe of nationalities? The ideas of the Enlightenment aged with their advocates. In the middle of the revolutions and the wars, the new generation looked to new horizons. They welcomed with interest the message of Emmanuel Kant, who demolished Cartesian philosophy and showed the limits of Reason. They listened to the first criticisms of the Revolution, its contradictions and its blind violence, and in particular to those made clearly and implacably by Edmund Burke (1729-1797). The new generation rose against militarism and coercion, symptoms of French hegemony. They did not feel at ease with classicism, favoured by Paris. Idolisation of Reason seemed to be a pretentious, sterile and out-dated attitude.

Intelligence, dedication and youth left the withered universe of the xviii[th] century and united under the banner of Romanticism. Intuition, instinct, feelings and spontaneity seemed to be the fountain of all life, creativity and hopes for the future. The French Republic and Empire had imitated the model of pre-Christian Antiquity in their institutions, language and emblems, architecture, painting and poetry. In contrast, the Romantic generation took as a point of reference the Middle Ages, the age of mystery, courage, loyalty and virtue. This led to a re-discovery of Christianity. The Catholic Church emerged renewed from the trials of the Revolution. The martyrdom and the courage of numerous priests and believers brought them respect and sympathy.

Romanticism was not only a remarkable intellectual and artistic innovation. It was also an explosion of talents rarely seen in history. It changed from top to bottom the cultural and political landscape in Germany, Britain, Spain, Hungary, Italy, Poland, Russia... More particularly, it contradicted the ideological and voluntary French concept of nation with its own idea, based on history and culture, which could be called deterministic. This romantic notion sprang from the ideas of Johann Gottfried von Herder, unveiled in his monumental work *Ideen zur Philosophie der Geschichte der Menschheit* (Ideas on the Philosophy of the History of Humanity), 1784. It was developed by numerous authors, mainly German, at the beginning of the xix[th] century. They argued that nationality was formed by the relief and the climate of the regions which had been its cradle, by millennia of shared experiences and trials. They felt that it reflected the *Volksgeist* (national spirit), which was considered

as being unique and inimitable and was found expressed in the most precious possession of every nation: its language. Man could only attain fulfilment and dignity by assuming his nationality. Cosmopolitanism, as it developed in the xviiith century, was seen as a form of cultural Frenchifying and as a synonym for all that was superficial and frivolous. Ernst Moritz Arndt set off a conceptual revolution when he gave a new definition of the German fatherland: *so weit die deutsche Zunge klingt* (as far as the German language rings out). Romanticism, which had incalculable political consequences, bore at the outset traces of very sincere populist, democratic and humanitarian leanings. It stimulated a passion for historical research and publications and an enthusiasm for ethnographical studies. Innumerable professors, students and artists laboriously itemized the languages, customs, beliefs and legends of country folk, whom they considered to be the real depositary of nationality. The Romantics also believed in fraternity between nations. Herder admired the Slavs and Mme de Staël the Germans, about whom she made the following remark: 'The Germans are like the scouts of the human spirit; they try out new paths, they test unknown means; how can one not be curious to know what they tell on return from their excursions into the infinite?'. The word patriotism took on new meaning everywhere. It no longer signified love of freedom in general, but first and foremost love of the nation, as expressed by the great Italian poet Vittorio Alfieri (1749-1803).

The rediscovery of the Middle Ages brought the Romantics face to face with the idea of a Europe made up of peoples aware of their distinct personality, but joined in spiritual and moral unity. In his essay, *Die Christenheit oder Europa*, the poet Novalis (Friedrich von Hardenberg, 1772-1802) concluded that the decadence and the division of Christianity had been the reason for the division of Europe. He claimed that a religious revival would set Europe back on its feet: 'It was a beautiful and brilliant age when Europe was a Christian land, when a single and unique Christendom ruled on this continent, which was articulated in a human fashion; a single common interest united the farthest-flung provinces of this vast spiritual empire. A single head, stripped of rich temporal possessions, led and united the major political powers.... Princes brought their disputes before the Father of Christendom and willingly placed at his feet their crowns and their splendour...' Wilhelm Josef von Schelling (1775-1854), friend and companion of Novalis, held similar views: '... the true unity can only be brought about through religion. It is not a question of domination of the Church by the state or vice versa, but of the need for each state to develop religious principles in such a way that union of all nations can be founded upon a community of religious convictions'. The brothers August and Friedrich von Schlegel published, between 1803 and 1805, a journal called *Europa* to promote the unity of the West in accordance with Romantic ideas. Mme de Staël, fascinated by the German cultural revival and completely won over by the new interpretation of the Middle Ages, wrote: 'The Crusades united the gentlemen of all countries, and transformed the spirit of knighthood into a sort of European patriotism which filled all souls with the same sentiment'.

Friedrich von Schiller also considered that Christianity was the basis of European unity, but did not interpret this idea in the same way as other German writers, especially of the young generation. Having remained a Protestant – unlike Adam Müller, Wilhelm Josef von Schelling and Friedrich von Schlegel, who became Catholics – he saw the Reformation as a powerful force which had swept away the barriers between the dynastic monarchies and

cleared a path for unity between nations: 'The Reformation broke down the partitions. Stronger, more immediate interest than national interest or love of the fatherland... began to rouse citizens, and even entire states. This interest was capable of creating ties between several states, even those furthest away from one another, whereas these same ties could disappear between the subjects of one state'.

French hegemony in Europe precipitated the crystallisation of national sentiment based on language and culture and was broken by the resistance of people inspired by this sentiment. Post-Napoleonic European leaders were aware of the potency of Romantic ideas. They tried to build a sort of Christian Europe. Their efforts led to the Holy Alliance between Austria, Prussia and Russia, which formed the core of the Quadruple Alliance, with Great Britain, and the Quintuple Alliance, with France. Some of the Romantics supported these initiatives, such as Friedrich von Schlegel and Josef Görres who acclaimed the Holy Alliance as the beginning of a 'European Republic'. But the majority of them were opposed to this system, which they considered as an incarnation of archaism, immobility and repression.

The confrontation with nationalities brought down the Holy Alliance. Nationalist sentiments had become the more powerful that they were now linked either with the ambitions of the middle classes or with the impatience of youth and the frustration of the military, who were cooped up in barracks after earlier glorious campaigns. A network of European secret societies grew up. Some of these, such as the Carbonari, had well-built structures and were able to coordinate their activities at international level. The insurrections which broke out in the 1820s in Naples, Spain, Greece and Russia were a forewarning of the upheaval of 1830. The revolutions which then set alight France, Belgium and Poland in the space of a few weeks demonstrated that Europe was in fact one profound unit of civilisation. The collision between the old and new worlds culminated in a progress of freedom in France and Belgium, but in a regression in Poland.

However, the bloody defeat which the Polish patriots suffered in 1831 in the war against Russia, and the severe repression which followed, did not discourage the advocates of nationalism. They doubled their efforts to overthrow the dynastic states and to free the people, with the end objective of a united Europe made up of free nations. The Italian patriots were in the front line of this combat. For example, Carlo Cattaneo (1801-1869), revolutionary, thinker and scholar, felt that the independence and the unity of his country was only one step on the way towards a 'United States of Europe'. Vincenzo Gioberti (1801-1852) held a similar view. His burning patriotism shone through in all the roles he filled, as priest, writer, diplomat, statesman. 'Europe', he declared, 'studied from the point of view of constitutional law, is at the same level as Italy, relatively speaking; in other words, it is made up of a number of states which require reciprocal union (without however losing their individuality)...' A final and crucial example is provided by Giuseppe Mazzini (1807-1872), a giant of Italian and European history, whose activity and influence made a great contribution to the collapse of the order resulting from the Congress of Vienna and to the birth of a new one. A nationalist theoretician, founder of the secret society *Young Italy*, which was feared by the monarchical powers all over the land, Mazzini created on April 15, 1834 the revolutionary organisation *Young Europe* with several Italian, German and Polish patriots. The aim of this organisation was to prepare for a union of free nations. Mazzini, generally considered as one of the most important fathers of

modern-day nationalism, was an ardent advocate of European union. He declared: 'Without the recognition of freely and spontaneously formed nationalities, there will never be a United States of Europe'.

The majority of German, Polish, Hungarian and Czech Romantic patriots were no different from their Italian counterparts. The great Polish poet Adam Mickiewicz (1798-1855), professor at the College of France, edited the Paris newspaper *Tribune des peuples* (Peoples' Tribune), which promoted both the national and European cause. The revolutions of 1848-49, which were as much a European phenomenon as those of 1830, represented a peak for the national movement.

The dream of harmony between nations gradually evaporated as time and the facts marched relentlessly on. Conflicts and hatreds between nations bubbled up in the whirlpool of revolution. The famous Viennese poet Franz Grillparzer enthusiastically welcomed the beginning of the 1848 revolution – he had long been opposed to the absolute monarchy of the Hapsburgs and was admired by his compatriots as an apostle of freedom – but a few months later he wrote a poem to commemorate the victory of the Austrian Marshal Radetzky over the Italians. The chauvinistic reflex proved to be stronger than solidarity with a people fighting against foreign oppression. The Hungarians who fought for their freedom against the armies of the Austrian Emperor found themselves up against the national aspirations of the Croats and the Romanians, and had to conduct war on two fronts.

Nationalist feelings were soon to reach white heat, leading to conflict everywhere in Europe. Irreconcilable territorial claims, historical memories and myths whipped up by demagogues, and conflicting economic interests kept tension at a dangerous level. In certain countries, where several nationalities had coexisted for centuries, such as the Austrian Empire which became Austria-Hungary in 1867, the class conflict became muddled up with nationalist feeling and accentuated the latter. Sense of national identity and solidarity with people speaking the same language and having the same culture gradually changed into a suspicious and aggressive nationalism. Rivalry between nationalities were similar to the ancient wars of religion and made the conflicts between dynastic monarchies appear as fleeting and benign events.

Moreover, certain statesmen, such as Otto von Bismarck, who basically were indifferent to nationalist feelings, which they considered as the gewgaws of poets, professors and other disreputable people, skillfully interweaved them with the interests of the state. This does not, however, mean that conservative governments were able to manipulate nationalism as they desired. It was a two-way affair. The state machinery, the army and the diplomatic corps absorbed the nationalist ideas and acted in consequence. Moreover, the slant of nationalism changed. At the beginning of the century, it had been populist and humanitarian, but by the end it had become exclusive and bellicose. It seemed to have learnt its lesson from specific historical events, such as the unification of Italy and that of Germany, both carried out by diplomatic trickery and military force rather than by a liberating surge of the people. It had also come under the influence of positivist, or 'scientific,' philosophy and the theories of Charles Darwin. The latter, popularised and projected onto the level of relations between national groups, made it seem that these relations were a continual process of natural selection. According to this type of thinking, war was a 'normal' and permanent phenomenon.

It should be added that nationality, originally understood as the community of language and culture, became at the beginning of the xx^th century

increasingly identified with race. As a result, the concept of nationality was enlarged and phenomena such as Pan-Germanism and Pan-Slavism appeared. Certain nations began to think that they had a world mission to carry out, that they should extend their influence and their culture to other continents, and impose the marvels of their institutions and their lifestyle on the peoples of other civilisations. In this lay the key to conflict and self-destruction.

The run-up to disaster. European socialists very early identified and strongly criticised the contradictions and the dangers of nationalism. Count Henri de Saint-Simon (1760-1825), one of the most famous early socialist thinkers, warned against the dangers of narrow patriotism. In 1814 he proposed in the essay *De la réorganisation de la société européenne* (Reorganisation of European Society), written with Augustin Thierry, that the nations of Europe should be united into a 'single political body'. He suggested creating a common market and a European parliament: 'Europe would have the best possible organisation if all the nations which it embraces, each of which is governed by a parliament, were to recognise the supremacy of a general parliament placed above all their national governments and invested with power to judge their differences'. Saint-Simon was convinced that the unity of Europe was a historical necessity. He gave the following laudable lesson in European spirit: 'The time will no doubt come when all the peoples of Europe will feel that points of general interest must be settled before getting down to questions of national interest; the problems will then become less difficult, troubles will be calmed, wars will die out; this is what we are tirelessly reaching out for; the current of the human spirit is carrying us to this!'.

Pierre-Joseph Proudhon (1809-1865), who placed his talent and intuition at the service of the social revolution, interpreted the awakening of nationalities as an inevitable stage in the evolution of humanity, but constantly warned against its dangers. He saw it as the source of the worst kind of demagogy and blind passion, as a factor which diverted energy from the objective of social liberation, acting as a catalyst of wars and as a handy pretext for refusing liberties or abolishing them. Proudhon bared the weak points in the nationalist theories of Mazzini. The great apostle of Italian independence and unity did claim a united Europe as one of his objectives. But he vehemently refuted the idea of a federalist Italy, as envisaged by Gioberti, and fought all his life for a 'single and indivisible' Italian republic in the Jacobin tradition. According to Proudhon, a federal Europe could only be built from political entities internally organised on federal principles: 'As the unitary system is the opposite of a federative system, so a confederation between large monarchies, and all the more so between imperial democracies, is impossible.... They tend to command, and not to compromise or to obey... It was in accordance with this thesis that I stated, in my last publication, that the first step to be accomplished towards the reform of European public law would be the creation of Italian, Greek, Batavian, Scandinavian and Danubian confederations as a prelude to decentralisation of the big states and to general disarmament. All nationalities would thus recover their freedom and a European balance, desired by all publicists and statesmen but impossible to achieve with big unitary powers, would be brought about'.

Karl Marx (1818-1883) was sceptical about European unification projects which did not include the objective of a proletarian revolution. He was convinced that national differences would become less marked as production and lifestyles were made more uniform and as a world market and international

Unable to contain socialism or nationalism, Bismarck became an obstacle to the emperor's policy and left the government (Drawing by Sir John Teniel, Punch, March 1890).

trade were developed. He saw social revolution as the only way of guaranteeing peace, introducing justice and promoting well-being. In theory, Marxist socialism was a global ideology. In practice, Europe became at the end of the XIXth and beginning of the XXth century the key area of its implantation and development. The movement took on the quality of a new type of European solidarity and seemed to hail the unity of the Old World under the red banner of the proletariat. The creation of the first workers' International in 1864 and the second in 1889, along with their conferences and resolutions, played a very important role in this evolution. The reformist strain gained a great deal of influence in the Marxist movement at the turn of the century, and socialist thinkers and leaders moved closer to pre-Marxist or non-Marxist European thought. It was no longer a question of erasing the past and building the future from a clean slate. In 1906, Karl Renner, one of the leaders of Austrian Social Democracy, wrote in *Grundlagen und Entwicklungsziele der österreichisch-ungarischen Monarchie* (Foundations and Development Objectives of the Austro-Hungarian Monarchy): 'Is an international state entity really beyond our imagination and our age? Will all of Western Europe not soon be obliged to unite to stand up to the Anglo-Saxon, Russian and Asian worlds which are becoming increasingly self-reliant?'

The socialist parties began to win more votes and regularly increased their parliamentary representation in all the Western European countries. Their accession to power by perfectly democratic paths seemed to be only a matter of time. The trade unions allied with the socialist parties moved into the foreground of social and economic life in the European countries and 'industrial solidarity', or coordination of strikes at international level, became a reality. At the dawn of the XXth century it therefore seemed, as Jean Jaurès said, that it was 'the actions of the socialist proletariat which were and would increasingly be the decisive force for the unification of Europe and the world'.

Socialism was not the only movement whose horizons stretched beyond national borders and which rejected the divisions between Europeans. At the end of the XIXth century and the beginning of the XXth, Catholic political parties were born, all rejecting the tenets of liberalism, socialism and conservatism. They fought against the anticlerical policies pursued by a number of governments in the last quarter of the century, but they also called for a fair social order and demonstrated their allegiance to Rome and their nostalgia for Christian Europe of the Middle Ages. They received inspiration from the encyclical *Rerum novarum* (Meeting New Problems) of 1891 and increased their political influence, particularly in Germany and Austria. These parties appeared as the natural allies of the idea of a united Europe.

It is therefore not surprising that at the beginning of the XXth century popular pacifism grew up in Europe. Many voices condemned war, which many people thought to be impossible. The socialists and the Christians of the different countries would surely not prove capable of exterminating one another? Would the governments dare to arm them? The business world also became pacifist, lulled by the internationalisation of production and trade and the interpenetration of national economies. It was believed that the industrialised countries would not go to war with one another because this would amount to economic suicide.

At the beginning of the XXth century Europe was at the peak of its development and prosperity. Its share of world industrial production was around 50%. Its population increased from 187 million in 1800 to 400 million

The Communist Manifesto of Karl Marx and Friedrich Engels in 1848, the first political document ever drawn up in all the official languages of the nine-nation European Community of the 1970s (Gerstenberg Archives, Frankfurt).

in 1900, i.e. at a rate much higher than in the rest of the world. Poverty and illness had been largely wiped out in Europe. It is calculated that purchasing power in Germany, Great Britain and France doubled between 1880 and 1914. The majority of Europeans were able to afford enough food, decent housing, education and medical care. The development of social legislation in the majority of countries offered a minimum of protection and security against the life's risk. Life expectancy, the best indicator of the health of a society, increased spectacularly. Economic and technical progress led to a stabilisation of the number of manual workers and a rapid increase of that of white collar workers. The latter rose in status to approach the middle classes, which were also growing rapidly. This evolution prompted Europeans into believing that progress would be continual, that the possibilities of science and technology were boundless, that standards of living would rise and that Europe would hold onto its leading position on the world stage.

Imperialism – a complex economic, military, cultural and psychological phenomenon – had transformed entire continents and sub-continents into the colonies of a few European states. Europe was the factory, the laboratory, the bank and the university of the world. The modernisation of certain countries, such as Japan, China or Turkey, was nothing other than the acceptance of European models in economic organisation, political and administrative institutions, education, the armed forces, lifestyles and ways of thinking. The world copied Europe, but Europe copied no one.

At the peak of its power and its prosperity, Europe tumbled over the edge, pushed by divisive forces. Pacifist ideas and the prospects of rediscovered unity were only superficial phenomena. Nationalism still held out a vast potential for psychological intoxication, for aggressiveness and destruction. Its forces were at work deep in Europe. It infiltrated economic and cultural life in a diluted

form. It even penetrated the political forces which in theory repudiated it. Did not socialist parliamentarians vote war credits in 1914? Nationalism poisoned relations between states with suspicions and fears, which became permanent obsessions among leaders. It made people believe in the inevitable and salutary nature of war. Nationalism was responsible for the fact that the Sarajevo incident on June 28, 1914, certainly tragic but little different from other such terrorist actions in previous years, blew up into the cataclysm of the First World War.

Europe, which had long been searching for unity, became a battlefield and a heap of ruins. All the European states lost the First World War. Their youth was slain. The cycle of economic growth was broken. Inflation ruined a large part of the population and undermined confidence, the basis of any normal economic activity. The rich became richer and the poor poorer. Optimism was destroyed by the horrors and grief through which Europe had lived. Poverty, despair and bitterness prepared the way for the unleashing of demagogy and the development of totalitarian movements. Years of coercion, arbitrary rule, psychological conditioning through the use of propaganda, and the restrictions imposed upon parliamentary institutions shook the political foundations of the West and opened the way to a serious crisis of democracy. The suicidal conflict between the European states had weakened their position in the world. Exhausted, impaired and anxious, Europe ceased to be a leader and a model for humanity. It began to imitate America.

The most perceptive Europeans realised that the need for Europe to unite in order to prevent further wars and simply to survive was more urgent than ever. The Pan-European movement between the two wars was a demonstration of this. But further cataclysms and regression had to come before the European dream slowly and painfully began to be translated into reality.

SELECTED BIBLIOGRAPHY

René Albrecht-Carrié, *The Unity of Europe*, London, 1966; Fernand Braudel, *Civilisation matérielle, économie et capitalisme, XVe-XVIIIe siècle*, 3 volumes, Paris, 1979; Hendrik Brugmans, *L'idée européenne 1920-1970*, Bruges, 1970; Federico Chabod, *Storia dell'idea d'Europa*, Bari, 1961; Carlo Curcio, *Europa, Storia di un'idea*, 2 volumes, Florence, 1958; Christopher Dawson, *The Making of Europe*, London, 1946; Luis Diez del Corral, *El Rapto del Europa*, Madrid, 1954; Jean-Baptiste Duroselle, *L'idée d'Europe dans l'histoire*, Paris, 1965; Pierre Gerbet, *La construction de l'Europe*, Paris, 1983; Heinz Gollwitzer, *Europabild und Europagedanke*, Munich, 1964; Oscar Halecki, *The Limits and Divisions of European History*, New York, 1950; Denis Hay, *Europe, the Emergence of an Idea*, Edinburgh, 1957; Paul Hazard, *La crise de la conscience européenne, 1680-1715*, 2 volumes, Paris, 1961; Friedrich Heer, *Das Experiment Europa*, Einsiedeln, 1952; Jean Lecerf, *Histoire de l'unité européenne*, 3 volumes, Paris, 1965, 1975, 1984; Georges Livet and Roland Mousnier, edited by..., *Histoire générale de l'Europe*, 3 volumes, Paris, 1980; Jerzy Lukaszewski, *Jalons de l'Europe*, Lausanne, 1985; Salvador de Madariaga, *L'esprit de l'Europe*, Brussels, 1952; Salvador de Madariaga, *Portrait de l'Europe*, Paris, 1952; René Pomeau, *L'Europe des Lumières – Cosmopolitisme et unité européenne au XVIIIe siècle*, Paris, 1966; Louis Réau, *L'Europe française au siècle des Lumières*, Paris, 1951; Pierre Renouvin, *L'idée de fédération européenne dans la pensée politique du XIXe siècle*, London, 1949; Gonzague de Reynold, *Qu'est-ce que l'Europe?*, Fribourg, 1941; Denis de

Rougemont, *Vingt-huit siècles d'Europe*, Paris, 1961; Armando Saitta, *Dalla Res Publica Christiana agli Stati Uniti d'Europa*, Rome, 1948; Dante Visconti, *La concezione unitaria dell' Europa nel Risorgimento italiano*, Milan, 1948; Bernard Voyenne, *Histoire de l'idée européenne*, Paris, 1964; Werner Weidenfeld, ed., *Die Identität Europas*, Munich–Vienna, 1985.

THE INTER-WAR PERIOD,
ZUSAMMENBRUCH
AND AFTER

*

Leo Tindemans

When the guns stopped firing on November 11, 1918, the resulting silence heralded the end of what was known as the 'Great War'. The conflict, which was expected to be a simple victorious march into enemy territory, had lasted more than 50 months. The price paid by Europe was huge. It lost more than 8 million men in battle, and the economic, material and financial infrastructure of the continent was in shreds. The psychological shock of the war was colossal: it was clear that a major chapter of history had been closed and that another was beginning.

THE LEAGUE OF NATIONS

The time had come to organise peace. Attempts were made by the signing of the Peace Treaties at Versailles, Saint-Germain en Laye, Neuilly, Trianon and Sèvres. A parallel can be drawn with the end of the Napoleonic Wars and the 1815 Congress of Vienna. However, there were a number of essential differences. The United States, a major non-European power, played a leading role at Versailles. In 1815, the Treaties of Paris were signed with defeated France, which was able to play a positive part in the 'Concert of Europe'. The situation was radically different in 1919: the Treaty of Versailles was a 'Diktat', a peace imposed on Germany by the victorious allies.

While the fighting was still going on in Turkey and Eastern Europe, a global organisation was set up, the League of Nations. The League's Covenant was

Demonstration in Berlin against the 'violent peace' of Versailles.

incorporated into the five peace treaties signed at the end of the war. The replacement of the Concert of Europe with the League of Nations was significant because it sought hopefully to create a Europe in which the big, almost colonial-type power blocs were replaced by a jigsaw pattern of smaller nation states. It resulted in a Balkanisation of the Old World, and the map of Europe was compartmentalized into 38 states. More than 8,000 kilometres of frontiers were added to those which existed before the war.

The system drawn up to preserve peace in Europe was based upon collective security, arbitration and disarmament. However, achievements were very modest in all three of these fields. The League of Nations was handicapped from birth by the absence of the United States, the Soviet Union and Germany. It rapidly became clear that Franco-German rivalry was at the heart of the European problem. Yet despite the tough peace conditions imposed upon Germany, which included considerable territorial losses, heavy reparations payments, temporary occupation by French troops and a permanent demilitarisation of the Rhineland, rapprochement between the two countries became possible a few years later at the initiative of the French and German Foreign Affairs Ministers.

Versailles, the traumatism of the German people. Demonstration against the reparations payments written into the Young Plan.

STRESEMANN AND BRIAND

Aristide Briand, French Foreign Affairs Minister from April 1925 to January 1932, and Gustav Stresemann, his German counterpart of the Weimar Republic from August 1923 to his death in October 1929, jointly drew up with Great Britain, Belgium and Italy the 1925 Locarno Treaties. Briand and Stresemann were awarded the Nobel Peace Prize for their initiative. Stresemann was perfectly aware of the fact that peace had not been totally won, since no solution had been found to the question of Germany's eastern frontiers. Nevertheless, the 'Locarno spirit' was very significant. It was present once again in August 1928 when the Kellog-Briand Pact was signed, which condemned war as a means of settling disputes between nations. The ideal of a united Europe was fostered at this time.

The outline of this ideal was provided by Richard Coudenhove-Kalergi, who in 1923 published a work on his Pan-European vision. He conjured up a picture of a Europe profoundly changed after the First World War by an internationalist, multiracial and cosmopolitan approach. Coudenhove-Kalergi's united Europe included neither the British Empire nor the Soviet Union. Pan-Europe would, he believed, act as a counterweight to powers such as America, the British Empire, the Slav bloc and the medley of Asian peoples. Count Coudenhove-Kalergi did not give precise details on the internal organisation of Europe, but he nevertheless stated that two representative assemblies should be set up and that the peoples of the European nations should be represented in an egalitarian manner in these. He felt that the nations of continental Europe should first conclude a security pact before proceeding to the creation of a Pan-European customs union and a single economic area. These were the conditions necessary for Europe to play a key role in the world. Coudenhove-Kalergi also tried, with the foundation of the Pan-European movement, to stir up a wave of grass-roots feeling for his ideas. The first positive achievement was the organisation in Vienna in 1926 of the first Pan-European Congress. It was followed by four other such conferences.

Gustav Stresemann addressing the League of Nations, Genève, September 5, 1929.

BRIAND PROPOSES A EUROPEAN UNION

Coudenhove-Kalergi's movement struck a chord with Aristide Briand, who made an enthusiastic yet prudent speech to the Council of the League of Nations on September 5, 1929. He spoke of the need to set up a kind of federal link between the nations of Europe. His proposal was accepted a few days later, and the French Government was given the task of couching it in a memorandum, which was then transmitted to the other 26 member countries. However, the memorandum on the organisation of a European Federal Union was surprisingly vague, both on the pact which should be concluded and on the creation of a mechanism or the definition of a programme and the way it should be implemented. In addition, there were few positive reactions over the next few months. The other 26 European members of the League of Nations debated the French memorandum in the General Assembly in September 1930. The result was the creation of a study committee to examine closely the question of European union. The committee, which was chaired by the Secretary-General of the League of Nations, Sir Eric Drummond, met five times. On March 7, 1932, Europe was deeply shocked by the news of Briand's death. The main creative force behind the project was gone. Briand's proposals had also been thwarted by a series of events. In September 1929, a few days after he put forward his proposal, the Wall Street crash took place on Black Thursday and Tuesday, October 24 and 29 respectively. Moreover, the General Assembly's discussion in September 1930 of Briand's proposals coincided with important electoral victories for the Nazi party in Germany. In the years to come, European life was marked by increasing national economic protectionism and by the emergence of nationalist movements. The totalitarian and dictatorial nature of the latter pushed the idea of European union very much into the background.

Nevertheless, the Briand project, even if it did not get off the ground, was the most representative political initiative in the inter-war period of the ideal of European union. Unfortunately, the ideal was too detached from reality, and many people concluded that the Briand proposal was only pie-in-the-sky, raising questions rather than providing serious answers.

The main questions were as follows: Was it necessary to include in any project the two Euro-Asian nations of the Soviet Union and Turkey? What

Richard Coudenhove-Kalergi, founder of the Pan-European Union, inspires Aristide Briand (photo autographed on October 14, 1929).

The break-up of Germany to supply French industry.

Slide of the Locarno Conference (October 1925).

were the extra-European responsibilities of the participating states? Should priority be given to political or to economic activities? In what way would the European institutions function? Should a representative 'European conference' be set up or an executive 'Permanent Political Committee' aided by a secretariat? All these questions give an inkling of the major concern of officials at the time, namely: how could European union be set up when the nation states wanted at all costs to preserve absolute national sovereignty?

THE RUN-UP TO THE WAR

While their dream was never translated into reality, a number of leading figures expressed their views on how a now compartmentalised Europe should have been unified after the First World War. For example, proposals of this type were made by the Luxembourg industrialist Emile Mayrisch, the French Minister Louis Loucheur and the Britons Arthur Salter and A. Duff Cooper. An Action Committee for a European customs union was also created. A number of leading political writers tried to promote the European idea. In French intellectual circles, magazines such as *'Esprit'* (Spirit) and *'L'Ordre nouveau'* (The New Order) were published. Denis de Rougemont, Robert Aron and Alexandre Marc were among the notable contributors. The impact of works by Gaston Riou *('Europe ma Patrie'* – Europe my Fatherland), Count Sforza *('The United States of Europe')*, Bertrand de Jouvenel *('Vers les Etats-Unis d'Europe'* – Moving towards the United States of Europe), Edouard Herriot *('Europe')* and other well-known names is difficult to quantify, but was considerable. And yet, the perception of the world held by these writers was in stark contrast to the realities of the time. 1936 was a crucial year in which people became generally convinced that the First World War had been no more than the first episode in a new 'Thirty Years' War', and that Europe was again to be swept into the throes of fratricidal conflict. Numerous Europeans tried to shake off this pessimism for a while. After all, they thought, was not the Munich Agreement (1938) the symbol of Hitler's desire for peace? The pacifist movement, symbolised by the 'broken rifle', became increasingly convinced that combatting the economic crisis was preferable to arming one's country.

Unfortunately, the pessimists' fears proved to be well-founded, and peace soon gave way to a terrifying massacre which lasted for five years. The western

The great deception of Munich (Hitler, Mussolini, Chamberlain, Goering in September 1938 in the Bavarian capital).

world seemed to be heading towards suicide. Only five countries were spared the conflict that drew in all of Europe from the Pyrenees to Moscow, from North Cape to Northern Africa. Europe became one big slaughterhouse. In our imaginations today we try to reduce this unprecedented catastrophe to the uniquely legal concepts of war crimes, crimes against peace and against humanity. However, even at the darkest moment of these sombre times, the small flame of the European dream continued to burn. Some people, such as Hendrik De Man, Pierre Daye and Francis Delaisi, even believed that the violent action of Adolf Hitler could result in European union. They were blinded by their convictions, for Hitler never wanted a federal Europe. His propaganda only exploited an attractive idea. His only goal was domination by the German Reich and all his conquests and annexations were linked to this objective.

A NEW DAWN

On the other side of the barrier were the Resistance movements. They found the courage, in extremely difficult circumstances, to reflect on Europe's future after the war. A famous example of this is the Ventotene Manifesto, which takes the name of the island where a large number of Italian opponents to fascism were imprisoned. The names of Ernesto Rossi and Altiero Spinelli have become inseparable from the Manifesto. The Manifesto was the achievement of a meeting organised in May 1944 in Geneva between representatives of the Resistance movements of Norway, Denmark, France, Italy, the Netherlands, Poland, Czechoslovakia, Yugoslavia and Germany. The Manifesto notably stated that freedom and civilisation could only be preserved on the European continent by the creation of a federal union. However, the Resistance movements worked in difficult circumstances, and the activities of some of them were limited to the national level. Others were torn by growing tension between Communist and anti-Communist trends. Their initiatives nevertheless had a decisive impact.

In London, which was the haven of a number of governments in exile, ideas on the organisation of peacetime society, which no longer seemed so distant, also flourished. The Polish General Sikorski and his colleague Jozef Retinger played a key role in discussions of the subject. However, the initiative of the Belgian Foreign Affairs Minister, Paul-Henri Spaak, had a more lasting result,

since it was at the basis of what subsequently became the Benelux economic union between Belgium, the Netherlands and Luxembourg.

It is striking to note that intellectual circles, Resistance movements and governments in exile all felt an overwhelming need to unify Europe.

When arms were finally laid to rest, men were again able to speak of reason, hope and ideals. Europe could not escape learning the lessons of the disastrous war. The entire continent had been the victim of unforgettable violence and unimaginable destruction. Europe emerged from this hell deeply shocked and faced with the vacuum which comes after the collapse of a system. There were legitimate fears that the Nazi dictatorship, which had been defeated at the price of enormous sacrifice, would be replaced by a Stalinist dictatorship. Europe was the melting pot for all the ideas, but the decisions were taken outside of its borders: in Moscow, Teheran, Yalta. After having ruled the world for centuries, Europe was itself divided into spheres of influence. The division of the Old World was the price which had to be paid to deliver Europe from tyranny.

However, the dream got a fresh chance. The signing of the Franco-British Treaty at Dunkirk in March 1947 was an unequivocal signal. This Treaty seemed to go much further than a simple extension of the 'Entente Cordiale'. Churchill's brave proposal, on June 15, 1940, for the creation of a Franco-British union, will never be forgotten. He suggested that defence, foreign policy, financial policy, the economy and citizenship should be united. This proposal unfortunately came too late, for French capitulation to Germany had already become inevitable.

The famous British diplomat Duff Cooper believed that the Treaty of Dunkirk laid the foundations of a European federation. However, his vision was much too large for that period in time. He saw Europe as including an African and Atlantic aspect. The hidden message behind this concept, which can justly be called 'grandiose', was not perceived by politicians.

'RATHER LIKE THE UNITED STATES OF EUROPE'

Winston Churchill had perfectly understood the new international reality. On March 5, 1946, he gave his famous speech at Fulton in the United States, when he spoke about the 'iron curtain' dividing Europe from Szczecin to Trieste. A few months later, on September 19, 1946, he gave a speech in Zurich which shook Europe. On this occasion, he called for the constitution of a federation

Europe ruined by the war.

which would be rather like the United States of Europe, of which Great Britain, the British Commonwealth, the United States and, if possible, the Soviet Union would be the friends and protectors. Again in September 1946, the first meeting of the European Federalists Union was held in the Swiss town of Hertenstein. Within this group, the dream of a united Europe had remained intact. Moreover, their vision of a united Europe still included both the Eastern and Western blocs, which would hold peaceful sway between the two superpowers. Less than one year later, in August 1947, the leaders of the movement were obliged to face up to reality and to reduce their objective to a united Europe without the Eastern bloc, but not against it.

There were a number of other initiatives at this time. Paul van Zeeland, one-time Belgian Prime Minister, founded in 1946 the European Economic Cooperation League, and Churchill formed in London in 1947 the United Europe Committee, chaired by Duncan Sandys. Count Coudenhove-Kalergi spent the entire war period in New York, and it was there that he organised in May 1943 the fifth Pan-European Congress. He decided to set up the European Parliamentary Union, which held its first conference in Gstaad, Switzerland, in September 1947.

Another change was seen in the fact that unification had become a priority for almost the entire European ideological spectrum. In 1947 a 'Socialist Movement for the United States of Europe' and the Christian Democrat 'Nouvelles équipes internationales' were formed.

However, this division of forces sapped the vitality of the movement for a united Europe. It was felt that there was a need to harmonise the activities of these groups and movements. As a result, the 'International Committee of Movements for a United Europe' was formed in Paris in 1947, again chaired by Duncan Sandys. All the various movements worked together within this committee to organise the European Congress in The Hague from May 8-10, 1948. It gave birth to the European Movement, its coordination body. This time, Europeans seemed to have learnt the lessons of the past. The dream had a chance of being translated into reality. Its geographical scale had been sharply reduced, but its advocates were at least able to get together in a democratic Europe to work in safety and peace towards the realisation of their ideal.

THE GEOGRAPHICAL NOTION
OF EUROPE
OVER THE CENTURIES

*

I. B. F. Kormoss

ORBIS TERRARUM DEMINUTA (1)

'We no longer inhabit the same planet as our ancestors: their world was immense, ours is small. For the first time in the history of our species, it is no longer true that land stretches 'as far as the eye can see'. Our earth in its entirety can be appraised in an inkling, it has been encaptured by photography, and the image of our family home can now be placed side by side with the image of our collective home. We become caught up in a spiral of expansion if we count the earth's people, but surveyed from afar the earth is perceived in a much narrower light'. (see B. de Jouvenel, Arcadie: 'Essais sur le mieux vivre' (Essays on a Better Life), Paris, Futuribles, 1970, p. 66).

This observation was made in 1959 at a time when the first satellite photographs taken in outer space were published. It marked the beginning of a new age in which mankind would have a new perception of space, of the physical area in which he could let his imagination wander.

Homo faber began his conquest of his living environment on a two-dimensional basis: progress was slow and difficult, and lasted from the prehistoric age into the twentieth century. Development went outwards in concentric waves around the original primitive settlements. The pace of development was determined by a combination of climatic changes and by the need to find food and ensure defence: primitive man moved gradually towards a communal lifestyle dictated by religious and civil powers.

The rate of advance depended upon the ease with which men came to perceive and understand the space in which they lived: this related to the level of technological development, and especially to means of transport and communication and instruments for measuring or magnifying objects. First on foot, then on horseback, next as a navigator, and finally as an astronaut, man gradually refined and developed his scientific instruments: for example, early on he measured things with rudimentary lenses, and later on he detected objects at vast distances by using the remote sensing properties of thermic waves.

De Jouvenel's 'narrowing' of perception is most clearly seen in the notion of *time*, of which *space* has become a function. The time factor has been reduced to zero for telecommunications. Television viewers throughout the world were able to watch at the moment it happened, on July 21, 1969 ,the landing on the moon of the American astronauts. Motive power (wind, river and muscle) was the only means of passenger and goods transport for millenia, but the steam engine arrived in 1830, upsetting rural life. It marked the beginnings of urbanisation and industrialisation and introduced notions such as speed and payloads and the quest to find ways of increasing them.

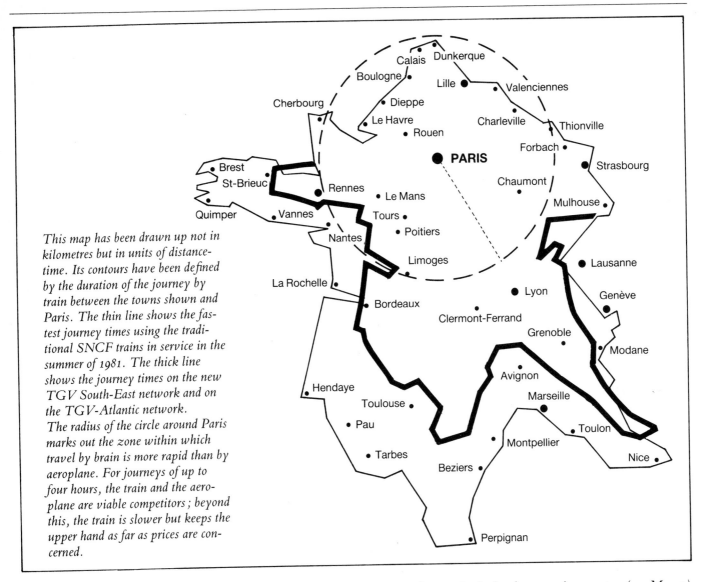

The map contains the following labels:

Calais, Dunkerque, Boulogne, Lille, Valenciennes, Cherbourg, Dieppe, Charleville, Thionville, Le Havre, Rouen, Forbach, Strasbourg, PARIS, Chaumont, Brest, St-Brieuc, Rennes, Le Mans, Mulhouse, Quimper, Vannes, Tours, Nantes, Poitiers, Lausanne, Limoges, Genève, La Rochelle, Lyon, Bordeaux, Clermont-Ferrand, Grenoble, Modane, Hendaye, Avignon, Marseille, Toulouse, Toulon, Pau, Montpellier, Nice, Tarbes, Beziers, Perpignan

This map has been drawn up not in kilometres but in units of distance-time. Its contours have been defined by the duration of the journey by train between the towns shown and Paris. The thin line shows the fastest journey times using the traditional SNCF trains in service in the summer of 1981. The thick line shows the journey times on the new TGV South-East network and on the TGV-Atlantic network.
The radius of the circle around Paris marks out the zone within which travel by brain is more rapid than by aeroplane. For journeys of up to four hours, the train and the aeroplane are viable competitors; beyond this, the train is slower but keeps the upper hand as far as prices are concerned.

1 / The map of France re-written by the high-speed train.

Countries and continents shrank, particularly along major routes *(see Map 1),* such as the Paris-Bordeaux-Hendaye and Paris-Strasbourg axes in France. This 'concentration' is continuing, and may even be accelerated by the introduction of high-speed trains on the Paris-Lyon-Lausanne/Geneva/Marseilles line, and on the Paris-Le Mans-Brittany and the Paris-Tours-Bordeaux-Hendaye lines. The railways changed the face of Europe in the space of 120 years, reaching their peak of expansion in 1950 *(Map 2)*. The railway network created several 'Europes', varying according to population density. The highest density was to be seen in Rhineland Europe and in Great Britain.

ORBIS ROMANUS: VIAE (2)

Archeological digs have revealed that the Roman roads which existed 1,800 – 1,900 years ago went one better than modern railways by standardising 'technical specifications'. (Nineteenth century European railway tracks were of assorted widths). The roads formed a close-knit and balanced network from Iberia through Gaul, Germania, Dalmatia and Macedonia to Asia Minor, and from Italy and through the Mediterranean islands as far as Mauritania,

Numidia and 'Africa Proconsularis', which now forms the Maghreb countries *(Map 3)*.

This allowed a definition of Europe comprising the entire Mediterranean basin, and a large 'hinterland' in current-day Tunisia and Algeria. However, it was a Europe limited to the north by two of the main rivers of our continent: the Danube and the Rhine, roughly linked between the present-day towns of Regensburg and Koblenz by the *limes* (Roman fortified frontier).

The Danube (*Ister* or *Istros* in antiquity) and the Rhine, which were the 'boundaries' of *one* integrated world, have since become major axes of *two* separate worlds, each in the process of their own integrations. The Danube is of vital importance for the South-West regions of COMECON (the USSR has been a Danubian country since 1945, following the annexation of Bessarabia), and the Rhine for the North-West continental regions of the Common Market. But this is as far as the analogy goes. The Rhine, a 'de jure' (Mannheim Act) and 'de facto' international river, flows into the North Sea, a key outlet for commerce and industry and an arm of the Atlantic. The Danube, on the other hand, is a 'de jure' but not 'de facto' international river, which flows into the

2 / *The very high density of the European rail network around 1950.*

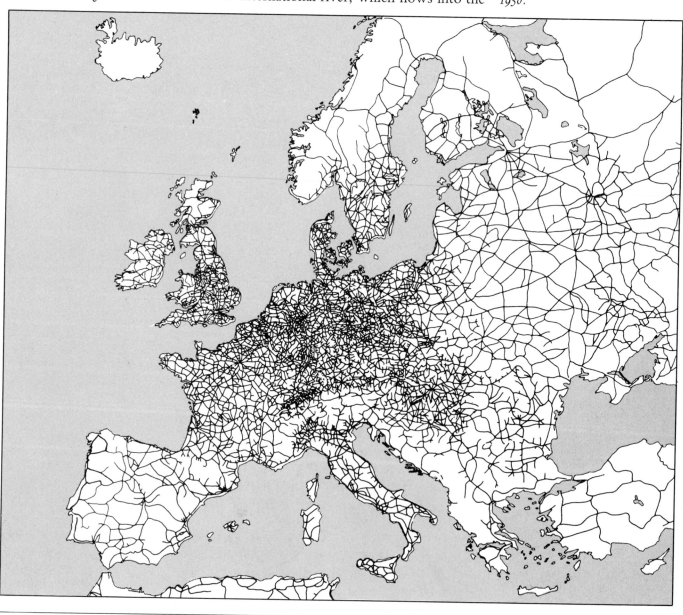

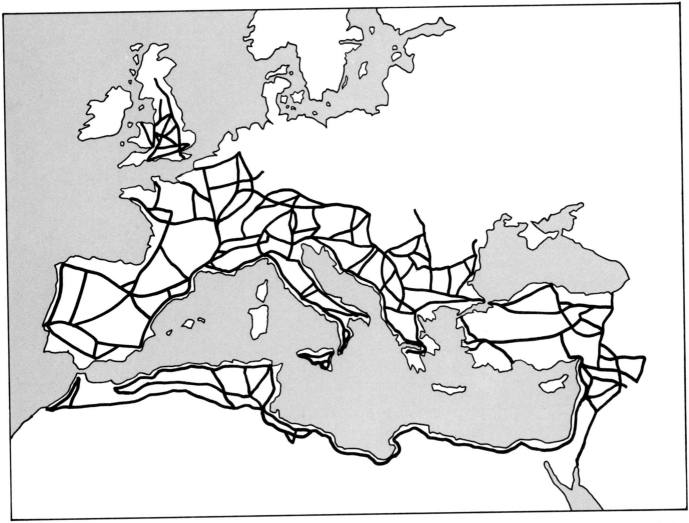

3 / The Roman imperium, unified by a close-knit and balanced network of roads.

Black Sea, hemmed in at two points by nature (the Bosphorus and the Dardanelles towards the Mediterranean and the Straits of Gibraltar or Suez towards the oceans) and by politics *(see Maps 8, 1963)*.

The ancient northern Rhenish border skirted the current site of Frankfurt (am Main) along the crests of the Taunus hills, before following the river to the South and then the line of the Neckar River towards the east between Stuttgart and Aalen. Located at strategic points along the Orbis Romanus, these densely populated regions now contain the towns of Rhein-Mainz, Rhein-Neckar and Stuttgart, with respectively 2.1, 1.0 and 1.9 million inhabitants, situated on the vital north-south axis of the Federal Republic of Germany.

Hadrian, who set the Rhenish border, also built *vallum Hadriani* (Hadrian's Wall) protecting 'Britannia Inferior' against the Picts inhabiting that part of northern Britain which is now the European nation of Scotland. All these borders defined in Roman times helped define the future shape of Europe. They were not always precise lines on a map or judicially defined, but were what one author described as 'subtle barriers richer in geographical virtues than in military significance, marking the zone where the West came up against the East, settlers against nomads.'(3) Further eastwards, Vidal de la Blache wrote of the Volga as being a barrier between 'the home of sedentary society and groups verging towards the unstable...the boundary marking the petering out of *civilised Europe*'.

'Europe: also called Eury-ôpé, which is close to Eury-ôpis. According to the word boôpis, Euryôpis should mean 'having a wide span of vision'. Others consider that the name Europe, like all the names which end in -ôpé, is a woman's name'.
Thesaurus, by Henricus Stephanus (5).

'In the same way as no-one knows whether Europe is surrounded by water or not, a mystery shrouds the meaning and the origin of the name. It is possible that the name was taken from the Tyrian Europa.... But it is certain that this Europa came from Asia and that she never set foot in the land which the Greeks now call Europe. She went only from Phoenicia to Crete and from Crete to Lycia'. Herodotus, Histoires IV, 15 (6).

The division of the globe into three parts was accepted by Herodotus, despite his preference for a two-continent system, in which Asia (including Africa, or Ancient Libya) would represent the East, the Persians and the Barbarians, and Europe would represent the West, the Greeks...the civilised world (7). The division into three continents was not, however, clear cut. The dividing line between Asia and Africa lay somewhere between the Suez Isthmus and the Nile River. However, the dividing line between Europe and Asia was even less well defined.

This triple subdivision of the 'Old World' is frequently used by the authors of *Orbis Christianus*, of whom Isidore de Séville is the most frequently quoted. The symbol of the unity between the three continents is provided by the so-called O-T map *(see Map 4)*. It is made up of a circle with the cardinal points

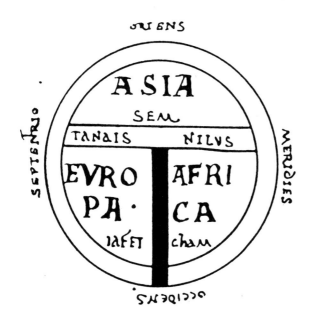

4 / The so-called 'O-T map' in the XIth manuscript of Saint Isidore.

Occidens-Septentrio-Oriens-Meridies, within which is another circle sub-divided into three by the rivers Tanaïs and Nilus. The rivers separated Asia and the two 'Mediterranean' continents: represented between Europe and Africa was the important but almost entirely land-locked sea, often called Mare Nostrum by the Romans (8).

The three continents are identified by the three sons of Noah, on the basis of Genesis (Chapters 9 and 10) and of the 'Civitate Dei' of St. Augustine, according to the meaning in Hebrew of the three names. Shem = nominatus (the named or the chosen), Japheth (width, enlarged) and Ham = calidus (fiery-tempered, impatient rather than wise) (9). The glossators of the Roman and Christian classics interpreted the reaction of the sons when Noah got drunk to apply value judgements to the continents, to the advantage of Japheth (Europe) and the disadvantage of Ham (Africa).

Many links still remain in mythology between Europe and Asia; the example of the 'abduction of Europa' is generally well known. However, details provided by Herodotus about Europa are less familiar. She came from Tyre (Tyrian, see quote above) in Phoenicia (currently the town of Sür in Lebanon, close to the border with Israël). From there she went to Crete, and from Crete to Lycia, the large peninsula of Asia Minor (= Turkey) between Rhodos (Rhodes) and the town of Altalea (Antalya).

It is tempting to interpret Europa's voyages as marking major steps in a system of settled land ownership and in the evolution of societies from the Fertile Crescent, situated between the Eastern Mediterranean coast (Phoenicia, Assyria) and Mesopotamia (Babel = Babylon), through the Minos culture (Minos being the son of Zeus and Europa) and the plateau of Asia Minor (Miletus, Troy) into island and peninsular Greece. Geographically *(see Map 3)*, the island of Crete is at the intersection of the dividing lines between the three continents. Politically and culturally long before the Romans and their 'Mare Nostrum', the Phoenicians and the Greeks had the Mediterranean world well under control, and even extended their influence beyond it to Gadez (= Cadiz), Tingis (Tangier), which were west of the Pillars of Hercules in the Atlantic, and to Istros (Constanta), Olbia (Odessa), and Theodosia (Yalta) to the east of the Bosphorus on the 'Pontos Euxeinos' (= Black Sea).

A pre-European division of the world existed. The Northern coasts of the Mediterranean east of Sicily fell into the Greek sphere of interest. The South and the East were in the Phoenician area, excluding Kyrene (Cyrenaica) and the delta of the Nile. The Phoenicians and the Greeks were 'face-to-face' in Sicily and South-East Spain (present-day Valencia, Alicante, Carthage), an omen of the confrontation between Rome and Carthage four centuries later.

Geographers had their own view of Europe. Strabo, a romanised Greek contemporary of Augustus and author of a complete 'Geography' in 17 volumes, adopted a highly modern approach. He interpreted geography according to human factors, with the environment, history, civilisation and the 'wisdom' of governments closely interacting. He wrote:

The Parthians and the Romans, by their conquests, have greatly widened our geographical knowledge. It had already been greatly enriched by the expedition of Alexander. Indeed, Alexander was responsible for discovering the greater part of what we now know as Asia, and of northern Europe up to Istros. But we owe our knowledge of all the western parts of Europe, to the Elbe which cuts Germania in two, and the regions which extend beyond Tyra to the Romans.... Finally, it is thanks to the Parthians that the lands occupied by the Scythians, of which previously little was known, are now better documented (10).
Let us speak first of all of Europe. Firstly because this part of the globe has the greatest variation of form, due to the climate, which is kind to industry and favourable to civilisation. Secondly because it imparts the greater part of its own advantages to the two others.

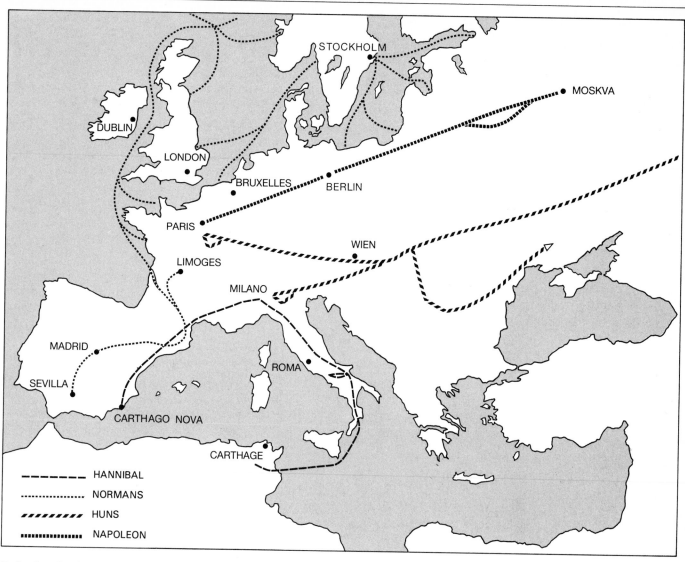

– – – – –	HANNIBAL	
··············	NORMANS	
//////////	HUNS	
▪▪▪▪▪▪▪▪▪▪	NAPOLEON	

Indeed, all of Europe is inhabited, apart from a small section which has remained deserted because of very low temperatures... The Greeks, by their wisdom of government, by their skill in the arts and their understanding of all the things which contribute to the goodness of life, have transformed the mountains and rocky hillsides which they occupy into flourishing settlements.

In a similar way, the Romans first conquered a people, often naturally very ferocious, ...then built up social relationships with people who up until then had been unsociable. They finished by civilising the most barbarian....

5 / *Hannibal, the Normans, the Huns, Napoleon: similar spans.*

To put Strabo into twentieth-century language, military conquest and development of land use, socio-economic and cultural institutions are the factors which mark out Europe.

Hannibal ante portas / A furore Northmannorum libera nos domine

The organisation of the *Orbis Romanus*, the extent of which can be seen on *Map 3* (under Hadrian, Emperor from A.D. 117-138), was not built in a day...nor even in a century. For a time, Carthage challenged Rome and had, in Hannibal,

one of the most impressive military geniuses in history, whose 'punica fides' (trickery, skulduggery) perplexed the Romans. He left Carthago Nova (now Carthage) in the winter of 219/218 B.C. with 40,000 men, including 10,000 cavalry and 38 elephants. He crossed the Ebro, the Pyrenees by the Perthus pass (where a motorway now lies), and then the Rhone, with the elephants on makeshift rafts covered with earth. Then he went up the Durance valley, and crossed the Alps in October 218 by the Geneva pass (1,850 m), which was covered with snow. Hannibal and his army marched in all about 2,500 km, the distance between Paris and Moscow covered by Napoleon in 1812-1813; *(see Map 5).*

The later *Orbis Christianus* was attacked by, among others, the *Huns*, who retreated towards the Don after the death of Attila in 453, and the *Arabs*, who, after having been beaten back at Poitiers in 732, kept their hold for eight centuries over certain parts of Spain. These attacks followed the division of the Orbis Christianus by Theodosius in 395.

The Empire of *Charlemagne* spread outwards from an initial core, extending over the territory roughly covered by the 1952 European Coal and Steel Community – excluding Brittany, Mezzogiorno, but including Switzerland and Austria. (*See Maps 8* comparing the years 800 and 1963). The prayer 'Oh Lord, save us from the violence of the Normans' was said many a time by nervous peasants anticipating Norman 'enlargement' towards the North and the East. The Normans, the Vikings and the Varangians all threatened and pillaged Charlemagne's empire, but they also traded with it. In a chapter with the evocative title 'La Sédentarité vaincue' (Defeat for the Settlements), Maurice de Lannou describes in his book, 'Europe, the promised land (pp. 156-159), the advance of these 'Barbarians' beyond the British Isles, the fringes of the Atlantic and the Mediterranean into the immense Russian plains, moving along the lines of the great rivers between the Baltic ports and the Black Sea (*see Map 5*).

Meanwhile, the Hungarians who, like the Huns came from the steppes of the East and were other victims of a frightened prayer, 'A sagittis Hongarorum libera nos Domine' (11) also settled and became Christians. As a result, Europe in the year 1000 (*see Maps 8*) included a large part of Scandinavia, excluding present-day Finland and the Lapp regions, a large part of western Russia, excluding Lithuania, the lands of the Pruzzes (to become the Prussians) and the territories of the Petchénègues (Siberian nomads) coinciding with what are modern Ukraine and Moldavia.

REX PATER EUROPAE, REX KAROLUS...
EUROPAE VENERANDUS
APEX (12)

The idea of an exact European 'core' as applied to the empire of Charlemagne was less clear-cut in the Middle Ages. Charlemagne, who was the Emperor of the West, reigned over lands which corresponded with the heritage of the Orbis Romanus, later to be transformed into an Orbis Christianus. There seems to have been a sense of identity between the two 'worlds', the ancient empire and the new one, summed up much later by Gregory VII in the eloquent phrase: 'Quibus imperavit Augustus, imperavit Christus'.

In the Empire, which some were beginning to call Europe, the princely rulers could not neglect the material and food needs of their subjects. When the

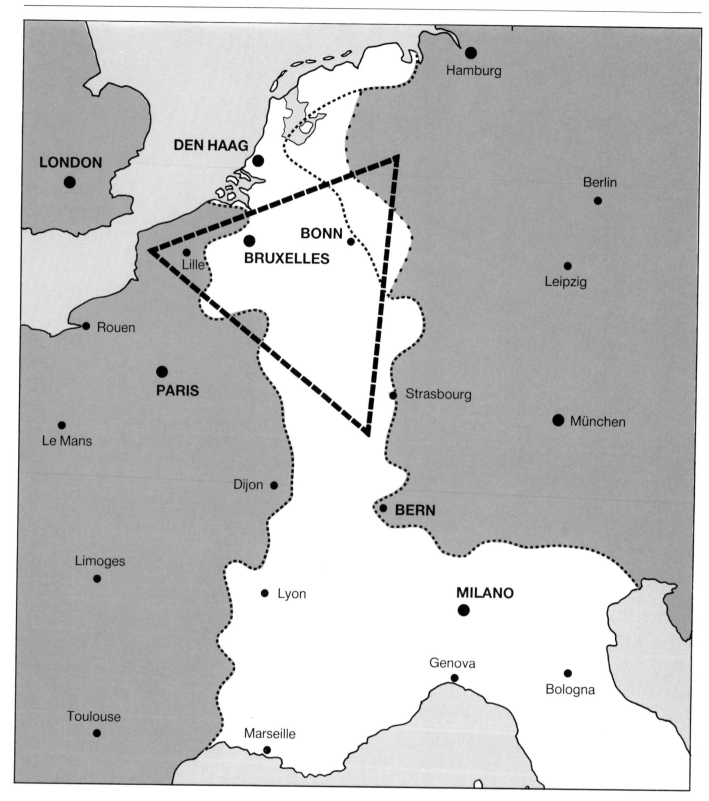

empire inherited from Charlemagne was divided by the Treaty of Verdun in 843, one of the main reasons for demarcating Lothair's share along the Rhine and southwards (13) was 'Propter vini causam'. Although Lotharingia only had an ephemeral existence as Europe's Middle Empire (843-870), it was located very favourably on the big isthmus between the North Sea and the nearest part of the Mediterranean coast (where Marseilles and Genova were the

6/'Lotharingia', geographical base of the ECSC.

leading ports and trade centres of the Western Mediterranean). The importance of the Rhine as a communication link cannot be over-emphasised. The ports of 'industrial Lotharingia' – the Dunkirk-Amsterdam belt passing through Zeebrugge, Ghent, Antwerp and Rotterdam – handle almost two-thirds of all modern continental EEC goods traffic. Moreover, its direct hinterland (*see Map 6*) is the 'heavy' triangle of the ECSC, the industrial base for the first stage of European integration.

Did this integration not, in fact, take place before its legal consolidation? This goes also for the Danube basin, in the form of the Austro-Hungarian empire. The Danubian Common Market was certainly not on the same scale as the EEC, but its socio-economic structures were as diverse, if not more so. It underwent strong economic growth at the end of the XIXth and beginning of the XXth centuries, but was not able to resist the centrifugal forces of its various nationalities during the First World War.

The Danube integration – *one* of several possible regional integrations – was an example of Europe in miniature.

✳

'Geographers in African maps
With savage pictures fill their gaps
And over unhabitable downs
Place elephants, for want of towns'. (Jonathan Swift)

'Euro-centrism' was certainly not the philosophy of the Middle Ages, which had inherited the concept of a tripartite world, symbolised on O-T maps (14) by Rome for Europe, Jerusalem for Asia and Carthage for Africa. However, the idea of a 'core' supposed outlying areas, which were less well perceived by authors and described rather imaginatively by cartographers, prompting the biting lines by Swift (1667-1745). What was true for Africa was also true for the polar regions, which were still circumspectly indicated (zona frigida ex parte poliartici) to the North-East of Europe in 1554 on the map of the world drawn up by the Portuguese Lopo Homen. Even the polar map dating from 1598 drawn up by W. Barents, who died on the arctic island of 'Nova Zembla' (now Novaya Zemlya) which he had just discovered, used only whales and compass cards to depict lands beyond the river Ob. A map of the same region (Septentrionalium Terrarum Descriptio) drawn up in 1595 by the younger son of G. Mercator, Rumold, is much more explicit. It has the inscription 'Asiae Pars' for the territories lying east of the mouth of the Ob.

There are almost 3,000 km (as the crow flies) between the mouth of the Ob and the mouth of the Don, which marked the southern limit between Europe and Asia for almost two millenia (from Herodotus to the XVIth century). Arguably, a comprehensive boundary between Europe and Asia could have been defined by a line beginning at the mouth of the Ob and ending at the mouth of the Don, just as the Orbis Romanus was separated from the 'Barbarians' along the 2,100 kilometre boundary between the months of the Rhine and Danube. But, in the end, no real boundary separates Europe from Asia, nor Asia from Africa. As Gonzague de Reynold (15) put it: 'The Arab world rubs shoulders with two continents, in the same way as the Russian world extends into Europe and Asia. Between Europe and Asia, Asia and Africa, Africa and Europe are intermediary, grey areas. Russia is a Euroasia; Spain, a Euroafrica; Egypt, a sort of Afrasia'.(16) The following summary of the formation of Europe was made by de Reynold:

The Europeans came from Asia. They brought with them the material base of our civilisation: wheat and its settled lifestyle. We owe them...domestic animals, agriculture, our first society....They prompted our transition from the savage to the barbarian state, then from the barbarian to the semi-civilised....The three big families of the European world, the Latins, the Germanics and the Slavs, then grew up.... History began.... From this moment onwards, Europe existed. It was not only a peninsula of Asia, but a daughter of Asia.

'FLORIDA... NOSTRA EUROPA NON MULTO INFERIOR' (17)

In America, there are 17 towns named London, 16 Paris, 14 Berlin, 14 Carthage, 13 Athens, 12 Berlin, 11 Brunswick, 8 Amsterdam, etc....

The circumnavigation of the oceans embarked upon by the Portuguese Admiral Magellan (1519-21) and completed, after his death in the Philippines in 1522, by del Cano provided material proof that the earth was round. The adventure of Magellan and del Cano was an extraordinary one, as unique as that of John Glenn and his fellow astronauts four centuries later. Both endeavours were achievements for technology and teamwork, although Glenn and company were able to return with visual proof of a third dimension inaccessible to Magellan.

The discovery of America and the colonisation of the 'terrae incognitae' was the work of Europeans – Portuguese, Spaniards, Italians, French, Dutch, British, Scandinavian: their exploits were the beginning of a 'Europe without frontiers' when Florida, Hispaniola and other new lands were taken advantage of to the full by Europeans.

A parallel can be drawn between the Westward advance of the U.S. and Canadian borders and the discovery and 'Europeanisation' eastwards of Siberia. Thus has Europe diffused outwards by great treks to the West and the East...

7/Map of J. Schöner (Nürnberg, 1523), describing the circumnavigation of Magelhaens.

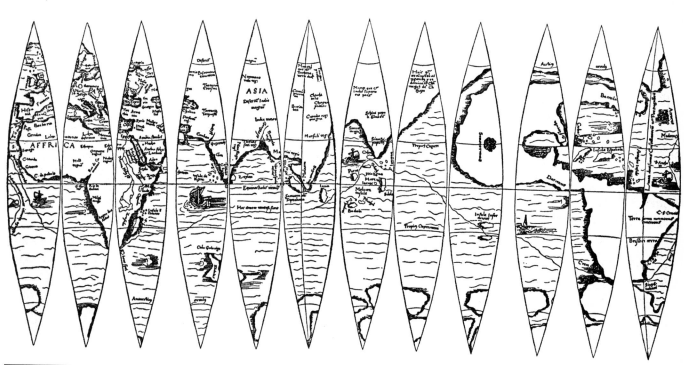

The idea of mankind's endeavours constantly radiating outwards from a European geographical core cannot be permanently sustained. Modern cosmonauts take off into space from Florida and Siberia, not from the West coast of Scotland, the Jutland Peninsula or the Spanish plains. But European intellectual and spiritual roots can be traced even in these challenging modern explorations, and the idea of the maps attached to this essay is to illustrate that, in the end, Europe is much more than a geographical notion. Its physical boundaries have fluctuated throughout time and there have been scarcely any limits to its maritime expansion, but ultimately Europe's boundaries are intellectual ones, determined by the degrees of influence and authority it wields in the world.

8 / Europe: a changing geographical notion.

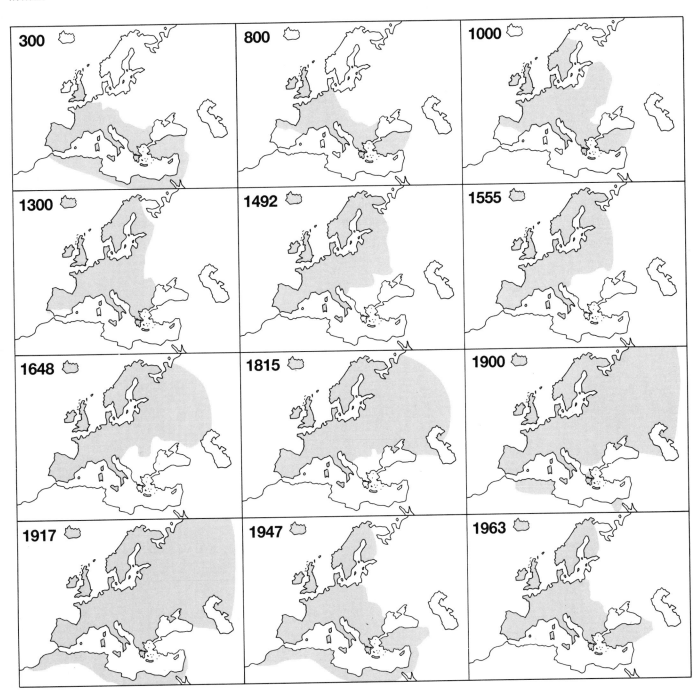

NOTES

1. The world is small.
2. The Roman roads.
3. Maurice De Lannou: *Europe, terre promise* (Europe, the promised land), Seuil, Paris, 1977, pp. 151-153.
4. Alcuin: *Interrogationes et responsiones in Genesim*, P.L. 100, Col. Inter 141. Quoted by D. Hay: *Europe, the Emergence of an Idea*, Edinburgh, 1957, pp. 38-39.
5. French text published in *Ecrits sur l'Europe* (Essays on Europe), Collection 'Ecrits', Seghers, Paris, 1963, 187 p., see p. 7.
6. *Ibidem*, p. 8.
7. See D. Hay, *op. cit.*, pp. 2-3. He adds: 'A.J. Toynbee deals trenchantly with Heredotus's part in defending the notion of an antithesis between Europe and Asia'. *A Study in History*, VIII, 708-11.
8. The term Mediterraneum Mare is first mentioned by Solinus, a contemporary of Ptolemy (IInd century B.C.), and it was often used as an adjective: '... mediterraneis sinibus quo usque Orientem Propellit' quoted by D. Hay, *op. cit.*, pp. 6-7.
9. 'Genus calidum, non spiritu sapientiae, sed impatientiae', *Ibidem*, pp. 12-13.
10. Land occupied by the Scythians was in the regions between the Bug and the Don, currently mainly in the Ukraine.
11. God, deliver us from the arrows of the Hungarians.
12. See W. Ullmann: *The Growth of Papal Government in the Middle Ages*, London, 1955, p. 95, quoted by D. Hay, *op. cit.*, pp. 51-52.
13. Escaut-Meuse-Saône-Rhône to the west, the Rhine to the east. 14. O = directed towards the Oriens (east); T = dividing lines of the three continents, in the form of a T, see map 4.
15. *Qu'est-ce que l'Europe? La formation de l'Europe* (What is Europe? The Formation of Europe) (Vol. 1), Egloff, Fribourg, 1944, 278 pp., quotation p. 50.
16. The author quoted also calls them 'Proto-Europe', or 'second centres of civilisation' which warmed and invigorated Europe.
17. 'Florida... not much inferior to our Europe,' Gemma Phrysius in *Cosmographia* (Apian) 1533, Ib., p. 117. Florida was discovered in 1513 on Palm Sunday ('Pascua Florida').

MAPS

1. 'Le Rail et le Monde' (The Railway and the World), n°26, July-October 1983, p. 29.
2. *Orbis Terrarum Europae*, I.B.F. Kormoss, published by De Visscher, Brussels, 1955.
3. *Westermanns Atlas zur Weltgeschichte*, pp. 26, 30, 31, 34, 36, 38, 39; Braunschweig, 1956.
4. O-T map from an eleventh-century manuscript of Saint Isidore of Seville (Andrews Collection, Royal Geographical Society).
5. From *Westermanns Atlas, op. cit., and others*, including Harms Neuer Geschichts- und Kulturatlas von der Urzeit zur Gegenwart, Atlantik-Verlag, Hamburg, 1950.

6. Extract from *Orbis Terrarum Europae, op. cit.,* with extra details on the boundaries of Lotharingia (843-870).

7. L. Bagrow, *Geschichte der Kartographie,* Safari Verlag Berlin, 1951.

8. Prof. Dr. H. Brugmans, published by de la Baconnière, Neuchâtel, 1965, and A.W. Sythoff, Alphen/Rijn, 1979, p. 217.

Adventure

THE COUNCIL OF EUROPE

*

Paul M.G. Levy

Founded in May 1949, the Council of Europe was the first European political organisation set up after World War II – eight years before the EEC. Now, almost forty years on, it is difficult to recall just what a revolutionary development was the council's birth (1).

Winston Churchill saw it as the realisation of an ideal he had developed in wartime (2). For Robert Schuman, the creation of the institution represented the fulfilment of his dreams (3). As far as the ten founding states – Belgium, France, Denmark, Ireland, Italy, Luxembourg, the Netherlands, Norway, Sweden and the United Kingdom – were concerned, 'body and expression' (4) had been given to a great hope: indeed, many of them felt that the true union of Europe had begun.

The first initiative for the creation of the Council of Europe was at an unofficial level. The European Movement – comprised of private citizens – had, at two post-war conferences, (5) recommended the setting up of *a European Assembly* and a *European Council of Ministers*. Governments took up the theme and the two institutions were created, forming together the Council of Europe.

*

The first session of the European Assembly of the Council of Europe was opened on 10 August 1949 in Strasbourg (6) by Edouard Herriot, the President of the French National Assembly and a long-time advocate of European Union.

The next day the Assembly was officially constituted. Paul-Henri Spaak, who had just lost his Belgian ministerial post after general elections, was elected President of the new Assembly (7). Although he was not a federalist at the time, he carried out his role with spirit and talent. However, he resigned on December 11, 1951, condemning the parliamentarians for failing to give adequate backing to national government Ministers who had come to seek their support for European political union (8).

The European Movement had visualised an Assembly made up of parliamentarians nominated by their governments and also of *other representatives* of society. But, as it turned out, parliamentarians from the ten founder states took up *all* the 100 seats and distributed them according to the division of political power within each country. Thus the European Assembly was modelled along lines more or less desired by governments.

The intention of the governments was to consolidate this *de facto* situation in the statute of the institution. But the members demanded that henceforth representatives in the Assembly be appointed *not* by national governments but 'by national parliaments or according to methods approved by these parliaments.' The Committee of Foreign Ministers of the Council of Europe agreed, and for a long time it was even thought that the Assembly might be elected by

Robert Schuman signs the Statute of the Council of Europe (London, May 5, 1949).

direct universal suffrage – but this has yet to be.

National governments wanted to keep tight control over the agenda in the Assembly. However, the members of the Assembly were not happy to be controlled by governments. They resisted and finally won the day.

There were other areas of friction. At the very first meeting of the Council of Europe, the Foreign Ministers of the Ten invited Greece, Iceland and Turkey also to join the Council. Greece and Turkey immediately accepted. But the ministerial initiative did not go down well with the Assembly, which had not been consulted (9). The parliamentarians insisted that they be consulted in future, and their wishes were respected a few weeks later in the case of the Federal Republic of Germany. Its joining in Spring 1950 – just five years after the end of the Second World War – was an important event in the construction of a more united Europe. The membership of the Federal Republic was essential to the Schuman proposal for the creation of a Coal and Steel Community, which, in April 1951, was to bring together in a supranational organisation six member states of the Council of Europe (10).

The Parliamentary Assembly, the first international parliamentary assembly in history, continued to demand more rights for itself. But on occasions the parliamentarians were more touchy than was justified. The Secretary General and the Deputy Secretary General of the Council of Europe had been nominated by the Foreign Ministers, and the Assembly suspected that both were in the pay of governments. In fact, the shared ideal of Jacques-Camille Paris and Aubrey Halford (11) was to build a united Europe which might one day be based on the wishes of the people expressed through the ballot box. Jacques-Camille Paris did his best to protect the institution which had been entrusted to him, and yet his profound attachment to federalism led him to criticise the Council of Europe's founding Statute, which he said was far too unadventurous. No one reproached him. Nevertheless, the Assembly did not rest until it was granted the power to elect the top three Council officials – the Secretary General and his Deputy and the Clerk of the Assembly.

The aims of the Council of Europe set out in the founding Statute were:
- to work for greater European unity;
- to uphold the principles of parliamentary democracy and human rights;
- to improve living conditions and promote humane values.

Although the Council's work is largely carried out through intergovernmental cooperation, the interests of the individual are its main concern.

The Council of Europe's Statute declares that each member state must recognise the principle of the rule of law and guarantee its citizens the enjoyment of human rights and fundamental freedoms. Any European state that accepts these democratic principles can apply to become a member. Since 1949 the membership has grown from 10 to 21 countries, representing practically the whole of non-communist Europe.

The *Committee of Ministers* is the decision-making body of the Council of Europe. The Committee decides what action should be taken on recommendations from the Parliamentary Assembly and on proposals from the various committees working within the Council's framework. It establishes the Council's work programme and approves its budget. The Committee of Ministers also provides a permanent forum for the member states to discuss a wide range of political issues.

The members of the Committee of Ministers each hold the Presidency in turn for a six-month period. Between meetings at full foreign minister level, their *Deputies*, diplomats who are accredited to the Council of Europe as permanent representatives of the governments, supervise the Council's regular work, meeting for about a week each month. They have practically the same decision-making powers as the Ministers.

The decisions of the Committee of Ministers take the form either of *Recommendations* to governments – policy statements proposing a common course of action to be followed – or of European *Conventions* and *Agreements*, which are binding on the states that ratify them. The Conventions are, in fact, multilateral treaties representing a general European consensus on a particular issue. After approval by the Committee of Ministers, they are opened for signature by the member states. To become effective in the member states, these Conventions must be transferred into domestic law. Once a government is able to comply with a Convention, it can *ratify* it, thus committing itself to respect the obligations laid down in it.

*Robert Schuman describing his plan
for the pooling of coal and steel
production to the Assembly of the
Council, August 10, 1950.*

The *Parliamentary Assembly* is a consultative body and has no legislative powers, but it is a major driving force within the Council of Europe. Its recommendations to the Council of Ministers have been the starting points for action in many key areas of the Council of Europe's work.

✳

At its conferences the European Movement had also proposed that a European Convention on Human Rights be drawn up and that a European Court be created to implement these rights. A number of foreign ministers objected, but after consultations between the Assembly and the Committee of Ministers the Convention (12) was signed less than sixteen months after it had first been proposed (13). Under the Convention the *European Commission of Human Rights* was created in 1953 and the *European Court of Human Rights* in 1958.

Saarland will not be European: press conference by Fernand Dehousse on the Saarland, accompanied by Paul M. G. Levy.

The Convention's ethos centres upon the rights of individuals, giving them the prerogative to bring complaints against the governments. It has provided an example to the rest of the world of how human rights can be respected. During the period when a group of army colonels seized power in Athens and suspended democracy, Greece was obliged to leave the Council of Europe (14) for failing to respect the rules of the club, and especially those concerning human rights.

The main rights and freedoms protected under the Convention on Human Rights are: the rights to life, liberty and security of the person and to a fair trial; right to respect for private and family life, home and correspondence; freedom of thought, conscience and religion; freedom of expression, including freedom of the press; freedom of association and assembly, and in particular freedom to join a trade union; the right to peaceful enjoyment of possessions; certain rights to education, liberty of movement and freedom to choose where to live; and the right to leave a country, including one's own.

The Convention prohibits: torture and inhuman or degrading treatment or

Winston Churchill speaking of the European Army to the Assembly of the Council, August 11, 1950.

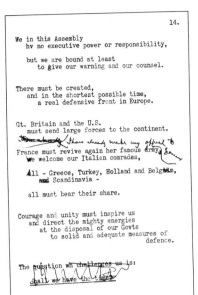

One page of Churchill's speech notes.

punishment; slavery, servitude and forced labour; criminal laws that are retroactively applied; discrimination in the enjoyment of the rights and freedoms guaranteed; expulsion of a state's own nationals or denying them entry, and the collective expulsion of aliens.

A recent Protocol provided for the abolition of the death penalty. By 1986, 19 of the current 21 members of the Council of Europe had accepted the jurisdiction of the Court of Human Rights as binding.

*

The early successes and the grand design of the Council of Europe adventure camouflaged inherent weaknesses. First and foremost, the Parliamentary Assembly had only consultative powers. Foreign ministers kept the decision-making powers and could act in most instances only on the basis of unanimity.

Moreover, within the ranks of the Parliamentarians there were wide differences of opinion on the European vision. To make a rough division, they were split between unionists and constitutionalists. The former desired only a loose union of Europe: the latter positively sought federation, although even they were not a uniform group. Members of national opposition parties were generally in a more comfortable position than members of majorities whose hands were tied by obligations to their governments. In 1987 similar tensions continue to exist in all the European institutions.

*

In 1949 the Parliamentary Assembly had committed itself to overcome the barriers to European integration. But the unification of Europe proved to be far more difficult than had been imagined in the enthusiasm which marked the Council's creation.

Very early on, at the ninth session of the Committee of Ministers in August 1951, they decided that any member state which wanted to opt out of a Committee proposal would have the right to do so. Thus the principle was established that any individual member state could move towards unity as and when it liked and at any speed it chose.

Elsewhere a bold initiative to achieve European unity quickly overtook the Council of Europe's own strivings. On May 9, 1950 Robert Schuman, acting for the French government, proposed to the Federal Republic of Germany first and foremost, but also to the other member states of the Council of Europe, that a European Coal and Steel Community be formed. It would be a practical and pragmatic organisation, but with a supranational authority.

This daring project raised both hopes and fears. But since only six of the 15 members of the Council of Europe opted to be part of the Coal and Steel Community, an effort had to be made to avoid any suggestion of a dangerous division of Europe: Robert Schuman therefore decided to unveil his plan before the Parliamentary Assembly of the Council of Europe and his fellow foreign ministers on the Committee of Ministers. The project was discussed twice by the Parliamentary Assembly (15) which warmly welcomed the ECSC plan. It was suggested that a Protocol to the ECSC Treaty should regulate relations between the new Community and the Council. This Protocol was signed on April 18, 1951, at the same time as the ECSC Treaty itself. The intent was to prevent a split between those who had opted for the new institution and the

states which, while remaining in the Council of Europe, did not immediately want to join the Coal and Steel Community.

Current conference room of the Committee of Ministers of the Council of Europe.

*

A number of crises arose which forced the Council of Europe to move beyond limits defined in its founding Statute, which stipulated that questions of national defence were not part of its competence (16).

Events in Berlin and Korea had to be confronted by the Committee of Ministers, and so the idea of a 'European Army' was born. During the session of August 1950 a number of members, and in particular André Philip, Paul Reynaud and Winston Churchill, recommended the 'immediate creation of a unified European Army under the authority of a European Minister of Defence, subject to proper European democratic control.' (17)

The idea was picked up and developed by the French government, particularly by the then Prime Minister, René Pleven. It resulted in the Treaty of the European Defence Community, signed on 27 May 1952 by France, the Federal Republic of Germany, Italy, Belgium, the Netherlands and Luxembourg, the six countries of the ECSC.

It also brought about, in 1952, a project for a European political union which, in the initial stages, would have been more important institutionally than either the Coal and Steel Community or the proposed Defence Community. But the idea for political union and the proposal for the Defence Community were both doomed to failure. The United Kingdom was unwilling to commit itself to any 'federal' links involving defence matters: Winston Churchill, in a House of Commons debate on 14 July 1954, regretted that the proposal was not of a less federal nature which would have allowed Britain to take part. And France itself, which had signed the Treaty of the European Defence Community, proved reluctant to establish the international army it called for. Pleven had proposed that, within the army, there would be no specifically national unit larger than a battalion: he believed this method might reconcile the French people to German rearmament. But he was wrong. On August 30, 1954, the French National Assembly refused to ratify the 1952 Treaty, thus destroying the European Defence Community before it ever got off the ground.

A new French Prime Minister, Pierre Mendès-France, accepted a new defence initiative proposed by the Parliamentary Assembly of the Council of Europe. This resulted in the setting up of the Western European Union (WEU) and was a much scaled-down version of the Defence Community idea (18) but which nevertheless built upon the 1948 Treaty of Brussels calling for mutual military aid in the event of outside attack upon either Belgium, France, the United Kingdom, Luxembourg, the Netherlands, Italy or the Federal Republic of Germany.

The Parliamentary Assembly continued doggedly to pursue the objectives spelt out in its earliest meetings in Strasbourg, namely the transformation of the Council of Europe into 'a European political authority with limited functions but real powers'. (19) This inspired many hours of debate in which the federalists argued that a European political authority had, of necessity, to be supranational. Others felt that an intergovernmental arrangement, within which representatives would take unanimous decisions, would be good enough. Gradually the general public lost interest in these long and inconclusive debates.

The Council of Europe therefore began to concentrate its energies on more pragmatic óbjectives. A list drawn up at the very beginning defined areas in which closer cooperation was possible under the Council's Statute, whose stated aim was 'to achieve a greater unity between its Members for the purpose of safeguarding and realising the ideals and principles which are their common heritage and facilitating their economic and social progress.' (20)

Some 120 Conventions and Agreements have resulted from this utilitarian approach, settling on the face of Europe a lacework of cooperation and agreed rules which have brought the European countries much closer together.

The European Convention on Human Rights continues to be the cornerstone of this system, making the rule of law and pluralist democracy binding obligations for member states of the Council.

Additions to the legal framework of the Council of Europe were provided by the European Social Charter, second in importance to the Convention on Human Rights, which guarantees the right to work, fair remuneration, equal pay for equal work, social security, medical aid, vocational training and the right to organise, bargain and strike. Other conventions have been concluded in the fields of law, the economy, education and teaching, science and environmental protection, public health, and inter-relations between central and local governments. The requirement for visas for travel between member states of the Council was scrapped and the passport system liberalised.

Another Convention provides a framework for cultural cooperation. Study grants have been created, exhibitions organised and the equivalent rankings of university qualifications widely recognised. A Convention on freedom of establishment has been concluded, along with a Convention for the peaceful settlement of disputes.

The initiative for the intergovernmental work in the Council of Europe often begins with a proposal from the Assembly, which is then referred by the Committee of Ministers to expert committees. If the work results in a draft Convention or Agreement it is then adopted by the Committee of Ministers and opened for signature and ratification by member states. However, this last link in the chain is weak, for no member state is compelled to ratify a Convention. Nevertheless, the list of ratifications is long.

From the beginning, the Council felt that the organisation should have a very open attitude to the rest of the world. Colonial problems were discussed in the context of the European Convention on Human Rights, and a number of states, such as the United Kingdom and the Netherlands, extended the application of the Convention to a number of their overseas territories. A bold 'Strasbourg Plan' was drawn up with the aim of resolving the difficult question of Euro-African relations ... but it was overtaken by the rapidly developing trend towards colonial independence in the fifties and sixties.

Though European nations under totalitarian rule were not represented in the Council, they were not forgotten. A proposal from the European Movement to set aside empty seats for these states was not taken up, but a special Committee on Relations with European Non-Member States was set up to monitor events in Eastern Europe and also in Spain and Portugal when they were under dictatorships.

In recent years annual participation in Assembly sessions by politicians from non-European democracies has been a regular feature. In 1983 the first

'Conference of Strasbourg' brought together members of the Council of Europe and representatives of other important democratic powers in the Americas, Asia and Oceania. The Assembly has frequently invited leading public figures to give addresses on such burning issues as the Middle East problem.

On several occasions the Committee of Ministers and the Parliamentary Assembly have expressed their desire to provide a general framework for European politics. The activities of the Council of Europe helped a number of European nations to approach and eventually join the new and more powerful European institutions.

✳

The Council of Europe today has 21 member states: Austria, Belgium, Cyprus, Denmark, France, the Federal Republic of Germany, Greece, Iceland, Ireland, Italy, Liechtenstein, Luxembourg, Malta, the Netherlands, Norway, Portugal, Spain, Sweden, Switzerland, Turkey and the United Kingdom (21). Finland and the Holy See are parties to the Council of Europe's Cultural Convention. The Council's European Youth Centre has also invited young people from Eastern Europe to participate in meetings in Strasbourg.

Strasbourg strives to be a centre of all that is most humane and cerebral in Europe. The Council of Europe is a centre for the exchange of ideas. Robert Schuman summed it up when he called it the 'testing ground for European cooperation.' (22)

This is what is symbolised by the flag emblem which the Council of Europe adopted in 1955: a perfect crown of twelve gold stars set against a deep blue background of the Western skies. Twelve is a numerical symbol of plenty and perfect union, and the gold stars themselves are the European peoples. In 1986 the European Community also adopted the flag as its own. (23)

The Council of Europe, under its new Secretary-General, former Spanish foreign minister Marcelino Oreja, will continue to demonstrate Europe's desire to be open to the world, that it wants to be a force for progress, freedom and peace, and a model of successful democracy.

Señor Oreja believes that the Council, the oldest and geographically the largest pan-European organisation, must play the role of permanent standard-bearer of European civilisation. It must give a special part to those non- EEC member-states who are now in the minority in the Council for the first time – following the accession to the European Community of Spain and Portugal – but who have become increasingly anxious to participate in European cooperation without being members of the EEC.

The fact is that if, one day, all the hopes of the founding fathers come about, they will have sprung from seeds first sown by the Council of Europe. Even with its imperfections, the Council remains the place where all West European democracies come together on an equal footing. While welcoming the major developments in the more geographically limited EEC, the Council's work continues to expand, taking into account the growing complexities of life in the late twentieth century.

NOTES

1. The Treaty establishing the Statute of the Council of Europe was signed in London on May 5, 1949. It entered into force on August 3, 1949.
2. It was on March 21, 1943, in a speech broadcast on the radio, that Winston Churchill outlined his plans for European organisation in the post-War era and

used the words 'Council of Europe' for the first time. In this speech he defined the goals which a European organisation should aim at.

3. France, which had Robert Schuman as Minister for Foreign Affairs, played an essential role in the intergovernmental consultation which culminated in the Statute of the Council.

4. This phrase was used by Edouard Herriot in his inaugural speech on August 10, 1949.

5. In The Hague in May 1948, in Brussels in February 1949.

6. Strasbourg was chosen as a symbol of European reconciliation. It had changed nationalities four times in the space of 75 years and it had lost men in the two World Wars on both sides of the Front.

7. The members of the Committee of Ministers are excluded from being elected to the Assembly by the Statute. Paul-Henri Spaak was, however, the first short-lived President of the Committee of Ministers on August 8, 1949, before his resignation was accepted as a Belgian Minister, and he then, as a Member of Parliament, was unanimously chosen as President of the Assembly on August 11.

8. On December 10, 1951, the Ministers – Adenauer, De Gasperi, Schuman and van Zeeland – appealed to the Assembly to call for the creation of a political union, which they were ready to accept.

9. The Assembly was only constituted two days after the first meeting of the Committee of Ministers.

10. Belgium, France, the Federal Republic of Germany, Italy, Luxembourg and the Netherlands.

11. Both excellent diplomats, the first French, the second British.

12. The inspiration for this project came from Sir David Maxwell-Fyfe (the future Lord Kilmuir) and Fernand Dehousse (future President of the Assembly).

13. The Convention was signed in Rome on November 4, 1950.

14. After it left the Council in 1969, Greece was only allowed to re-enter once the dictatorship was deposed in 1974.

15. In August and November 1950.

16. On the basis of Article 1, paragraph (d) of the Statute.

17. Assembly recommendation of August 11, 1950.

18. The Western European Union (WEU) was formed by an extension of the 1948 Treaty of Brussels to include the Federal Republic of Germany and Italy. The signatories of the Treaty of Brussels were Belgium, France, the Grand Duchy of Luxembourg, the Netherlands and the United Kingdom.

19. The main formulators of the proposal to the Assembly were André Philip (French socialist) and Kim Mackay (British Labour Party).

20. First Article of the Statute.

21. In accordance with the Protocol to the Council of Europe, the countries are given in English alphabetical order, since the Statute was signed in London. It is in this order that Ministers succeed to the Presidency of the Committee, and that the flags are flown.

22. Speech by Robert Schuman on December 10, 1951 to the Assembly of the Council of Europe.

23. See on the question of the origin of the European flag the brochure by Robert Bichet (*Le Drapeau Européen* – Besançon, 1985) and the work by Paul M.G. Levy (*Sauver l'Europe* – Duculot, Paris-Gembloux, 1978).

THE MARSHALL PLAN
AND THE OEEC

*

Guy de Carmoy ·

After liberation from German occupation, Western Europe severely lacked basic goods and raw materials. Capital equipment had been partially destroyed, and means of payment were scarce. The neutral states – Switzerland, Sweden and Portugal – were in a relatively better position, as was Great Britain. Economic activity was 50% paralysed in France, Italy, Belgium and the Netherlands, and almost at a standstill in Germany.

Western Europe was in a situation where it was obliged either to reduce its imports and postpone industrial reconstruction until a later date, or increase imports and exhaust foreign currency reserves.

In 1946-47, the US Treasury lent a great deal of money to the United Kingdom in order to place the pound sterling back on its pre-war footing of reserve currency. However, in August 1947, a payments crisis forced the UK to suspend convertibility of the pound. Italy received food aid from the United States, and France borrowed from it on a number of occasions.

In light of the serious economic situation in Europe, the United States decided to replace bilateral aid by an international organisation managing all aid to Europe. This led up to the Marshall Plan and the creation of the Organisation for European Economic Cooperation (OEEC).

THE MARSHALL PLAN

The Truman Doctrine, unveiled on March 12, 1947, was a reaction to British back-tracking on aid promised to Greece and Turkey in 1945. Truman did not mince his words. He declared that the United States had a duty to help the free nations direct their own destiny as they thought fit. Moreover, he stated, the first priority for the US had to be economic and financial aid, essential for economic stability and the preservation of the political order.

The Doctrine was originally intended as an all-embracing concept. However, the splits which appeared between the Soviet Union and the Western world at the Moscow Conference in March 1947 convinced President Truman that the two sides would eventually come to blows on peace questions. Consequently, a plan was hastily and secretly drawn up by General George Marshall, then Secretary of State. The basic principles of this were outlined in his famous speech on June 5, 1947 in Harvard. He maintained that US policy was not directed against any country or any doctrine, but against hunger, poverty, despair and chaos. The objective was, he emphasized, to set the world economy back on its feet and to create the political and social conditions indispensable for the existence of free institutions. The United States delegated the task of working out the programme for economic recovery to the Europeans. They were to begin with a meeting to draw up the balance of Europe's resources and requirements.

However, it still had to be decided whether US aid would be for all of

Two worlds are born in Europe. The reconstruction of the West with Marshall aid, the dominance of one ideology in East Germany.

Europe, both western and eastern, including the Soviet Union. Viatcheslav Molotov, Soviet Foreign Affairs Minister, was received in Paris on June 27, 1947, at the invitation of the French and British Governments. Molotov categorically refused to allow the creation of a study group to analyse the requirements of the European states. The Soviet Union refused to accept the idea that Germany, other ex-enemy states and neutral states should also be allowed to benefit from US aid. He was afraid that the Eastern European states would fall under Western influence if they received aid. The US offer was rejected on July 2 by the Soviet Union and, on its orders, by the satellite states. Consequently 'a profound rift opened up in Europe' (1).

As a result, the Marshall Plan took on two quite separate aspects. On the one hand, it was an expression of US solidarity with Western Europe. On the other, it became a weapon in the ideological war of the free world against communism (2). The final break between the Soviet Union and the United States was provided by Molotov's exit from the Paris Conference. 'After the failure of the Moscow Conference at the beginning of 1947, the West finally had to recognise that a joint aid programme for all of Germany was an impossibility' (3).

From July 12 to September 22, 1947, the Western European states met in Paris to draw up an inventory of their resources and requirements. They agreed to request 19 billion dollars in aid from the United States. In December of the same year, the US paid out 'interim aid' to France, Italy and Austria, which were experiencing severe balance of payments difficulties.

In his message to Congress on December 19, 1947, President Truman declared that the US considered European recovery essential for the United States, and that it did not want to see nations give way to despair and succumb to totalitarian regimes. The US economic cooperation law was approved by Congress on April 3, 1948. It created an American body for monitoring the aid, and stipulated that the bilateral agreements to be concluded between the United States and each of the beneficiary European countries would contain a clause specifying that that country would participate in an organisation for collective management of the aid. Finally, it transferred a total of $17 billion to the European States, designed to tide them over until June 1952.

THE ORGANISATION FOR EUROPEAN ECONOMIC COOPERATION

The Organisation for European Economic Cooperation, the body to be charged with managing Marshall aid, was set up in Paris on April 16, 1948. Sixteen European states were members: Austria, Belgium, Denmark, France, Greece, Ireland, Iceland, Italy, Luxembourg, the Netherlands, Norway, Portugal, Sweden, Turkey and the United Kingdom, along with the commanders in chief of the three western occupation zones in Germany. The Federal Republic of Germany joined soon after its creation in 1949. The United States and Canada became associate members in 1950. Spain was originally excluded due to its political dictatorship, but eventually became a member in 1959.

The new organisation was a sort of permanent international forum for inter-governmental consultation. Mutual cooperation was one of the stipulated aims of its members. They agreed to reduce restrictions on trade and monetary transactions, set up a multilateral trade and payments system and study the possibility of setting up a customs union or a free trade area. The United States would have liked a powerful organisation. However, the United Kingdom was only prepared to accept a body controlled by a Council of Ministers which operated a unanimity voting system. The compromise agreed was that the abstention of one member should not prevent decisions, provided that the one member was not affected by the subject in question. The Secretary General (this position was occupied by Robert Marjolin from 1948 to 1955) was also given the right to present proposals to the Council of Ministers and to suggest possible compromises in cases of deadlock (4).

There were two main phases in the activity of the OEEC. In the first phase, the main objective of the organisation was to liberalise trade and intra-European payments. The second was the much more stormy phase and was dominated by debate between the advocates of a customs union and those of a free trade area.

The practice of bilateralism had paralysed intra-European trade since 1945. The shortage of goods and the low level of monetary reserves prompted each state to strive to balance its trade with each of its partners, so that credit operations were reduced to a minimum. In 1949, the decision was taken within the OEEC to reduce tariffs representing a certain percentage of member countries' goods imports. The percentage was set at 50%, and was to be raised gradually each year. In 1950, the OEEC set up the European Payments Union (EPU). The EPU allowed member states to settle intra-European debts on a multilateral basis. It was also a credit body, paying out loans to member states or collecting funding from them in units of account, depending on their respective positions. The volume of trade grew rapidly as a result of this automatic mechanism. However, the smooth running of the system was disrupted by the monetary and financial policy pursued by the French. France's position was dictated by the wars in Indochina and Algeria. As a result, the re-establishment of European currency convertibility, which could have taken place in 1955, was postponed until 1958, when France carried out a monetary reform placing it on an even keel with the rest of the European states (5).

The Messina Conference in 1955 was the scene of a diplomatic battle between two different concepts of a more united Europe. It was a preparatory meeting which culminated in the signing of the Treaty of Rome, establishing the European Economic Community (EEC) between six European countries,

namely France, the Federal Republic of Germany, Italy, Belgium, the Netherlands and Luxembourg. The main clash over the future face of Europe was between France and the United Kingdom. The UK would have preferred a free trade area to the customs union set up by the Treaty of Rome. The British Government proposed in 1955 that the powers of the OEEC be reinforced. It also requested that the question of relations between 'the Six' and the remaining Western European states be discussed by the OEEC Council of Ministers. In 1956, the Council set up a special working group to examine possible procedures for a multilateral association between the future customs union and the other European countries. Negotiations got properly under way in October 1957. The economic pros and cons of a free trade area versus a customs union, eventually leading to a vast common market, were pitted against one another. The United Kingdom argued especially virulently for the first option, which would allow it to maintain preferential links with the Commonwealth and protect its own agriculture.

However, the true nature of the question was political rather than economic. Would not 'little Europe', in the form of a customs union centred upon France and Germany, have greater cohesion than the states attached to the United Kingdom, within and outside of Europe, by monetary and trade links? Did the new organisation not stand a good chance of becoming the main European 'voice' in the dialogue with the United States? The negotiations begun in 1957 were suspended due to the French political crisis in 1958. General de Gaulle visited the West German Chancellor Adenauer in November 1958 and assured him that France would not use the safeguard clause to opt out of the dismantling of customs controls provided for in the Treaty of Rome. In return Germany agreed not to insist upon the re-opening of negotiations with the United Kingdom on a free trade area.

The United Kingdom wanted to obtain assurances that the principle of non-discrimination in trade between all the OEEC member states would be respected. France, on the other hand, wanted a difference in treatment between EEC goods and non-EEC goods. The radical monetary reform which took place in France in December 1958 allowed it to free its trade to such an extent that the majority of the UK technical objections were no longer founded. The UK finally gave up all hope of a single multilateral system within the OEEC, and in November 1959 in Stockholm set up the European Free Trade Association (EFTA) with the remaining European countries which were not members of the EEC: Sweden, Norway, Denmark, Switzerland, Austria and Portugal (6).

Shortly after the creation of EFTA the decision was taken to reform the OEEC by enlarging its geographical scope to embrace the entire western world. With the entry of Canada and the United States, the OEEC wound up its purely aid function, as the European currencies regained their convertibility. The trade functions of the OEEC were also greatly limited, since it had been largely superseded by the EEC and EFTA. The name changed to the Organisation for Economic Cooperation and Development (OECD), which was offically set up in November 1960. It was given the task of coordinating aid from the Western countries to the developing world. A number of other industrialised countries have since joined, transforming the OECD into a club of market-economy industrialised countries.

The club owes its formation to the rapid economic recovery in the European countries. The situation was neatly summed up by Raymond Aron in 1973: 'My opinion of the Marshall Plan has not changed in 25 years; I still see it as generous, enlightened and effective' (7).

SELECTED BIBLIOGRAPHY

1. Jean Monnet, *Mémoires*, Fayard, 1976, p 315.
2. Guy de Carmoy, *Les politiques étrangères de la France 1944-1966* (French Foreign Policy 1944-1966), La Table Ronde, 1967, p 85.
3. Raymond Aron, *République Impériale, les Etats-Unis dans le monde 1945-1972* (Imperial Republic; the United States in the World Arena 1945-1972), Calmann-Lévy, 1973, p 58.
4. Pierre Gerbet, *La Construction de l'Europe* (Building Europe), Imprimerie Nationale, 1983, pp 81-83.
5. Guy de Carmoy, *op. cit.*, pp 88-92.
6. idem pp 134-137, 402-404.
7. Jean Monnet, *op. cit.*, p 60.

THE SCHUMAN PLAN
AND THE ECSC

*

François Fontaine

The European Community was born one day when everyone had given it up as a lost cause. It seemed that everything had been done to try to bring the European nations together in a peaceful organisation: the Treaty of Brussels, the OEEC, the Council of Europe, the imminent European Payments Union, and other such excellent initiatives, described in the preceding chapter. Yet the crux of the matter had been forgotten, or deliberately left to one side: decision-making power. In each of these initiatives, power had been rendered hypothetical by leaving national governments the right to place a veto. No-one wanted to give ground, and therefore no progress was made. Everything was negotiable in the European institutions, except for sovereignty, and everything except the common interest was placed first.

Did anyone think of cutting the Gordian knot? The answer would seem to be enigmatic. Statesmen built innumerable European castles-in-the-air during this period. But nothing came of any of them. This ambiguity was to be found even in the best intentioned federalist projects of the time. Even Aristide Briand, who took the idea to the highest political degree, stopped short. His project for a European federation left the almost sacred privileges of the nation states intact. The internationalist rhetoric was very spirited, but the ancient frontiers did not budge one inch. Everyone felt in a rather baffled way that an essential piece of the puzzle was missing. The most daring constructions lacked solid foundations, and the magnificent cupolas of the palace of Europe remained in the architects' briefcases.

They would have remained there for another generation if a situation had not arisen which necessitated action. After the First World War, the victors believed in the illusion of their own superiority, but after the Second adversaries were rapidly and paradoxically transformed into allies. Attempts to turn the clock back to the spirit of the Treaty of Versailles were ill-fated. French aspirations over the Saar produced deadlock in Franco-German relations. Moves to hold down once and for all coal and steel production in Germany failed miserably. The Marshall Plan, which set a precedent, had, as early as 1948, created new prospects and a new creative outlook in Europe as a whole. It was time to revise old economic and political conceptions. But the nation states dragged their feet and were unwilling to change their old ways, even although they periodically led to disaster.

The nation states which still believed in the virtues of diplomacy – force having fallen into disrepute – continued to hope that History would carry on along its traditional path. France seemed to be stringing out its inevitable demise, and Great Britain refused to renounce its imperialist destiny. Germany, where political awareness had just been re-born, fought to loosen the bonds of occupation. It was watched with a stern eye, for there was some indication that it was trying to win tactical advantages in the West and in the East. Advantages could be drawn from an unstable situation; nothing was more fragile than the

new-born balance of powers between the two superpowers, fresh from a combat where Europe and, at the heart of Europe, Germany were at stake.

European politicians gradually became aware that the Old World was no longer a key nerve centre. It had been transformed into a passive battleground for the rivalries between East and West. The United States and the Soviet Union had traded in their peripheral roles to come to the centre of the European stage and were ideologically and militarily present. Each was sorely tempted to try to push the other back, especially since both now had an atomic bomb (the Soviet Union first exploded one in 1949), and a regulatory void for nuclear weapons still existed. Berlin was overhung with a sense of latent catastrophe, which might be accidentally let loose at any moment. An inveigled or demoralised Germany could once again destabilise Europe and the world.

Luckily, it had at its head a man who was both imbued with Western culture and democracy and who was a staunch patriot: Konrad Adenauer. He was intransigently patriotic, but this never got the upper hand over his European convictions. However, there was a risk that the country would be dragged too far into the counterbidding not between East and West, but between the occupying powers. In 1950, the independence of which Adenauer had dreamed, full control over Germany's economic resources and even the rebuilding of an army were all within his reach.

Such prospects just five years after the end of the war were too much for France, which hardened its position and stood on its dignity when pressed by its Anglo-American allies to lighten the burden of Germany's reconstruction and its defence. Paris continued to call for annexation to France of the Saar and for the maintenance of restrictions on German heavy industry. The man responsible for behind-the-scenes diplomacy, French Foreign Minister, Robert Schuman, was, paradoxically, best placed to understand the German mentality. His cultural background and his origin – an Alsace-Lorrainer born German –

Konrad Adenauer and Robert Schuman in 1950.

Robert Schuman with Jean Monnet in 1950.

made him well suited to the job. Yet at the beginning of 1950, Adenauer and Schuman were not on speaking terms, at least not face to face. An unreal dialogue was carried on through a series of middle men.

In April, Adenauer gave an interview to an American agency. He declared that 'the French and the Germans will undoubtedly sit down *one day* around the same table, in the same building, to work together and assume their joint responsibilities. A big step forward will take place'. Schuman echoed this sentiment: 'Transfer of sovereign power will one day be a reality, but *not for a long time yet*'.

Deadlock was complete, and France was the most to blame. One month later, the Allies were due to meet in London to settle the problem of German sovereignty once and for all. Schuman was aware of the fact that he was going to be totally isolated, and was seriously troubled by this thought since he had accepted the brief, delegated to France by the British and the Americans, of making constructive proposals. Given the urgency of the situation, he hurriedly looked around for a solution, and one fell into his lap by a lucky combination of circumstances.

Destiny was shaped by Bernard Clappier, head of the French Foreign Affairs Minister's departmental office. He had met Jean Monnet, France's General Commissioner of the Plan, a few days earlier. Monnet gave him a copy of a project which he had secretly drawn up with Etienne Hirsch, Pierre Uri and Paul Reuter. The project, so recently completed that the ink was hardly dry on the blueprints, was radical in that it treated the problem at its roots, namely national sovereignty. Symbolically, the roots went even deeper, to the coal and iron in the Ruhr and Lorraine soil, masses of which had been extracted in times past to manufacture weapons. In the future, they would be jointly worked, and no nation state would have the right to expropriate them to make war with another. They would, on the contrary, be put to peaceful ends. Monnet's idea, quickly accepted by Schuman, was both noble and ingenious. It provided the spark that was lacking in all the other initiatives.

The method proposed for its fulfilment was also rather original. There was no point, it was felt, in negotiating a revolutionary project through diplomatic channels, for it would soon be buried and forgotten. The plan would be

ORAVIT, DOCVIT, CHRISTVS, FIT VICTIMA, VICTOR

Das newe Testament.
auffs new zugericht.

I.N.R.I.

Doct: Mart: Luth:

Witeberg.

Gedruckt durch Hans Lufft.

1 5 4 6.

Preceding page: The end of unity in the Christian world and of the supremacy of Latin (Luther, Das neue Testament, 1546, Wittenberg).
Above: Francis I receives Charles Quint in Paris in 1540, in the presence of the papal legate, Cardinal Alessandro Farnese (fresco by Taddeo Zuccari, Palazzo Farnese, Caprarola).

Above: Turks defeated at Lepanto by the united fleet of Spain, Venice, Genoa, Malta and the Vatican (fresco by Andrea Vicentino, Palazzo Ducale, Venice).
Below: The Peace of Westphalia of 1648, ending the Thirty Year's War but consecrating the division of Europe and notably of the Netherlands (Copy of Gerard Terborch, Rijksmuseum, Amsterdam).

*George Washington in 1773 with the 13-star banner in Princeton, symbolising the
states of New England (Painting by Charles Wilson Peale, 1779, the Capitol,
Washington). On the right: Napoleon Bonaparte, Emperor
(painting by Ingres, 1810).*

The Quintuple Alliance, allegory on the Paris Peace of May 30, 1814, forerunner of the Congress of Vienna.

1830, the year of revolution in Europe.

1848: Republican riots in front of St. Paul's Church in Frankfurt, where the first national German parliament sat.

revealed publicly a few days before or even on the eve of the conference in London. It would not be the main point on the agenda, but it would certainly steal the spotlight from the conference. The project not only got over the German problem, but re-balanced Europe and Europe's relationship with the rest of the world and, finally, pointed Europe in a new direction. The rest of this chapter will deal with how the idea was born, how it was implemented and what its fate has been.

✳

It has been said that Jean Monnet had been mulling over this project for a long time, and indeed evidence of its germination can be traced far back in his notes. Other daring initiatives throughout his career foreshadowed the move. His philosophy revolved around bringing men to work together, pooling their resources, and building the foundations of far-reaching political ambitions. However, what became known as the Schuman Plan is essentially a child of its time, of the atmosphere at the beginning of 1950.

The plan cannot really be classified as a piece of improvisation, but it is true that urgency brought it into the world. It was the work of an optimist, conceived in dramatic circumstances. It met the needs of the moment, and also provided the foundation for one of the hardiest institutions of our age. Inventors have the art of integrating contradictions. And inventors of uplifting political systems are a rare species indeed. For once, it is possible in Monnet's case to trace the development of the political idea of one of these founding fathers. Jean Monnet related in his 'memoires' in full detail the conception of the 'Schuman Declaration' of May 9, 1950. He felt it could inspire the creation of a more advanced political system, and it can certainly be drawn upon even now when faith in the modern EEC occasionally flags.

Monnet conceived a very powerful political idea, whose richness is still being drawn upon and developed today. Continuity can be seen in the work method which seemed so strange at the outset but has now become second nature to all

Declaration by Robert Schuman in the 'Salon de l'Horloge', Paris, May 9, 1950.

Europe's major joint enterprises. The method created by Monnet in the first days of the Schuman Plan constituted a break with all the traditional approaches to international negotiations. Previously, each state had come with a set brief, and sought to score points off the others. This all changed, and a code of conduct founded upon common interest replaced it. The proposal on May 9 was the first test. Germany, Italy and the Benelux countries gave their wholehearted acceptance. The United Kingdom proved unable to accept the change in the rules of diplomacy, and only came to the European Community table twenty years later.

This community of interests first consisted of the Conference of the Six, which drew up the ECSC Treaty, and then embraced each successive institution created by this Treaty. The Luxembourg-based High Authority, the Parliamentary Assembly and the Court of Justice were given the task of managing and supervising the execution of joint projects. The activities of the ECSC were concentrated upon the coal and steel industries, which at that time were the backbone of the European economy and the centre of international rivalries. It was an excellent choice for demonstrating the superiority of integration procedures over individual action. It was important that there should be success in this limited yet significant test case chosen by Jean Monnet and Robert Schuman. Their move was not an arbitrary one. The coal and steel industries were a symbol of war or peace, destruction or prosperity, depending on whether they were viewed from the narrow national perspective or from the broader European one.

The attitudes of the millions of inhabitants of the Old World had to be changed. Jean Monnet began the immense task within the first teams set up in Luxembourg in August 1952. The High Authority was a melting pot for producing a new kind of 'European citizen'. All illusions of superiority or even rivalry between fellow workers, no matter what their nationality, had to be swept away. Sceptics came to witness for themselves this phenomenon and today the workers who are building a tightly-meshed society are many and multifarious. The exclusivity of coal and steel has long been forgotten. The European Coal and Steel Community was rapidly conceived and born into a closely confined environment. Yet it had great ambition. The history of the birth of the European Community contains some lessons which can be put to use in its maturity.

The ECSC demonstrated to Europe the superiority of joint institutions and regulations. Day after day, a work method, jurisprudence and democratic consensus grew stronger. There is no space in this essay to recount the

successes and misadventures of its development. There is no point in trying to analyse the immense legal and economic activity to which this first community, the 'testing ground' of Europe, gave rise. Attention should rather be focussed upon the far-reaching venture of the Common Market, to be discussed in the next few chapters. The quintessence of the whole European Community adventure is to be found in the ECSC Treaty, which was in turn inspired by the declaration of May 9, 1950. The fact that nothing fundamentally new has been invented since is less a sign of the lack of imagination of the ECSC's successors than of the visionary power of the founding fathers, perhaps born of saturation with horror after the two world wars.

✳

However, the Old World had to live through a number of hair-raising crises before loyalty to the old historical divisions began to erode. The Korean War and a new stormy period in East-West relations raised their ugly heads even before the Six had the time to draw up the ECSC Treaty. But the storm gradually passed over Europe, and the European states continued their work unperturbed.

The knock-on effects of the ECSC made themselves felt, with the United States doubling its efforts to convince its European allies that Germany should play a larger part in the defence of Western Europe. The furore over German rearmament, which threatened to break out once again, was stopped in its tracks by the dynamics of the Schuman Plan. Jean Monnet went back to square one, and tried to transform the fear of a German army into confidence in a joint European army, commanded by international institutions. This was the genesis of the Pleven proposal, and then of the European Defence Community (EDC) plan. It was given an extra boost by Adenauer, who had the wisdom not to play upon the idea of power and independence for his country, but to stick

Jean Monnet, Robert Schuman and Walter Hallstein among others, in front of the building of the High Authority in August 1952.

resolutely to the European option. The European commitment of Germany was not questioned.

Yet the problems for the EDC were only fleetingly solved. The EDC seemed to strengthen the integration system, since it was composed of the same institutions as the ECSC. It began on a high note, and many thought that it would give impetus to a move towards irreversible federalism. A plan for a political Community already existed, and the finest constitutionalists spent their time devising a remarkable edifice for this. But whereas in Luxembourg, the ECSC High Authority, presided over by Jean Monnet, was exercising its authority in the single market and in the international arena, the stalwarts of nationalism decided to put up firm opposition to any new projects. Conservatives and reformers joined forces to prevent Europe from extending the field of its compentence. The EDC sadly spiralled downwards, culminating in the final collapse of the project in the French National Assembly on August 30, 1954.

The real interest of this historical sidekick concerns the effects which it had on the process set up by the ECSC. The path towards supranationality taken by the first Community had turned out to be a dead-end. Had the 'Europe of tangible achievements, the first stage of European federation', as heralded by Robert Schuman come to a halt or retreated? For a short while, this seemed to be the case, and the resignation of Jean Monnet from the ECSC appeared to confirm it. However, as will be seen in the next chapter, this resignation opened the way for the Messina Conference which, scarcely a year later, set Europe back on the tracks. Clearly some people's determination to hand down to their children a world free of the disorder through which they had lived had survived intact. The means to accomplish their task had been buffeted or sometimes destroyed by the sheer force of resistance. The new Community initiative was to be less ostentatious, but with a wider and more diverse sphere of action. It was to be both more and less ambitious, and it was this inherent contradiction which was to create problems for the Common Market soon after its promising start.

The first ingot of 'European' steel. Messrs. Spierenburg, Etzel, Finet, Coppé, Potthoff, Wehrer, Giacchero and Daum of the High Authority, among others.

'The French proposal is politically inspired. It even has a moral aspect', declares Konrad Adenauer (on the right) talking to Jean Monnet.

The Declaration of Robert Schuman on May 9, 1950 will be a source of reflection for many a year to come. His phrase: 'Europe cannot be built in a day, and it cannot be built in one go. It will rest upon concrete achievements, creating a *de facto* solidarity' demonstrates a pragmatism which, in the modern day and age, is a superior form of political philosophy. The EEC has to this day more achievements than failures to its credit, and the Community which exists today would never have been created but for this gradualist approach. It is now the only course considered possible. But the following chapters may give the impression that Europe has missed a number of historical chances since 1950 of accelerating the integration process. The concept of full integration formed an integral part of the original blueprint, implicit in the Declaration of May 9, explicit in the spirit of the Federalists. Jean Monnet told Adenauer that the grasp towards European integration 'is essentially political. It even has a moral aspect'. 'Indeed', concurred the German Chancellor, 'it is the moral responsibility which we have towards our people, and not the technical responsibility, which we must bring into play to make a reality from this vast pool of hope'. Nearly forty years on, the sentiments of Monnet and Adenauer remain extraordinarily topical.

The EDC, the WEU,
Messina, Val Duchesse, Rome

*

Count Snoy et d'Oppuers

The EDC – European political union
and the Beyen Plan

Europe was given fresh inspiration by the success of the Schuman Plan, which led to the signing on April 18, 1951 of the Treaty of Paris setting up the European Coal and Steel Community with six member states. A supranational solution was thought to be the answer to all the fundamental problems facing the construction of Europe.

This was the case, for example, in 1950, when the need to remilitarise Germany became an urgent issue. In June 1950, the United States felt justified, by the Korean War and growth in the Soviet threat, in requesting that Germany make an important contribution to the military defence of Western Europe.

However, memories of the war were still vivid in people's minds, and there was a very strong reaction against the idea of rearming Germany. Reaction in France was so antagonistic that the French Government, headed by René Pleven, suggested that a European army be created rather than a German national army. It would include, under a single commander, military units from the member countries. The Pleven Plan, blueprinted by Jean Monnet, was approved in principle by the French National Assembly on October 24, 1950. It went on to be accepted by the North Atlantic Treaty Council, Germany, Italy, Belgium, Luxembourg and finally, the Netherlands (in October 1951). Lengthy and exhausting negotiations then took place. The Pleven Plan was adopted by the United States in the summer of 1951, but the idea of immediately recruiting German volunteers was dropped.

René Pleven, addressing the European Parliament, relaunches Jean Monnet's idea for the creation of a European Defence Community (1953).

The concept of the European Defence Community included also the political principles of a common external policy and a common market. The former was written into Article 38 of the draft Treaty on the suggestion of Alcide de Gasperi, then Italian Prime Minister. The latter formed part of a plan for a customs union, put forward by Jan Willem Beyen, Dutch Foreign Affairs Minister.

The Treaty creating the European Defence Community was signed in Paris on May 27, 1952. The institutional system was to be along the same lines as the ECSC, with a Commission (an executive body made up of nine members), a committee of national ministers, a Parliamentary Assembly and a Court of Justice. The European army was to contain 40 divisions (14 French, 12 German, 11 Italian and 3 from the Benelux countries). National military forces would be in addition to this, with the exception of Germany.

The Strasbourg Assembly was to be responsible for filling in the small print of Article 38 (political integration). A kind of federal European power was to be created, which would include a two-chamber parliament, a European Executive Council, a Council of National Ministers and a Court of Justice.

These institutions were gradually to absorb those of the ECSC and the EDC.

The Beyen Plan (a common market) was discussed in Rome in 1953, but no successful conclusion was reached, due to political difficulties in France concerning the ratification of the new European Defence Community Treaty. Its ratification in the five other signatory countries did not meet with any significant obstacles, but in France a morass of problems was encountered. The fear of a German army and of loss of identity of the French national army, the proposal for the creation of a federal European power overseeing the nation states, the precarious situation of the French army in Indochina and reservations of the UK about the EDC were enough to provoke successive postponements of the adoption of the Plan by parliaments under the Pleven, Pinay and Mayer governments.

France requested that amendments to the Treaty, in the form of additional protocols, be made in an attempt to appease objectors in the National Assembly and to preserve France's leading role in the Community. The other signatory states were not keen to agree to the French request, but, preferring to adopt a conciliatory stance, did so at the Conference of Rome on February 25, 1953. However, when the amendments were dissected, it became clear that the protocols were incompatible with the original treaty, which had already been ratified by Germany and the Benelux countries.

Hoping to assuage the worries of the French Parliament, France then tried to obtain supportive position statements from Great Britain and the United States (in the framework of NATO), but these were not forthcoming. When Pierre Mendès-France stepped into the shoes of Prime Minister Laniel, he announced that the EDC project would be put before the French parliament after the end of the war in Indochina. A new draft project with a large number of amendments was finally presented at a conference held in Brussels beginning on August 18, 1954. However, it fell through, despite a plaintive appeal to France from President Eisenhower. On August 30, 1954, a procedural motion postponing discussion of the proposal *sine die* was adopted by the French National Assembly by 319 votes to 264.

THE WEU

The National Assembly vote marked the end of a period of fervour and enthusiasm for the construction of Europe. The rejection by one of the major signatory states of the Treaty of May 1952 brought not only the failure of the European Defence Community plan, but also compromised the adoption of a project for political union, as provided for in Article 38 and in the negotiations on the Beyen Plan. Moreover, the problem of the status of a German Army, which, by 1954 had become more urgent than ever, was still not settled.

The UK Government called a meeting in London on September 27, 1954, in which the six signatories of the 1952 draft Treaty, along with the United States, Canada and Great Britain, participated to try to settle the military problem. The meeting decided to extend the Treaty of Brussels which, in 1948, had created a defensive alliance between five European countries: Germany and Italy, the former enemies, had been excluded. Since times had changed and the former enemies had become allies, they were now taken into the fold. Force numbers were to be limited and the United Kingdom committed itself to maintaining on the continent until 1998 four army divisions and tactical air forces. The Treaty of Brussels was thus transformed into the 'Western European Union' (WEU), comprising the six countries of 'Little Europe' and

the UK. Ratification procedures were accelerated, and the WEU became official in April 1955. Germany was therefore given the right to a conventional army, without any nuclear weapons, within the framework of an alliance which had no 'Community' spirit in the traditional sense. A new initiative was needed before further moves were made to unify Europe.

THE EUROPEAN INITIATIVE RESUMES

The new thrust came from the three Benelux Governments. They were convinced that their customs union experiment, begun in 1948, had a decisive contribution to make to European integration. They had overcome a number of inevitable problems arising from a lack of harmonisation of basic policies. The secret of their pragmatic solutions was to be found in their refusal to bind themselves to the logic of pre-conditions. Their common position had increased Benelux authority in the international arena. They had profited from it to gain acceptance of their position in the Havana Charter and the GATT, Article 24 of which exempts 'common markets' from the non-discriminatory trade rules.

Within the OEEC, the Benelux countries capitalised on the benefits of multilateral liberalisation of their internal trade and the multilateral nature of payments. The Benelux Governments felt that the vast potential of their countries, arising from their geographical situation at the crossroads of European communications and the delta of the major Western European rivers, could only be exploited within the context of European integration.

Moreover, they were worried by the trend in France and Germany towards close, preferential bilateral cooperation, which would be detrimental to Benelux competitiveness. This prompted them to start up research on September 15, 1954, in parallel with the WEU negotiations, into possible ways of relaunching the drive towards European integration. Jean Monnet, President of the ECSC High Authority, resigned from his post to have complete freedom to join in the new initiative.

The problem was analysed in the following light: nationalist reactions had sabotaged the plan for a European army. Therefore, proposals for European integration should not be too ambitious. Transition would have to take place in gradual stages, with less emphasis being placed on the supranational nature of the new institutions which would replace national institutions. Moreover, any idea for reducing the importance of national armies and the symbolic power attached to them was dropped. The advocates of unification agreed that a 'softly-softly' approach was required.

Jean Monnet advocated European union in new fields such as energy, transport, and front-line industries. The Benelux countries preferred the kind of integration which they themselves had implemented. However, nothing could be decided before the ratification by national parliaments of the WEU process, and sources in Paris indicated that the Government of Pierre Mendès-France would not welcome anything with a European tinge to it.

However, the Mendès-France administration fell on February 5, 1955, and was replaced three weeks later by the Government of Edgar Faure, with Antoine Pinay as Foreign Minister and Robert Schuman as Justice Minister. Chances of successful negotiations with the new government were considered much more promising.

The Benelux Governments speeded up their work, and on April 2, Paul-Henri Spaak, the Belgian Foreign Affairs Minister, asked Chancellor

Adenauer and his Bonn colleagues, France's Pinay and Italy's Martino, to fix a meeting of ECSC Foreign Affairs Ministers to examine the possibility of extending the powers of the Community to cover all energy production, atomic energy and the transport sector. He suggested that an international conference be organised, chaired by Jean Monnet. However, the initiative got a cool welcome from the three other statesmen, and was turned down.

As a result, the Benelux Ministers met in The Hague on April 23 and decided to submit a joint memorandum to their ECSC colleagues at the end of May. It recommended that an international conference be organised, with the participation of all the OEEC members. The issues for discussion would be: European integration in the transport and atomic energy sectors and the creation of a free European trade area, which would eventually become a customs union. The text of the Benelux memorandum was finalised on May 6, and sent to ECSC Ministers.

The Ministers agreed to meet on June 1 and, since Minister Martino was obliged to remain in Sicily for regional elections, they decided on the venue of Messina.

THE MESSINA CONFERENCE

This conference provided an opportunity for movement towards European integration to be relaunched. Sicily in spring provided both a pleasant place and time for a meeting. Franco-German negotiations on the status of the Saar had reached a conclusion acceptable to both sides one week earlier. The Whitsun holiday the previous week-end had calmed the nerves of all the delegations and, after the rush of previous weeks, a holiday atmosphere prevailed.

The meetings began at 4 pm in the Messina Town Hall. The first task was the appointment of a successor to Jean Monnet as president of the ECSC High Authority. René Mayer was very rapidly chosen. Then a relatively discreet exchange of views took place on the memorandums presented by the German, Italian and Benelux Governments. The foreign ministers of the three Benelux countries held consultations and agreed not to stand in the way of any preferences expressed by their colleagues for sector-by-sector integration or general integration. Their main objective was to put all their negotiating weight behind any procedure which would result in the adoption of some kind of project.

Messina Conference: Benelux relaunches Europe (June 1, 1956). From left to right: J. Bech (Luxembourg), filming the photographers, P.-H. Spaak (Belgium) and J. W. Beyen (Netherlands).

Experience had shown that technical objections too often degenerated into unyielding conflicts, which only political negotiation would settle.

After two meetings and all the welcoming speeches, neither option seemed to stand a good chance of being adopted. Negotiations only started to hot up during a night session, from 2 am to 5 am, in the Hotel San Domenico in Taormina.

The outcome was positive. Ministers agreed that an international conference chaired by a political figure should take place. It would study proposals for sector-by- sector integration (transport, energy, nuclear energy) and examine the possibilities of creating a common market, either through a free trade area or through a customs union. The six member countries would participate in this conference, along with the United Kingdom, in its role as a 'member of the WEU, and associate member of the ECSC'.

Other states could participate, provided that notification was given before October 1, 1955. An Intergovernmental Committee was set up to draft a general report on behalf of the foreign affairs ministers.

Messina: (from left to right) Jan Willem Beyen, Gaetano Martino, Joseph Bech, Antoine Pinay, Walter Hallstein, Paul-Henri Spaak.

During the second half of June, the Ministers appointed Paul-Henri Spaak to chair this committee. They had originally intended to appoint someone with fewer demands on his time, but Spaak's international authority was incontestable.

THE SPAAK REPORT

The Messina Conference had agreed that the Intergovernmental Committee would submit a general report on October 1, 1955, and would in the meantime draw up interim reports. The time required for such an important subject was severely underestimated. An interim meeting finally took place in Noorderwijk in September 1955, and another in Brussels in February 1956. It became clear that sector-by-sector integration would be more difficult than originally thought, except in the case of nuclear energy.

On the other hand, a global approach seemed feasible, and documentation appeared to demonstrate that a customs union would be more effective than a free trade area for the creation of a common market.

The United Kingdom found this position difficult to swallow, because of its preferential customs system with the Commonwealth countries. The UK representative, R.F. Bretherton, Under Secretary of State at the Board of Trade, ended his participation in the committee activities. The heads of the six other delegations, Professor Carl Friedrich Ophuels, Ambassador of the Federal Republic of Germany, Baron Snoy et d'Oppuers, Belgian Secretary General at the Ministry for Economic Affairs, Ludovico Benvenuti, former Minister and Italian Member of Parliament, M. Félix Gaillard, former Minister and French Member of Parliament, Lambert Schaus, Ambassador of the Grand Duchy of Luxembourg and Professor Verrijn Stuart for the Netherlands, meeting under the chairmanship of Paul Henri Spaak, decided to draft the final report to the foreign affairs ministers on the basis of concordance of views which had appeared during their discussions.

The final editing work was entrusted to a small team at St.-Jean-Cap-Ferrat (France). It was made up of three experts: Pierre Uri, ECSC official and associate of Jean Monnet, Hans von der Groeben, a West German official, and Albert Hupperts from Spaak's departmental staff. The heads of the delegations had not committed their governments to anything at this stage. They worked

independently with a view to reaching unanimous agreement on methods for the attainment of the objectives proposed at Messina. These were then presented to governments as a basis for negotiation.

The document drawn up has gone down in history as the 'Spaak Report'. It was presented to a meeting of the ECSC foreign affairs ministers in Venice on May 29-30, 1956.

The conference lasted less than two hours. The report was adopted without discussion, on one condition. This was that the future treaties for the Common Market should include a chapter providing for the integration of the colonies and the overseas territories in any future economic entity. This was a concession to France.

The Spaak Report was divided into three parts: The Common Market, Euratom, Sectors requiring urgent action (energy, air transport, post and telecommunications).

The third section was treated in a summary manner, and the proposed institutional framework barely mentioned. For both the Common Market and Euratom, the report suggested a council of national ministers, taking decisions on the basis of a qualified majority, an independent Commission, a Court of Justice and some sort of Parliament.

THE CONFERENCE OF VENICE AND VAL DUCHESSE

The Conference of Venice provided the impetus for the launch of the new initiative, and gave the idea of European integration considerable credibility. Until then, there had not been much international coverage of the negotiations outside of the six participating countries. The Conference of Venice decided to adopt the proposals of the Spaak Report as the basis for negotiations on a treaty which would set up a generalised Common Market and another which would create a European nuclear energy organisation. With this purpose in mind, the Ministers called an international conference in Brussels on June 26, 1956 under the chairmanship of Spaak. The Venice Conference invited any countries which desired to join or associate themselves with the new initiative. The chances of success seemed much better in 1956 than in the previous year.

This was why, six weeks later on July 19, 1956, the OEEC Council met at ministerial level, and decided to discuss the 'creation of a free trade area comprising the customs union and OEEC member countries not participating in the union'. This was the first historical appearance of the idea of 'two-speed Europe'. The boldest countries would proceed towards integration, with the invitation to join them open to all of free Europe.

However, this is to jump ahead. First came the February 1956 Brussels conference. The 1955 Intergovernmental Committee had met in the renovated buildings of the 'Compagnie de Trieste' in rue Belliard, in the very centre of the city. The Belgian Government looked around for a calmer and more relaxed setting for the new negotiations. It asked the 'Donation Royale' for the use of the Val Duchesse Castle and its beautiful gardens, situated in countryside on the edge of the city.

It was here that the Treaties of Rome were drawn up. They were entirely inspired by the Spaak Report. A number of heads of delegations had been changed for the new phase of negotiations. Gaillard had been replaced by Maurice Faure and Robert Marjolin for France. Attilio Cattani and Roberto Ducci had taken over from Benvenuti for the Italians, and Hans Linthorst-

Val-Duchesse: the Spaak Committee writes the draft of the Treaty of Rome.

Homan replaced Verrijn Stuart for the Netherlands. However, the constructive spirit was maintained.

Difficulties abounded, but the threats overshadowing Europe in 1956, such as the Suez affair and the Soviet military occupation of Hungary, lent urgency to the negotiations. Some answer had to be found to the French request for a harmonisation of labour costs between the Common Market countries before the implementation of free competition. Bilateral talks between Adenauer and Guy Mollet on November 16, 1956 provided a solution. It was agreed that the social objectives would have to be attained before moving on to the second stage. Free competition would be brought in by a vote, for which unanimity would be required, at the end of the 4th and 5th years, easing to a qualified majority from the 6th onwards. The question of the French monetary situation, which necessitated export aid and import taxes, was settled in October 1956 by the adoption of protective clauses.

Finally, the call for consideration of the overseas territories in the Economic Community was settled by three principles, inherited from the regime introduced for the Congo Basin in 1885: free import of goods from overseas territories, non-discrimination and the provision of development aid.

There was a clash of interests between France and Germany, with the former having preferential links with certain territories and the latter not possessing any colonies. Germany had no desire to be associated in international opinion with the former colonial powers. The answer was provided by a meeting between heads of government on February 21, 1957, which laid the foundations of what has gradually become the EEC's development policy under the Yaoundé and Lomé Conventions. The Treaties were completed very rapidly, and were signed in Rome on March 25, 1957.

Speed was of the essence if advantage was to be taken of the favourable political situation. Even so, there were a number of nationalist hiccups, even in Belgium. The Belgian Prime Minister, after he had read the Treaties closely, refused to delegate full signing powers to the relevant officials. It took the threat of a ministerial crisis to bring round Achille Van Acker, who had always been lukewarm about European integration. However, the mutiny was only among the old order, which gradually gave way to the new.

THE TREATIES OF ROME AND THE ASSOCIATION
OF THE OTHER OEEC COUNTRIES

The Treaties of Rome were solemnly signed on March 25, 1957 at 4 pm in the Horatii and Curatii Hall of the Capitole Palace. All the bells of the Eternal City rung out the glad news. After signing the Treaties, Paul-Henri Spaak declared: 'This time, the Western nations have not lacked courage and have not acted too late. Unhappy memories and perhaps errors have spurred them on, have given them the necessary courage to forget old quarrels, overturn out-dated traditions and think and act in a new manner to bring about the biggest voluntary and controlled transformation in the history of Europe' ('Combats inachevés' – The Battle goes on – II, page 99).

Yet the Six still had to counter the risk that the clubbishness of the European Economic Community, the European Atomic Community and the European Coal and Steel Community might provoke further division of free Europe, which had already been reduced by Yalta and Prague to the OEEC countries. Consequently, the OEEC Council began in July 1956 to study ways of bringing about an association of the EEC and non-EEC groups. Experts concluded that a free trade area covering both the European Economic Community and the remaining OEEC member countries was technically feasible.

On the basis of the experts' findings, the OEEC met at ministerial level on February 13, 1957 (a few weeks before the signing of the Treaties of Rome). It decided to open negotiations for the establishment of a free trade area 'associating on a multilateral basis the six members of the Common Market and the remaining member countries of the OEEC'. It further proposed that Peter Thorneycroft, President of the OEEC Council and UK Chancellor of the Exchequer, should coordinate the activities of specialised working groups and carry out the same function for the free trade area as Spaak would for the Common Market.

On March 8, 1957, the OEEC Council opened the negotiations by setting up three working parties.

On the left: signing ceremony of the Treaty of Rome, March 25, 1957. On the right: signatures of the Treaty.

Television makes its debut: Eurovision debate on the Treaties of Rome (Strasbourg, early 1957 with Michel Debré, Paul Struye, René Pleven, Jean Fohrman and the journalist José Kullmann (FR 3)).

Talks got off to a fairly rapid start, but were then slowed down in the second half of 1957 so as not to hinder parliamentary ratification of the Treaties of Rome.

The unhappy procrastination over the European Defence Community comes to mind here! But the OEEC Council decided as early as October 19, 1957 to set up an intergovernmental committee at ministerial level. It was chaired by Reginald Maudling, UK Paymaster-General.

A practical difficulty was posed by the need for the Common Market countries to present a common position. This would have required lengthy and difficult negotiations between the six member states, particularly since the Treaties of Rome had entered into force on January 1, 1958. On the other hand, the application of the Treaties gave rise to trade discrimination, which heightened the impatience of the other European states.

Equanimity was restored when a report defining the common position of the Six was drawn up and adopted during a conference in Venice on September 20, 1958 between the EEC member countries and the Commission.

The document was known as the Ockrent Report, named after the Belgian Ambassador and head of the OEEC delegation. It was finalised by the EEC's Ministerial Council and sent to all the OEEC member countries on October 17, 1956. It carried the signature of Professor Müller-Armack, Secretary of State of the Federal Republic of Germany, who was then President of the Community Council.

French concerns had been largely taken into account by the five other delegations, and France raised no objections to the report.

The EEC report was discussed on two occasions by the OEEC Council, first at the end of October, and then on November 14, 1958. There was a great deal of tension in the air, but no forewarning of French unilateral action on November 15. At the end of the Council, a bombshell was dropped by French Information Minister, Jacques Soustelle, who announced that France did not accept the idea of an association of the Common Market with the remaining OEEC countries. The reason given was that this association would not apply a common external tariff.

In making this move, France both rejected the proposition which had been

officially accepted by all the OEEC countries and negated the Ockrent Report which had been officially transmitted to all the OEEC countries on October 17, 1958. The French Government acted totally in isolation, contacting neither the other OEEC member countries nor any of the Six! This brutal break in negotiations, spelt out at a press conference, had de Gaulle's mark on it, and it was to be seen again in the entry negotiations for the UK in 1963 and in successive years.

The idea of an association was therefore shelved indefinitely, and Europe split once again. The 'European Free Trade Association' (EFTA) was set up by the Treaty of Stockholm on November 20, 1959, between seven OEEC countries. At the time, EFTA had a total population of 87 million, compared to 164 million for the Common Market. The OEEC countries did not act out of spite towards the EEC, but were concerned that integration of national economies would make the EEC states much stronger. However, the situation rectified itself with time, and a number of EFTA countries joined the EEC in the 1970s and 80s.

The launching of the
European Economic Community:

rapid take-off,
years filled with hope

*

Hans von der Groeben

The initial situation

Walter Hallstein, President of the EEC Commission.

The Treaty setting up the European Economic Community entered into force on January 1, 1958. Many people felt it to be unsatisfactory. It did not fulfil the hopes of the European federalists who wanted the creation of a United States of Europe. And yet, since the European institutions were given a certain degree of economic power based on European law, it was also rejected by those who felt that national sovereignty should be kept intact: these Europeans felt that sovereignty had been seriously violated by the Treaty of Rome.

Under the Presidency of Walter Hallstein, the nine members of the European Commission were given the task of setting up a European Community, a Common Market, in accordance with the directions of the Treaty of the European Economic Community. Within this framework, they were to present the Council of Ministers with explicit proposals. The Treaty gave the Commission the necessary powers to fulfil these tasks; the political goal was only generally outlined in declarations of intent. The failure of the European Defence Community and the rejection of political unification by the French Parliament had demonstrated that there could be no hope of rapid political integration. The first step was therefore to extend to all sectors of the economy the integration which began in 1952 with the creation of the ECSC. An internal European market had to be created as a preliminary. The conditions for such an extension existed. Politicians, economists, trade unionists and scientists in the forefront of new ideas all agreed that the protectionism of the past should not be allowed to re-surface and that the advantages of a market economy could only be fully exploited in a large-scale market, a common market at European level.

The members of the Commission and of the Council of Ministers only had extremely limited powers to promote integration. The lack of means was acute for political integration in the economic, foreign and defence policy sectors.

It is of prime importance that the Community's initial working conditions be kept in mind. In order to correctly judge the results and failures of integration, the room for manoeuvre which the EEC Treaties gave to politicians should not be over-estimated. This would be to commit an error frequently seen both in the past and present.

THE BEGINNINGS

Despite the limitations of the Commission's powers and the restrictions of the Treaty, the members of the Commission set to work with confidence. When the Treaty was negotiated, a small group of politicians and senior civil servants emerged who were enthusiastic, convinced of the European idea, and led in masterly fashion by a great European, Paul-Henri Spaak. It was clear that they could accomplish a great deal, provided that the politicians were not guided solely by national considerations but also by Community objectives in the political, economic and scientific fields. From the outset, the Commission considered its work as political, although it was fully aware of the limits imposed upon it by the Treaties.

The first task was to implement those clauses of the Treaty which provided for considerable intervention in affairs which, up until then, had been exclusively regulated at national level. At the beginning the provisions were nothing more than ink on paper.... They had been thought up at the discussion table and analysed by national governments; but now the time had come to breathe life into them. Many observers thought at the time that the obstacles would prove to be too large and that the 'nationalist' tendencies of the politicians and officials would be too strong. They predicted that the attempts would fail. However, it became clear that the provisions of the Treaty were realistic, that they were suited to the economic backcloth and corresponded exactly to hopes for a rational creation of a large-scale, liberalised market. The ideas were even accepted by political or economic groups which had previously looked upon them with reticence. Naturally, this did not mean that opposition to the Community had died out, or that it would not plague its future development.

THE COMMON MARKET

Negotiations to create a true Common Market certainly turned out to be long, but it was without any serious difficulty that progress was made in the first decade towards a customs union and free movement of goods and persons. Steps were also taken towards the liberalisation of services and the right to freedom of establishment. However, barriers to the free movement of capital remained and were even fortified when national monetary policy required this. On June 1, 1968, one year before the scheduled expiration of the transitional period, the Common Market became a reality. It not only covered industrial goods, but also agricultural produce, thanks to the agricultural policy put forward by Sicco Mansholt.

After the introduction of common external customs tariffs and EEC regulations on external trade in agricultural produce, the foundations of a common trade policy were laid.

The elaboration of a common competition policy was one of the key elements in the creation of a large internal market in Europe. The conditions for fair and efficient competition within the Common Market needed to be created. Significant measures have included the outlawing of cartels for the purpose of market domination and the abuse of economic power by a company or a group of companies; the regulation and control of subsidies; the harmonisation of legal provisions, particularly in areas such as product safety, technical standards and health protection; and standardisation of tax systems. Worthwhile results were obtained in all these fields in the period up to 1970,

Sicco Mansholt, architect of the Common Agricultural Policy.

when the transitional period ended. The competition provisions of the Treaty were generally accepted, since they corresponded to the requirements of the member states and of the economic interests concerned.

The EEC's Court of Justice and the legal system which it established have played a fundamental role in the Community from the very beginning. The Court, in its interpretation of EEC regulations, saw the Treaty as a sort of Constitution which had to be placed in an organisational setting. A clear example of the intent to make progress towards integration was the immediate application of European law, the priority given to this law over national standards and the establishment of fundamental laws recognised in all the member states of the European Community.

PLANS FOR THE FUTURE

The intuition of the founding fathers of the EEC has proven to be correct. The Commission has demonstrated its ability to work for a future beyond the stage of simple economic integration to the more ambitious objective of European political unification.

It was thought at first that this goal could be easily attained, and the disappointment when this proved not to be the case was magnified at a time when the clouds on the horizon were already looking very dark. When the Treaty of Rome was signed all the governments were agreed on the objectives and the means to attain them, but within months the French government of General de Gaulle declared its opposition to any hint of supranational integration. France under de Gaulle wanted, like the other member states, reinforcement of Europe's position on the political and economic fronts, but it wanted to achieve this objective through simple cooperation between fully sovereign nation states. Apart from this, all the provisions of the Treaty were respected and an EEC-wide Common Market grew up covering agricultural produce. However, when steps were taken to draw up the Common Agricultural Policy, it became clear that divergent national interests could stand in the way of integration if positions were adopted solely in accordance with national criteria.

The agricultural proposals drawn up by the Commission called for free circulation within the Common Market, unification of customs policy, joint financing and a preferential system to be applied to EEC production. The proposals took into account the need for protection of European agriculture, but were also intended to allow internal market forces to have full play. This had a beneficial influence on geographical balances, on the viability of investments and on the division of employment. Care was taken to avoid abuse of guaranteed prices: guarantees were planned only for the cereals, sugar beet and dairy sectors. The Commission's proposals included measures to prevent overproduction and the wasting of financial resources.

Although normally the Agricultural Ministers had difficulty in agreeing, they got together continually to extend the market regulation system to include other agricultural products. And in the European Parliament there were few Members willing to argue for a free market economy in farm produce.

This led to the present situation which is characterised by large-scale surpluses of many farm commodities. If the expensive EEC surplus products are to find outlets on the world market, large subsidies have to be paid. The EEC's finances are being frittered away on unproductive expenditure and cannot therefore be invested in more important areas, such as research, training,

regional policy and development policy. In 1958, the author of this text, along with a number of colleagues, attempted to amend the agricultural system by tying it to market prices and by only paying agricultural subsidies in the form of direct payments to boost the incomes of smaller and poorer farmers. The project did not get beyond the Commission, where it was rejected by a majority of the Commissioners.

The French government argued that the Common Agricultural Policy must be set up simultaneously with a Common Market in industrial goods. The German government was reluctant to embrace the new agricultural policies because its agricultural trade lobby and many small farmers, representing a significant part of the electorate, feared the competitive edge that France would have because of the lower prices of that country's farm products.

The integration process continued to deteriorate as France began making demands bordering on ultimatums in a number of fields. Soon member governments of the EEC were acting solely according to national interest, or what passed as national interest, rather than for the sake of the Community.

Living in a dream world, the Community continued to plan for full implementation of the Treaty of Rome. Apart from directions specifically laid down in the Treaty, paper proposals were made for medium-term economic policy, monetary policy, the creation of a European patent system, harmonisation of direct and indirect taxes, industrial policy and the creation of a regional policy fund.

POLITICAL INTEGRATION

Progress towards completion of the Common Market brought the Commission and the Council face to face with a crucial problem: how were questions left unsettled when the Treaty was concluded in 1957 to be dealt with? The Commission quickly understood a point which national politicians took longer to comprehend, namely that the future of integration depended largely on the manner in which these gaps were filled. Unresolved problems included the enlargement of the European Community to include other states, the unification of economic policy and the methods to be adopted to achieve political integration.

The United Kingdom had refused to participate in the negotiations culminating in the Treaty of Rome, since leading British politicians felt emotionally

The Belgian Presidency of the Council in 1961. From left to right: Charles Héger, P.-H. Spaak, Henri Fayat, Maurice Brasseur and (standing) Ambassador Joseph Van der Meulen.

Hans von der Groeben 131

detached from mainland Europe: they were also wary of participating in a Community whose rules were seen as a threat to British independence. After it became clear that the Community worked, the UK changed its mind and in 1961 submitted a request for entry. Reactions to the UK's application differed in the founder states. Influential politicians and economists in the Federal Republic of Germany, the Netherlands, Belgium and Italy felt that British entry was desirable, and even necessary, if the economic and political division of Western Europe was to be avoided. However, in the light of the previous scepticism of the UK, a large number of Europeans felt priority should be given to economic and political consolidation of the European Community as it stood, and that enlargement should only be considered at a later date. General de Gaulle felt that the narrower framework of an EEC limited to the six founder states would be more favourable for his own policy of maintaining an EEC in which the member states retained as much autonomy as possible and for reducing its economic, political and military dependence on the United States as far as was feasible. For de Gaulle, the United Kingdom was the Trojan Horse of the United States. On January 14, 1964, he placed before his European partners a 'fait accompli'. Without consulting any of them, he announced that France was withdrawing from UK entry negotiations which were in full swing. This unilateral position was in complete contradiction to the norms of behaviour which had grown up in relations between member states. It led the integration process into serious crisis, which was only very gradually resolved, and left its mark on the future development of the European Community.

During the Treaty negotiations (1956-1957), hopes of harmonisation of economic and monetary policy had to be abandoned in the face of German fears that the EEC institutions would act in an interventionist manner and threaten the market economy principle. Neither the French nor the German governments were willing to grant new powers to the Community institutions, and without the support of Paris and Bonn it was impossible to draw up common economic and monetary policies. It soon became clear, as the articles of the Treaty were gradually implemented, that without harmonisation of national economic policies the Common Market could only be half-finished and might even crumble.

The Commission continually recommended better coordination of economic policies and greater harmonisation. It was thought that this could only be achieved once the political integration process had begun. However, things did not happen this way, for opinions on the objectives of political integration grew increasingly divergent.

The majority of Commission members were not so naive as to believe that it was possible to create a federation of states from nothing, simply by concluding a treaty. But they thought that the success of economic integration would provide a firm base for future political development and that the *modus operandi* of the Treaty of Rome could be applied also to political integration. The economic vocation of the EEC's Council of Ministers presented clear political opportunities, and the Commission felt it would be the ideal body to weave in foreign and defence policies with the economic integration process. This prompted the Foreign Affairs Ministers into holding political consultations in 1958 and 1959. Here again, General de Gaulle had his own individual ideas. He proposed the Fouchet Plan, based on purely inter-governmental political cooperation. The six member states were not able to reach agreement on this proposal. The Dutch delegation said that rules of supra-nationality, as specified in the Treaty of Rome for economic relations, had logically to be

'We have one foot over the edge and we are holding on to a tuft of grass' (P.-H. Spaak before the failure of entry negotiations with the UK, January 29, 1963, interviewed by journalists, including Guido Naets).

Continuity: (from right to left) Robert Schuman, Jean Monnet and Walter Hallstein.

applied also to political questions; if this was not to be the case, there could be no reason to refuse membership of the EEC to the United Kingdom or other Western European countries. The French government was not prepared to accept either of these premises.

There were two important conclusions to be drawn from this episode. On the one hand, all plans for the extension of economic integration to the political field had failed. On the other, the French attempt to limit or reduce the supranational core of the Community to mere political cooperation had failed. This is why, in subsequent years, the French adopted a strategy of rendering ineffective any provisions of the Treaty of Rome which did not correspond to France's conception of the Community and of opposing all proposals which aimed to strengthen EEC institutions. It also explains why the French Foreign Affairs Minister, Couve de Murville, rejected both the direct election of the European Parliament and the extension of the Parliament's powers. Contrary to what was stipulated in the Treaty, France was not willing to follow the line taken by a majority of the Council of Ministers on important questions. The Commission was refused political status and came to be considered as a purely utilitarian and technical body.

In the Luxembourg Compromise, the five other member states had to give way to French demands in order to preserve the Community. They did not, however, renounce the essence of the Treaty on the legal front. Paris countered by practising the 'empty chair' policy in EEC institutions for six months, hoping that such a war of attrition would force its partners into accepting its diktat. It was only after General de Gaulle retired from politics that the EEC was able to repair the damage and tackle all the many problems which had had to be shelved: the relaunch began at The Hague summit in 1969.

CONCLUSION

To what extent should we be satisfied or disappointed by the results that the EEC has achieved? Should we resign ourselves to the possibility that the EEC

will always have limitations? Those of us involved from the beginning hoped, in our brightest dreams, that the political unification of Europe would be completed in the space of one generation. We hoped that a Europe which was unified would recover its confidence, preserve its culture, find fresh inspiration, assure its own defence and win the respect of the rest of the world for its political importance stemming from its human resources and its spiritual potential. Given the powerful idealism of our dreams, it has to be said that the success of the EEC has been very limited. We underestimated the strength of the instinct for survival of the nation states and the willingness to cling to national myths. We believed that the experience of two world wars had taught even more to the European nations and their leaders than became apparent. However, the achievement of our dream is clearly going to take some time yet. New concepts and ways of thinking take time to become simple facts of life. Realising Europe's full potential is, in fact, a difficult task.

Nevertheless, many victories have been won. Progress in the post-World War Two period has been spectacular when compared to the inter-war years, and the European Community has shown itself to be a viable enterprise. We now live in an economic community, although it is incomplete. We have an outline of European law, within the framework of which steps have been taken towards blending and unifying national law. We have created a community of states living in peace. The legal systems and jurisdiction of these states is now based upon more than international law. The states have taken the process further, and harmonised their laws to a certain extent. Even more importantly, there is a continual growth of cultural, artistic and scientific exchanges. The economic network of the Community is becoming increasingly dense and the strength of relations between the peoples of Europe is for ever growing. Cruel criticism and open hostility towards the Community have given way to new manners of thinking, characterised by acceptance by citizens from individual countries of their neighbours' differences, and, at first, strange customs. Mutual understanding and transnational friendships have grown, and that has to be very encouraging. It is at the level of day-to-day life that the foundations of new trust are to be found. I believe that, despite all the obstacles, politicians will succeed in re-organising Western Europe while respecting all its many traditions and characteristics. Our cultures will then be reinforced and Europe will be able to play its fullest possible role in world affairs.

SELECTED BIBLIOGRAPHY

Complete information on the origin of the European Community and the history of its creation can be found in the following works:
Robert Lemaignen, *L'Europe au Berceau – Souvenirs d'un Technocrate* (Europe in the Cradle – Memories of a Technocrat), Paris, Plon, 1964.
Hans von der Groeben, *Combat pour l'Europe* (The Fight for Europe), Brussels, 1984. French translation of the book 'Aufbaujahre der Europäischen Gemeinschaft', Baden-Baden, 1982.
Hans Jürgen Küsters, *Die Gründung der Europäischen Wirtschaftsgemeinschaft* (The Foundations of the European Economic Community), Baden-Baden, 1982.

CRISIS AND CONFRONTATION

*

Pierre Gerbet

The first few years of the European Community were packed with achievements, but they were also fraught with tension and crises which left a deep mark on the construction of Europe.

General de Gaulle, who returned to power in June 1958, did not share the beliefs of the founding fathers of Europe. Although he understood the urgent necessity of economic, political and strategic union in Europe, he thought that the Community was going the wrong way about it. He criticised the supranational nature of the European Coal and Steel Community and more particularly of the European Defence Community. He did not clarify his position on the Treaty of Rome, but was very hostile towards EURATOM and not very convinced of the need for a common market. Was he going to call into question the existence of the three Communities? There was a great deal of apprehension among the advocates of Europe that this would be the case. However, de Gaulle accepted the economic aspects of the Communities, although he rejected their institutional and political objectives.

De Gaulle made a great contribution to economic Europe by bringing France into the Common Market. Whereas financial and economic difficulties suffered by the waning Fourth Republic had threatened the effective application of the Treaty of Rome, economic and monetary reforms in December 1958 put France in a position to face the competition of its partners and to begin dismantling its customs barriers. De Gaulle had been convinced – in particular by his Finance Minister, Antoine Pinay – of the need for the French economy to open up to the outside world and to develop with the stimulus of competition. The Common Market gave France the chance gradually to dismantle its traditional protectionism, within the limited framework of the customs union composed of six countries, surrounded by a moderate common external tariff.

This was the reason for de Gaulle's rejection of the British proposal for a large free trade area, within which the Common Market would lose some of its significance. It also explains why he accepted an acceleration of tariff removal among the Six, on the condition that the common external tariff was set up at the same time. He obtained this in the face of Dutch and German reservations. France never sought to go back on these moves towards union, even in difficult periods. In the serious crisis of May-June 1968, it refrained from introducing temporary import restriction measures and did not hold back on the complete opening up of the Common Market on July 1 of the same year. At the same time, de Gaulle put all his weight behind the elaboration and implementation of a Common Agricultural Policy. The Treaty of Rome only laid down the principles for this sector of policy. Such a policy was clearly in French interests, but was also requested by the Netherlands and by the EEC Commission – despite German reservations – and it constituted a powerful instrument of economic integration.

Although he accepted economic integration, de Gaulle made it plain that he did not like the means chosen to achieve it. He stated his preference for a Europe of nation states over the ideal of a supranational Europe.

After the collapse of the EDC, the federalist objective was not so clearly stated. The Treaty of Rome only set the modest objective of laying 'the foundations of an ever closer union among the peoples of Europe', and did not define the precise nature of the proposed union, nor the mechanisms by which it should be achieved. But it set up, as did the Treaty of Paris, institutions which were independent of governments (Commission, Parliamentary Assembly, Court of Justice) which, in the eyes of some, were the embryo of true European power which would naturally grow with the development of the Communities. De Gaulle denounced the whole idea at a press conference on September 5, 1960:

'What is Europe? What are the pillars upon which we can build? Its nation states are certainly very different one from the other, and each has its soul, its history, its sadnesses, its glory and its ambitions. But it is the nation states which alone have the right to order and have the authority to act. It is nothing but a wild dream to imagine something which is efficient, which can act and which will be approved by the peoples apart from and above the states.... True, it has been possible to set up certain bodies which are more or less extra-national. They have technical qualities, but they do not have and they cannot have authority and, consequently, political authority.... It is totally natural that the nation states of Europe have at their disposal specialised bodies to prepare and, if necessary, to follow up their decisions, but decision-making power belongs to the state. Decisions can only belong to states and can only be taken by them through cooperation'.

At the same time, de Gaulle was also preparing a strategy, set out in secret instructions addressed to his Prime Minister, Michel Debré. These were published in 1985 in his 'Lettres, notes et carnets, juin 1958 – décembre 60' (Letters, Notes and Jottings, June 1958 – December 60, Plon, pp 398-9). De Gaulle stated: 'The integrationists will only accept *confederate Europe* gradually. But we should be careful not to throw fat on the fire..... As for the various Communities, we must not give the impression of directly attacking them or the Treaties. If we succeed in bringing about a confederate Europe, the Communities will be *ipso facto* put in their place'.

The first stage required, in de Gaulle's opinion, the establishment of political cooperation between the Six. This was the object of the project entitled 'Union of States' proposed by France in the form of the Fouchet Plan. It suggested the creation of a Council of Heads of State and Government which would take decisions by unanimity voting in the fields of foreign policy, defence and culture and all matters not covered by the EEC Treaties.

France's partners recognised the desirability of political cooperation between states to facilitate economic integration and to increase solidarity, on the condition that it was given a Community character. Italy and the Benelux countries were very attached to a system which gave them guarantees against possible Franco-German hegemony, the seed of which could be seen in the *rapprochement* between General de Gaulle and Chancellor Adenauer. The Five wanted an independent Commission to be attached to the Council, like that of the Communities, whereas de Gaulle was calling for an inter-governmental

General de Gaulle welcomed by Chancellor Konrad Adenauer at the Bonn European Summit of July 18, 1961.

General de Gaulle dit not share the ideas of the 'fathers of Europe' (press conference on September 5, 1960).

Commission. They also called for the inclusion of a revision clause which would allow the introduction at a later date of a degree of supranational power, but de Gaulle refused this outright. In addition, de Gaulle was calling for the competence of this Political Union to be extended at a later date to include the economy. This would, according to his plan, have allowed subordination of the Communities to the body of inter-governmental cooperation taking decisions by unanimity voting. However, France's parties refused to jeopardise the building of Europe in this way. More profound differences of opinion became apparent on the relationship of any Union of States with the North Atlantic Treaty Alliance and on the participation of Great Britain (see below).

De Gaulle's plan to organise a system of political cooperation distinct from the Communities, and even against them, to 'put them in their place' finally came to grief in April 1962.

He then adopted a strategy which he had been keeping in reserve, namely a direct offensive on the 'first fruits of integration'. He had already begun implementing this stategy prior to 1962. He rebutted the High Authority of the ECSC in 1959 when there was a serious coal crisis, by rejecting the measures which it proposed. France was joined on this occasion by Germany, which was also hostile to this supranational 'interventionism'. De Gaulle also succeeded at the end of 1961 in ousting the President of EURATOM, Etienne Hirsch, who was considered too supranational in attitude.

France had good relations with the European Commission of the EEC at the outset. The Commission had done a great deal to develop the Common Agricultural Policy, and both were agreed on the need for an economic community which went beyond free trade. But de Gaulle was irritated by the fact that the Commission considered itself as the forerunner of a future European government. The Community is not a state, he declared. He opposed the Commission's attempt to accredit ambassadors overseas, and was irritated by President Hallstein's protocol behaviour. At the same time, he refused to allow the European Parliament to be elected by direct universal suffrage.

After the failure of the Fouchet Plan, de Gaulle stiffened his tone. In a press

Maurice Couve de Murville with the UK negotiators Edward Heath (on his left) and Christopher Soames (on his right), March 22, 1962.

conference on May 15, 1960, he strongly attacked supranational ideas and poured scorn on what he termed 'stateless people'. He accused the advocates of a supranational Europe of being in the pay of the United States, and the United States of being the true force for federalism in Europe. This brutal declaration caused a great deal of upset in the Five and in France itself, where a number of ministers, led by Pierre Pflimlin, withdrew from the Pompidou Government. Jean Monnet's Action Committee for the United States of Europe spoke for the Europeans. A declaration issued on June 26, which had a resounding impact, denounced de Gaulle's 'spirit of superiority and domination' and extolled the complementary nature of the Community method to inter-governmental cooperation for the construction of Europe. 'This method is totally new. It does not include a central government; but results in Community decisions within the Council of Ministers. It is able to do this precisely because proposals for a solution to joint problems are made by an independent European body, which allows removal of the need for unanimity. The Parliament and the Court of Justice underline the community nature of this entity. This method is the true 'federating force' in Europe'.

The test of strength came in 1965 over the funding of the Common Agricultural Policy. France wanted a financial Regulation which would assure the autonomy and the durability of the agricultural policy. The Commission proposed one, but attempted to tie this to acceptance by de Gaulle of a revision of the Treaty which would have increased the powers of the Parliament and the Commission itself. This package of proposals led to disagreement among the Five, and was rejected by the French Government. De Gaulle brought the EEC into crisis by practising the 'empty chair' policy in Brussels. French officials no longer participated in EEC activities. Was France going to withdraw from the Common Market and thus deal a fatal blow to European construction? There was a great deal of emotion and anxiety not only in the Five, but also in France. The irritation of sectors of the population in favour of Europe, and in particular the farmers, led eventually to de Gaulle having to face a second ballot in the December 1965 presidential elections.

De Gaulle did not, however, intend to bring about the break-up of the EEC, whose usefulness to France he recognised. He wanted to use the crisis not only to resist granting the Commission and the Parliament a wider role, but to place a question mark over the use of majority voting in the Council of Ministers. Even though such a system was stipulated in the Treaty, de Gaulle judged it to be a threat to national sovereignty. The Five, on the other hand, considered it to be indispensable for reasons of efficiency, if national opposition was to be overcome and deadlock in the decision-making process avoided.

MEMBER STATES AGREE TO DISAGREE

After more than six months of crisis, the Six reached agreement on January 30, 1966 to co-habit once again, but with each member state holding on to its own concept of Europe. This is known as the 'Luxembourg Compromise', which is to all intents and purposes a declaration of disagreement. It does no more than give a summary of the two different approaches to decision-making on matters of prime national interest for one or more member states. The Five reaffirmed their commitment to the letter of the Treaty, and said that the maximum should be done to reconcile different points of view before moving on to a majority vote, whereas France declared that discussions should continue until unanimous agreement was reached.

General de Gaulle demands departure of Walter Hallstein (June 1967).

The French Government did not succeed in getting an amendment of the Treaty, but it was clear that if the remaining partners tried to use majority voting, a new crisis would arise. Thus the principle of majority voting was maintained but its application became rather risky. Most of the time, it was not used in areas where the Treaty stipulated that it should be used. The consequences for the Community were very serious. In practice, each member state maintained a veto. This may have been justified if essential interests were at stake, but it eventually began to be used for all matters, since member states alone decided whether or not a matter was of extreme national importance to them. The practice of unanimity voting was abused, and began to be used in all areas. The Council of Ministers consequently had increasing difficulty in taking decisions, even minor ones.

At the same time, the Commission found itself rebutted. The Five had not accepted France's demands, which would, to all intents and purposes, have resulted in control of the Commission by the Council of Ministers and a limitation of the Commission's right to initiate proposals. The original nature of the Commission, namely its independence and its right to propose initiatives, was preserved. However, the member states did adopt a 'code of good conduct' for application to the Commission which stipulated that the latter should no longer try to force the hand of national governments, or regard itself as a European government. The role of the Commission was nevertheless diminished, not so much by this rapping of its knuckles as by the use of unanimity voting. It could no longer put forward daring proposals which had the backing of some member states despite the reservations of others. It was obliged to draw up proposals which would be acceptable to all, even to the states with the most reservations. It was to play more the role of honest broker than of the 'driving force' of the Community. The fact that the French Government had obtained the departure of Walter Hallstein increased the Commission's caution. Hallstein had for ten years played an essential role in the implementation of the Treaty of Rome, and had considerable prestige and

authority. Finally, in 1967, the two Commissions of the EEC and EURATOM and the ECSC High Authority were fused into one executive power, the European Commission.

The French Government and de Gaulle's followers felt that, as a result of the 'Luxembourg Compromise', the Community had become more realistic and therefore more efficient. The Europeans, on the other hand, felt that they had been weakened and that the system had been brought closer to mere inter-governmental cooperation. The economic integration process would therefore go no further than the creation of an imperfect customs union and the implementation of agricultural policy. It was very difficult to get beyond this stage. The EEC was ill-prepared, in the seventies, for the international monetary crisis, the oil crisis, the halt in growth and rising unemployment. Joint action proved impossible to organise or was insufficient. The cost of the weakening of the EEC institutions turned out to be very high.

After de Gaulle fell from power, opposition to a supranational United States of Europe became less strong, but the inter-governmental aspect of the EEC became more accentuated as the institutions developed. His successors stuck to the idea of a Europe of nation states, and considered that a European Government could not be engendered by a technical body – meaning here the Commission. Nation states continued to act upon unanimous decisions. Georges Pompidou began organising meetings of heads of state and government on a regular basis, and Valéry Giscard d'Estaing succeeded in 1974 in transforming these into a regular feature of the EEC landscape. These summits were named the European Council and became the supreme body of the EEC. By way of compensation, direct universal suffrage was introduced for the European Parliament in 1979. Despite the budgetary powers of the latter, it can only exercise a very limited influence on EEC legislation as decided by the Council of Minsters. Nothing was done to increase the powers of the Commission.

EUROPEAN EUROPE OR ATLANTIC EUROPE?

Fundamental differences over the end objective and dimensions of a united Europe divided the Six to a much greater extent than differences of opinion over the method of integration and the institutions. De Gaulle felt that in order to exist Europe must assert its own personality, define its role in international relations, have its own foreign policy and even be able to defend itself. He wanted a 'European Europe', more detached from the United States, which would be capable of playing a role between the two superpowers and negotiating with the East the reunification of Europe. France, which was the only major power among the Six, would take the leading role. Europe, for de Gaulle, was less an end in itself than an instrument of French policy. This was why political cooperation was interesting, for it would allow France to direct its partners and to implement a foreign and a defence policy which would be based upon French ideas.

However, this grandiose vision did not tempt the other member states, who attached an absolute priority to the Atlantic Alliance and did not want to break away from the United States or give up the US nuclear umbrella. This seemed much more credible than the French nuclear force whose use was, anyway, reserved by de Gaulle for defence of the national territory. They further considered that a policy of 'third force' between the East and the West would be dangerous and might result in the United States pulling out of Europe,

Franco-British Summit on May 20, 1971: Edward Heath, Georges Pompidou and Jacques Chaban-Delmas.

which would leave it vulnerable to Soviet pressure. France's partners therefore remained militarily and politically attached to Atlantic Europe and to the United States.

During discussions of the Fouchet Plan, the Five requested that the defence policy of the future political union be drawn up 'within the framework of NATO' (Netherlands) or 'contribute to the reinforcement of NATO' (the other member states). De Gaulle, on the other hand, was opposed to the very mention of the Atlantic Alliance in the text of the draft Treaty.

These fundamental differences were also reflected in attitudes towards the United Kingdom. The latter wanted to enter the Community, since the obstacle of supranationality had been removed by de Gaulle. The Five were in favour of letting Britain enter. Since it was to be a Europe of States, a British-style Europe, there was no reason not to let the UK join! Italy and the Benelux countries further felt that the UK would redress the balance slightly, in the face of the strong Franco-German friendship, and would act as a guarantee of Atlantic orthodoxy. It was precisely for these reasons that de Gaulle refused to let Britain join. He wanted to create a political union with just the six original member states but, in the absence of Great Britain, Belgium and the Netherlands refused to continue the Fouchet Plan negotiations.

A few months later, on January 14, 1963, de Gaulle, speaking at a press conference, delivered a spectacular rebuff of the British application. He criticised the British for having placed their nuclear force under US control and declared that a Community enlarged to include Great Britain and other candidate countries risked dilution into the huge free-trade area proposed by President Kennedy. Europe would no longer be able to remain 'European'.

This veto strongly irritated France's partners, who had not been consulted, and sharply changed the Community atmosphere. The fears of the Five concerning French foreign policy were confirmed in March 1966 when France withdrew from the military integration of NATO. Their desire for British entry

was heightened as a result. Great Britain requested entry for a second time in 1967, encouraged by the 'Luxembourg Compromise' on the practice of unanimity voting. De Gaulle again vetoed British entry, even refusing to negotiate, for fear that the Five would show themselves to be too favourable to British membership, in particular since Britain now declared itself willing to accept the Treaty of Rome, which had not been the case when its first application was made.

De Gaulle still felt that additional members and their various interests would create running problems for the Communities, and that they would eventually be transformed into a free trade area. The other member states reacted vigorously to de Gaulle's individualistic stance. The German Government sought a way to avoid crisis, but Italy and the Benelux countries moved closer to Great Britain in order to try to exert pressure on France through the WEU. Community activities ground to a standstill.

PRESIDENT POMPIDOU FACES UP TO REALITY

After the departure of General de Gaulle, President Pompidou was finally obliged to accept the EEC's enlargement in order to break the deadlock and obtain a financial Regulation, or law, in relation to the Common Agricultural Policy. France could no longer reject both supranationality and Great Britain. Pompidou felt that British membership of the EEC might serve to redress the balance against a Germany which had become economically too strong and to stengthen the trend towards a Europe of States.

Differences of opinion over foreign and defence policy remained, but they became less accentuated as Franco-American relations improved and the other members of the Atlantic Alliance finally accepted the French nuclear policy. Cooperation was able to begin in the field of foreign policy, on the basis of unanimity voting. Defence was excluded, hence the limitations of the Community's action in this sphere. The dichotomy between European Europe and Atlantic Europe stopped plaguing the EEC, and it could begin to seek identity and to express it in the international arena.

How the Community

faced the

new challenges

*

Emanuele Gazzo

The late sixties marked much more than the end of a decade for European integration. As Jean Monnet put it: 'We have changed era'. At the conference of heads of state and government in The Hague on December 1-2, 1969, the six founder member states of the Community began a new adventure. As Robert Schuman put it in his declaration on May 9, 1950, they took a 'leap into the unknown'.

The historical significance of the December 1969 decisions is to be found in the three objectives which the Community set itself. These were as follows:

1. The *completion* before December 31 of the first transitional period (which ran for twelve years beginning on January 1, 1958).

2. The economic, political and institutional *reinforcement* and *extension* of the Community.

3. The *enlargement* of the Community (this point caused bitter controversy) to include four countries which had applied for membership, namely the United Kingdom, Ireland, Denmark and Norway.

These three objectives were interconnected, with no enlargement being possible before completion of the first stage. Member states knew that enlargement could fail if reinforcement of Community structures did not take place. Everyone recognised that the building of Europe required *fresh impetus* if Europe was to face the future with dynamism.

Study of the history of European unification shows that the words 'fresh impetus' or 'recovery' crop up frequently. It indicates both that the Community process has come up against difficulties which cannot be resolved by existing methods and that the will exists to try to overcome the difficulties. The Community needs this fundamental dynamism if it is to survive. Pauses and bursts of activity are a normal part of the Community process, which can be compared to a runner who slows occasionally to catch his breath. The word 'recovery' was already on everyone's lips in 1953 when the project for a political Community was adopted by the ad hoc Assembly and again in 1954, immediately after the failure of the European Defence Community. This recovery led directly to the Messina Conference and the signing of the Treaties of Rome. In 1963, after the failure of the Fouchet Plan, negotiations with the United Kingdom opened; in 1966, after the crisis provoked by the French 'empty chair' policy, the establishment of a common external tariff was accelerated and the Kennedy Round completed. This cycle has continued into more recent Community history.

How did Europe arrive at the crossroads of The Hague in 1969? Where did it succeed and how? Where did it fail and why?

At the time, not everyone was aware of the fact that whereas *completion* on the one hand and *enlargement* on the other were routine activities, new concepts such as *reinforcement* and *extension* were fundamental to the future of the Community. Europe had to add other common policies to the Common Agricultural Policy.

To take just the major examples of what had to be done: European Monetary Union; a common energy policy; development of nuclear research and of technology in general; preparation for reform of the Common Agricultural Policy; and the creation of a social policy. The bases of political cooperation also had to be laid and the powers of the European Parliament reinforced, particularly in budgetary matters.

Until 1969, the Community had been rather like a train which just had to be set on well-placed rails. It stopped at certain spots and observed generally accepted rules of conduct. Decisions were almost always taken unanimously. The customs union had more or less been completed and internal frontiers were theoretically open. In other words, what was called *negative (or passive) integration* had taken place. However, the time had come to advance to *active integration*.

This new entity, although inspired by accepted principles and supposedly accepted objectives, had to stand on its own two feet. The Community had to find the best path to take, define the stages of its development and make difficult political choices. The Community could probably have done with an interim period, giving it time to reflect upon the new objectives and the institutional instruments which would be necessary to attain them. Two perceptive men, Altiero Spinelli and Jean Monnet, actually suggested this. In 1972, Spinelli declared: 'It is no longer possible to disguise the fact that the current institutions of the Community...are no longer suited to the new dimensions and tasks of the Community and must be modified, probably on a very large scale'. Almost at the same time, Jean Monnet called for the 'birth of European power' and wrote: 'The vicious circle whereby the EEC is not equipped to meet the common interests of its member states must be broken.

Group photo of the Summit of The Hague, December 1-2, 1969. Sitting from left to right: Mariano Rumor, Willy Brandt, Georges Pompidou, Piet De Jong, Gaston Eyskens, Pierre Werner.

A traumatising period for the French; after having defeated Napoleon III, William I proclaimed himself Emperor at Versailles, January 18, 1871. (Painting by Anton von Werner, 1877, Bismarckmuseum, Friedrichsruh).

The red banner of the proletariat unfurled over Europe: 'The evening of the strike'
(Painting by Eugène Laermans, 1893, Musée royal d'Art Moderne, Brussels).

The Six get off the ground.

'In the Hague we changed era': the Summit of December 1-2, 1969
in the Ridderzaal.

Paris Summit, October 19-20, 1972.

Signature of the Accession Treaties, at the Palais d'Egmont, Brussels, on January 22, 1972: 1 / Edward Heath and Geoffrey Rippon for the UK. 2 / Jack Lynch and Patrick Hillery for Ireland. 3 / Jens-Otto Krag and Ivar Norgaard for Denmark.

Dictatorships fall and Europe embraces the south: 1 / Felipe Gonzalez signs on June 12, 1985 for Spain; 2 / Georges Karamanlis signs on May 28, 1979 for Greece; 3 / Mario Soares signs on June 12, 1985 for Portugal.

The European Investment Bank occupies a prime position on the financial markets.

The existing European institutions do not have enough force to accomplish the tasks lying before them'. He concluded by calling for the creation of a provisional European Government. Awareness of this lack of sufficient authority led, at a later date, to the creation of the European Council of heads of state and government.

At that time, it was believed that the euphoria created by the enlargement of the Community would give it sufficient inspiration to launch its 'reinforcement'. Unfortunately, this proved not to be the case. The absence of internal cohesion and of Community spirit, coupled with external factors (most importantly the deterioration of the world economic situation), resulted in the project for Economic and Monetary Union coming to grief.

Nevertheless, after The Hague conference, the community took measures to complete the transitional period. These were the subject of feverish negotiations which began on January 1, 1970. Financial regulations were adopted, and a number of decisions in principle were taken. As a result, the Council formally adopted on April 21, 1970 the decision by which 'own resources' were gradually handed over to the Community. By January 1, 1975, the Budget was totally financed by these. On April 22, 1970 a Treaty was adopted which amended the Treaties of Paris and Rome to give the Parliament additional budgetary powers. These powers were further reinforced by the Treaty of July 22, 1975, which set up a Court of Auditors.

These Treaties in fact ratified the tripartite system, proposed by Hallstein in 1964, whose rejection by France led to the 'empty chair' policy in 1965 and the Luxembourg Compromise 'arrangement' of January 1966. Five years had been lost, and the Community had been dealt a serious blow. The 'Luxembourg Compromise' heavily impaired the efficient working of the institutions.

A green light was then given to the opening of negotiations for enlargement. Talks with the United Kingdom opened on July 21, 1970 and ended on June 23, 1971. The formal signing of the entry agreements took place on January 22, 1972 in the *Palais d'Egmont* in Brussels. A referendum then took place in Norway on EEC membership, but unlike the British, the Irish and the Danish, the Norwegian people voted against. On January 1, 1973 – twenty years after the creation of the ECSC by the six founder countries – the Community gained three new member states. It was no longer the 'little Europe' of the fifties, but had become the leading trading power in the world. But it is doubtful that the new members increased either the cohesion of the Community or the will of its member states to proceed towards true integration.

'The institutions must now be given a new dimension' (Altiero Spinelli).

THE UPS AND DOWNS OF THE EARLY SEVENTIES

When Franco Maria Malfatti succeeded Jean Rey as President of the European Commission at the beginning of July 1970, he knew that two main tasks lay before him:
– successful conclusion of the negotiations on enlargement;
– strengthening of Community institutions in order to avoid damage being done by enlargement.

Although he succeeded on enlargement, reinforcement of the Community failed to get off the ground. The fact that the two did not go hand in hand resulted in heady quarrels which rocked the Community boat for at least twelve years.

The major priority for reinforcement was the Economic and Monetary Union (EMU). Its establishment and the creation of a European reserve fund

were written into the conclusions of The Hague, along with a deadline: December 31, 1979. As of today, this objective not only has yet to be achieved, but does not even constitute a priority. When Governments signed the Single Act in February 1986, only its preamble mentioned the declaration of the heads of state and government in October 1972 on the 'gradual realisation' of the EMU.

And yet the European Commission had played a leading role in this field even before enlargement. The Community of Six in the sixties was a relatively congenial economic entity. The gradual completion of the customs union led to economic harmonisation. Organisations were set up, 'medium-term economic programmes' submitted for approval by governments, and short-term economic policy measures taken. The world economy went into slump towards the end of the sixties, which made the attainment of the EMU even more essential. However, at the same time states were much more inclined to be introspective and to adopt measures at national level.

On March 6, 1970, a Committee chaired by Pierre Werner, Luxembourg's Finance Minister, began drawing up the project of economic and monetary union, to be completed in several stages. This project, which was submitted to the Commission in October of the same year, recommended a ten-year completion period, with three stages, culminating in the creation of a 'centre of European monetary power' (in other words a Central Bank and a joint reserve fund). On March 22, 1971, the Council gave an assurance of political will to begin retroactively the first stage on January 1 of the same year. They agreed that three ministerial sessions per year would examine the evolution of the EEC's economic situation and adopt short-term policy guidelines.

However, this coincided with monetary havoc on the international markets. The gold convertibility of the dollar was formally suspended on August 15, 1971, but this was merely recognition of a *de facto* situation. The monetary system set up at Bretton Woods in 1944 was breaking down completely. The devaluation of the dollar marked the beginning of a phase of general

Economic and Monetary Union planned for 1980: the president of the Commission, Jean Rey with Pierre Werner.

EMS announcement, at the European Council of Copenhagen (April 7-8, 1978): James Callaghan, Valéry Giscard d'Estaing, Helmut Schmidt, Hans-Dietrich Genscher.

fluctuation. The EEC continued to pay lip service to its desire for union. The Summit of October 1972 proclaimed the 'irreversibility' of economic and monetary union and insisted on the transition to the second phase on January 1, 1974: but already in April 1973 the Commission, whose President since January of that year had been François-Xavier Ortoli, admitted that this goal would not be attained.

'The Community is crippled', Ortoli declared. 'The key word is uncertainty, and it generates Community inertia which results in uncoordinated reactions and introspection'. Europe had not noticed that the world was changing and, when it did, adopted an 'every man for himself' policy. In a report drawn up by a group of experts, Robert Marjolin concluded that 'the EEC set out towards economic and monetary union without having any precise idea of what it had undertaken and without the political will of the member states'.

THE EUROPEAN MONETARY SYSTEM

It was only when events bore witness to the EEC's inability to integrate and the need for an injection of European will that two heads of government heeded the impassioned plea made by Roy Jenkins, the new President of the European Commission, in Florence on October 27, 1977. Valéry Giscard d'Estaing and Helmut Schmidt called for substantial progress to be made in monetary integration at the European Council in Copenhagen in April 1978.

Decisions taken in Bremen in July 1978 and in Brussels in December of the same year led to the creation of the European Monetary System (EMS) based on a common currency, the European Currency Unit (ECU). It was equipped with an exchange mechanism which set limited fluctuation margins for EEC currencies. The EMS obliges member states to intervene when their currency reaches a certain threshold of divergence above or below the central rate. Consensus is required for any adjustment of the parities. Interventions must be

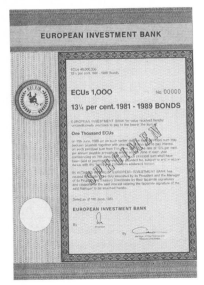

Investments in ECU become possible.

coordinated in order to avoid serious deflationary effects resulting from adjustments of one currency.

The EMS has acted as a stabilising force, and has reduced the frequency of necessary adjustments over the years. However, the absence of the pound sterling from the exchange mechanism has reduced its credibility and its effectiveness. It also bears witness to the UK's reluctance fully to commit itself to European integration. Moreover, the objective of economic integration has only partially been attained.

THE FOREIGN POLICY FRONT

If, economically speaking, economic and monetary union was a prerequisite for the strengthening of the EEC, on the political front enlargement should have been accompanied by 'progress in the field of political union'. The Hague declaration had proposed exorcising the memory of the stinging failure of the Fouchet Plan in 1962, which would have given the Community true political leadership, and introducing regular consultations on major international topics and necessary follow-up measures.

In October 1970 the 'Luxembourg Report', introducing 'political coopera-tion', was formally adopted. This cooperation is essentially about exchange of information, consultations with a view to better mutual understanding of major international problems, moves to strengthen EEC solidarity, coordina-tion of positions and, where possible and desirable, joint action. It was agreed that ministerial meetings, to be prepared by a Political Committee, would take place twice a year. A second Report (Copenhagen, July 23, 1973) reinforced the structure of political cooperation by increasing the frequency of the meetings to four times per year. A third Report (London 1983) marked a move towards a more precisely defined area of consultation. Finally, provisions on European cooperation in foreign policy were included in the EEC Single Act of February 1986. It was explicitly stipulated that the member states 'would attempt to formulate and jointly implement an EEC foreign policy'. The Single Act incorporates the content of the Luxembourg, Copenhagen and London Protocols, but also introduces a number of innovations. It stipulates that the European Commission is to be a full partner in political cooperation at the level of Directors and experts, and that ministerial meetings should be held at least four times per year.

The Single Act therefore transformed European political cooperation from the level of diplomatic protocols to an integral part of the EEC Treaties.

Political cooperation: Viscount Etienne Davignon, then Political Director at the Belgian Foreign Ministry, takes up the Fouchet Plan.

MOVES TOWARDS EUROPEAN UNION

The Paris Summit on October 19-22, 1972, under the Presidency of Georges Pompidou, can be termed the 'Summit of Optimism'. The EEC was on the verge of enlargement, and an impressive list of objectives in a wide range of fields was drawn up. This Summit was also responsible for setting the supreme objective of *European union* of the member states by the end of the decade. Simultaneously in London, the Labour Party announced that once in power it would re-negotiate UK membership.

Meanwhile, monetary crises were aggravated by the oil crisis. The indu-strialised countries, and in particular those in Europe, were dealt a sharp blow by the 'first oil shock' during the 1973 Middle East war. Europeans were deeply divided. The disappointment which followed the promises of the

For the British channel Granada TV, journalists take the place of 'their' Head of State or Government to re-enact the Dublin Council.

'Summit of Optimism' prompted Jean Monnet to suggest that a provisional European government be set up by the European leaders. But the leaders in question had already lost their personal prestige. At the Copenhagen Summit in December 1973, the cracks surfaced. Each country tried to protect its own short term interests. The Netherlands was abandoned to the vengeance of the oil sheiks. A conference in Washington on energy highlighted the divisions between the Europeans, and the International Energy Agency was set up without France.

According to Kissinger, 1973 should have been 'European Year'. Instead it was the year of missed opportunities. Within a few months Heath, Brandt and Pompidou lost power. The Labour Party leader Harold Wilson took over in London, and charged Foreign Secretary James Callaghan with announcing at the Council in Luxembourg on April 2, 1974, that the UK wanted to re-negotiate its entry conditions. Pompidou was succeeded by Giscard d'Estaing, who organised a summit in Paris on December 9-10. This summit injected a fresh burst of energy into the EEC when the participants decided to set up a European Council, an extra-institutional body, to increase the powers of the European Commission and to use majority voting more frequently. They also re-asserted their commitment to economic and monetary union, agreed to set up a regional policy, to take measures to favour employment and, most importantly, to introduce, at the latest in 1978, direct suffrage for the election of the European Parliament. The heads of government committed themselves to examining how to avoid 'unacceptable situations', a Euro-euphemism for

'I want my money back' (Margaret Thatcher to the Dublin European Council, November 29-30, 1979).

the problem of the UK's EEC budget contributions. They re-affirmed their allegiance to European union and called upon Leo Tindemans, Belgian Prime Minister, to submit a report on this matter before the end of 1975. The European integrationists were happy....

The first 'European Council' took place in April 1975 in Dublin, and it set up a 'correcting mechanism' for member states' contributions. The UK therefore got what it wanted, but a spoke had been put in the wheel of the EEC's procedures. The Pandora's Box of budgetary claims had been opened, and EEC orthodoxy had been violated. However, the Labour Government was happy with the outcome, and a referendum demonstrated its action was approved by 66.9% of the British population.

The budget quarrel raised its ugly head again in 1980, when the correction mechanism was suspended. Margaret Thatcher, who came to power in 1979, bluntly declared at the European Council in Dublin at the end of November 1979: 'I want my money back'. She was offered 500 million Ecus, but wanted 1,500 million. In Luxembourg, one month later, she re-stated this claim. The quarrel was not just over money, but over the nature of the Community and its mechanisms. The other member states had to admit that the Common Agricultural Policy was swallowing up too great a share of the budget, that structural policy was in a financial straitjacket and that industrial and technology policies were non-existent. They agreed that budgetary imbalances existed, but not that these required solution by reimbursement. The 'UK problem' weighed upon the EEC from Council to Council and from summit to summit. The President of the Commission, Gaston Thorn, spoke of a Community 'identity crisis'. After the problem was provisionally settled for 1980 and 1981, the Council gave the Commission what became known as the 'May 30, 1980 Mandate'. The Commission was asked to present proposals which would lead to a permanent solution.

CHAOS REIGNS

A complete history book could be written about the events which were engendered by the Mandate of May 30, 1980. The theory of a perfectly logical, all-round solution proved to be untenable. A number of problems arose, placing before the EEC a list of contradictory priorities which could not be simultaneously resolved – the funding of the budget, including an increase in the VAT ceiling on 'own resources'; the question of budgetary discipline; the budgetary powers of the European Parliament; the Common Agricultural Policy, its cost and necessary reform; economic union, with the reinforcement of the EMS and introduction of 'new policies'; the creation of a true single market; trade policy and negotiations for the entry of Spain and Portugal; all these were jumbled up together.

A comprehensive solution was the logical way-out, since it would have benefitted the entire Community, including the United Kingdom. But discussions became bogged down in endless conflicts, resulting in general frustration. In the course of at least five years, relations between the ten member states (the nine former members had been joined by Greece) were tainted and the image of Europe projected to the outer world was of reactionary pettiness. This proved the inability of the institutions to face up to serious problems. It was in part in reaction against this deterioration in the EEC that the German Foreign Minister Hans-Dietrich Genscher launched a political revival of the EEC in 1981, in collaboration with his Italian colleague Emilio Colombo. However, this made no impact on the political mood. The diplomats sealed Genscher's and Colombo's work with a so-called 'solemn' Declaration which was made public in Stuttgart on June 19, 1983, but which is better known for its restrictive footnotes than for its contribution to political union.

After European Councils at Stuttgart, Athens and Brussels had failed to find an answer to the problem of UK budget contributions, a solution of sorts was provided by the European Council of Fontainebleau in June 1984. The 'mediocrities of the past', as President Mitterrand put it, were buried, but the price of reconciliation was admitting the justification of compensation for 'budgetary imbalances'. Once this had been done, it was certain that the problem would again arise on future occasions. The Fontainebleau agreements were given effect at the summit of March 1985 in Brussels after more acrimony. This was the summit at which the entry of Spain and Portugal was decided, the Integrated Mediterranean Programmes set up and 'own resources' increased to 1.4% of member states' VAT collections, with the possibility of raising the level to 1.6% in 1988.

European Union: which form? (Leo Tindemans, July 9, 1975, speaking to the European Parliament).

HIGHLY MODEST SUCCESS

Despite the difficulties which it faced between the first and the most recent enlargements, in an economic and political environment which was for the most part difficult, the EEC had attempted to make progress towards integration, particularly in the economic and social spheres. Consultations began to take place more frequently and were more to the point. A Regional Development Fund was set up in 1975 and has gradually been strengthened. The Regional Fund is currently allocated around 7% of the budget. A similar sum goes to the Social Fund, the scope of which has also expanded. However, there has been no real evolution in industrial policy since 1970. There was only

piecemeal application of the 1973 Action Programme on industrial policy and technology. On the other hand, the FAST, ESPRIT, RACE and BRITE programmes have allowed the creation and the channeling of transnational cooperation into the high technology sectors in a fairly satisfactory manner. EEC activity in the steel sector has helped the industry adapt as best as possible to one of the most serious crises in its history: a great deal of restructuring has taken place, with the use of minimum prices, production quotas, and import and export controls. The EEC has done much to promote rational use of energy, and in particular to reduce dependence on external sources. It has also tackled the problem of environmental protection, and in 1975 gained acceptance of the 'polluter pays' principle. The EEC has monitored in an increasingly diligent manner air, water and noise pollution. The Community has played an active role in the North-South dialogue, and has started up a Euro-Arab dialogue. Its association with the ACP States is an example of development aid on a stable and contractual basis.

The EEC has participated in the GATT negotiations and has drawn up a closely woven network of cooperative, preferential and non-preferential agreements. It has concluded free trade agreements with the EFTA member countries (Austria, Iceland, Norway, Sweden and Switzerland) and is currently looking at ways of developing closer cooperation with this group.

SPINELLI LEAVES HIS WORK UNFINISHED

When he left the Presidency of the European Commission, François-Xavier Ortoli said the EEC had survived, but 'the strategy of Europe should, all the same, be re-thought'. The hopes which had been raised by the fresh attempt at economic and monetary union, by the creation of the EMS, and then by the use of direct universal suffrage in 1979 for the election of the European Parliament were rapidly dashed.

The Parliament, devoid of real power, proved to be a mere talking shop. Despite the high quality of certain debates, it was in the budget battles that the Parliament gained attention. The political and technical dimension which the budget problem had taken on, the spiralling growth in the cost of the Common Agricultural Policy, growth in unemployment all coincided with the new enlargement. One year was required for completion of the first enlargement negotiations (after 9 years of 'quarantine'), but enlargement to Greece took four years to negotiate (despite the fact that it was already associated to the EEC), and nine years of talking were required for the entry of Spain and Portugal. In 1985, with the prospect of twelve member states just around the corner, the need for a new strategy was more obvious than ever. The EEC needed to re-gain confidence in itself and in its institutional, financial and political means of action.

Altiero Spinelli in front of the Crocodile restaurant in Strasbourg where in 1980 he called a meeting of federalists elected to the European Parliament.

Two types of action to give fresh impetus were initiated. The first was based on a perceptive initiative by the Parliament, taken under the direction of Altiero Spinelli and his 'Crocodile Club' in 1980. It led to an historic event on February 14, 1984, the adoption by an exceptional majority (231 for, 31 against, 43 abstentions) of a draft treaty setting up European union. The adoption of this bill was the main political achievement of the European Parliament's first directly elected term of office, and provided it with an objective for its term beginning with the 1984 elections.

The second was based on the fact that 'incomplete Europe' had lost a great deal of its competitiveness on world markets and seemed incapable of creating

The European Council of Milan on June 28-29, 1985: fresh impetus.

new jobs or of uniting what was still a fragmented internal market. The date fixed for unification of the market – 1970 – had long since passed. The European Council of Copenhagen in 1982 analysed the problem in depth, prompted by insistent demands from economic and social groups for action. Jacques Delors, who took over the Presidency of the Commission at the beginning of January 1985, made the completion of the internal market the main aim of what he termed the 'launching pad for recovery'. His other objectives included reinforcement of technological cooperation, monetary cooperation, economic cohesion and the 'social dimension'.

It was clear to all and sundry that if the institutional mechanisms continued to function as they had been doing up until then, Delors' goals would never be attained. The Council had been employing unanimous voting, or abusing the 'veto', and as a result paralysis had set in. Should the Treaties be amended? Should the draft adopted by the Parliament be taken on board, thus achieving a 'qualitative leap' towards union?

The opportunity for decisive action was offered by the Milan Council of Europe at the end of June 1985. The heads of state and government declared their support for the Commission's 'launching pad for recovery'. They studied an in-depth report by the 'Dooge Committee' on the draft treaty for union drawn up by the European Parliament, and also a rather vague report on how to achieve a 'Citizens' Europe'. They agreed that basic reform of the EEC was indispensable. However, they were divided on what exactly to do. Finally, by a majority vote, they decided to call an 'Intergovernmental Conference' which would be given the task of amending the EEC Treaty in order to change

decision-making procedures and give the EEC new scope for action.

The Intergovernmental Conference was held in Luxembourg in the second half of 1986. It culminated in the drawing up and signing (in February 1986) of the 'Single European Act'. This introduced amendments to the EEC Treaties and set out provisions for European political cooperation.

The Act was scheduled to enter into force on January 1, 1987, but was delayed by Irish constitutional problems relating to formal political cooperation. The European Parliament considers – and all the evidence points to this – that this Act will not achieve European union. The Parliament also said union was more necessary than ever and that it would not take place without more dedicated attempts at integration (in particular economic and monetary union) and without the granting of a co-decision role to the European Parliament. The Parliament has therefore decided to continue the fight, and has requested that its institutional committee draw up a new strategy before the third European Parliament elections in 1989.

The Community is still incomplete. Many of its citizens even wonder whether it exists. A true Europe will not come about until the will of nations and political perception allow it to take a decisive and courageous step culminating in the creation of a real European power.

Reality

THE EUROPEAN
MOVEMENT

*

Claus Schöndube

In politics, innovation does not just fall from the sky. There is always a long evolution. New political ideas are conceived when some people become dissatisfied with the political structures within which they live and begin to look around for better ways of organising society. New ideas gradually emerge from criticism of the existing order. The ideas are usually rather vague at first, but may eventually come to constitute viable social and political options.

No matter how brilliant, the new ideas cannot be imposed upon society. In Chapter 6 of *The Prince*, published in 1532, Machiavelli noted how difficult it was to win acceptance of new organisational concepts: 'It must be considered that there is nothing more difficult to undertake, or more dangerous to handle, than the introduction of new ideas. For the person introducing the ideas becomes the enemy of all those who benefit from the old order, and is lukewarmly defended by those who would gain advantages from the new order. The lukewarm nature of the advocates is due to fear of their adversaries, who have laws on their side, and in part to the mistrust of men, who only believe in new things when they have a tangible experience of them. It follows that each time the enemies have a chance to attack, they will do so by supporting the old regime, whereas the other side will defend the new idea in a lukewarm fashion, so that it collapses along with them' (1). A few centuries later, in 1861, the English philosopher, John Stuart Mill, elaborated on this interpretation. He declared that those who succeed in convincing the majority that a new form of government or of social organisation should be given preference have undoubtedly passed the most difficult stage in the political process (2).

PIONEER MOVEMENTS

These remarks are of particular relevance to the European idea, whose aim is the specific political attainment of universal peace and law. Almost seven hundred years ago, in 1306, the French jurist Pierre Dubois proposed to his King the first plan to unify Europe, as part of a scheme to urge the sovereign to undertake a new crusade. However, almost 650 years went by before the first achievements were seen in this field. During this time, the dream of an international pacific order based on law and justice did not die. Its advocates included statesmen (the Comte de Sully, William Penn), philosophers (Jean-Jacques Rousseau, Immanuel Kant) and poets (Ernst Moritz Arndt, Victor Hugo). Hugo dedicated his lifetime (1802-1885) to the ideal of a united Europe. His speech at the opening ceremony of the second international congress on peace in Paris on August 22, 1849 is unforgettable: 'The day will come when the weapons will drop from your hands! The day will come when war will seem as absurd and will be as impossible between Paris and London, between Petersburg and Berlin, between Vienna and Turin as it would be today

»Wie sollen wir uns da
die Hand geben?«

»Simplizissimus«, 1912

*On the left: Europe of yesteryear:
'How can we clasp hands?'.
On the right: 1979, the first
European elections.*

between Rouen and Amiens, between Boston and Philadelphia. The day will come when France, Russia, Italy, England, Germany, all the nations of the continent, without losing their distinct qualities and their glorious individuality, will tightly merge into a superior unit, and you will form a European fraternity, just like Normandy, Brittany, Burgundy, Lorraine, Alsace and all our provinces merged into France. The day will come when the canonballs and the bombs will be replaced by votes, by universal suffrage of the nations, by the true arbitration of a large sovereign senate, which will be to Europe what the Parliament is to England, what the Diet is to Germany and what the legislative Assembly is to France!' (3).

Many men and women, of greater or lesser notoriety, have kept in existence down the centuries an organised European movement. They dreamt of a united Europe, but the time was not ripe. Nation states had to come first. The powers of Europe flaunted their national sovereignty and their legality as an excuse to provoke conflict and to use war as a tool which could reinforce their political power. The new ideas were occasionally brought to the notice of these powers, but they were put down with irony and heavy scorn, or their advocates were prosecuted for treason. This, for example, is what happened to the Abbot of Saint-Pierre (1658-1743), who dedicated almost half of his life to the European idea. He drew up a peace plan for Europe and sent it to Frederick II of Prussia. In a letter to his friend Voltaire, the King made his opinion plain: 'The Abbot of Saint-Pierre, who holds me in such esteem as to honour me with his correspondence, has sent me a beautiful work on the way in which peace can be restored in Europe. It is very practical: to succeed it only requires the consent of Europe and other such minions' (4).

Immanuel Kant, in his book 'Eternal Peace' (1795), argued that it was only possible to create lasting peace on the basis of 'federalism' between free states. He had already demonstrated the difficulty of the enterprise in an essay entitled 'Outline of the History of Humanity at World Level'. He wrote in 1784: 'The most important problem which nature obliges the human race to resolve is that of the creation of a civil society regulated by legality.... This problem is both the most complex and the last which the human race will succeed in resolving.... The problem of the creation of a perfect social organisation

depends directly on that of international relations between states based on legality; the former can only be solved after the latter...' (5).

However, nearly two centuries passed before Kant's ideas became political fact in part of Europe. Europe waded through a sea of blood and injustice before the idea was transformed into reality. For this to be achieved, men had to be found who, ignoring all the frontiers and social barriers, fought for the European ideal. As David Hume remarked: 'The creation of a large state or society, whether monarchical or republican, on common legal foundations, is such a difficult undertaking that no human being can reach this goal uniquely using reason, whatever his power. For the goal to be attained, several men must pool their reason, they must let themselves be guided by their experience. Time must accomplish its work and finish off their efforts; errors must become clear and the lapses which inevitably blemish the first attempts be corrected' (6).

Such a pooling of efforts occurred in the European Movement which took its current form and name on October 25, 1948. However, preliminary mention needs to be made of the pioneer movements which carried out the groundwork on which the European idea grew up after the Second World War.

One of the first movements was born in the context of the search for peace in the second half of the XIXth century following Napoleon's earlier thwarted attempt to unify Europe by force. Although not all the wings of the peace movement advocated the idea of a European federation, many did so. They considered that it was the only way of creating real peace in Europe. Some statesmen listened, and one result was the organisation in The Hague of the Peace Conferences. However, there were no positive conclusions.

It was only after the First World War, which weakened all the European countries, that the European idea made its first real entrance on the political stage.

A range of groups and associations, among the most important of which was the Pan-European Union, founded in 1922 by the Count Coudenhove-Kalergi, convinced some leading politicians of the need for a European association. The French Foreign Affairs Minister of the time, Aristide Briand, made the proposals his own. On September 5, 1928, he delivered a famous speech to the League of Nations, whose powerlessness had by then become blatantly obvious. He suggested that a federal association of all the European states be set up. The German Foreign Affairs Minister, Gustav Stresemann, took the same line shortly afterwards, placing his main emphasis on the potential economic benefits. On May 1, 1930, the French Government issued a memorandum calling for a European federal organisation. The document received a mixed welcome, particularly since, in the meantime, Stresemann, a leading supporter, had died. Moreover, the situation in Europe had changed. The world economic crisis and other events had stirred totalitarian elements into life and reinforced nationalist sentiments.. Any hope of seeing this project consolidated was destroyed in 1933 with the rise to power of the national-socialists in Germany.

The true foundations of the European Movement were laid by resistance groups fighting against fascism and nazism. When Germany's troops were unleashed on Europe, the Resistance organised itself, as had already happened in the fascist states of Germany and Italy, to fight against dictatorship and occupation. In hushed tones in the concentration camps or on the Italian island of Ventotene, where many were in exile, or more openly in the forests of Limousin, and indeed everywhere in Europe, the men and women of the Resistance discussed the perversity and obsolescence of a European political

system which continually generated wars. The Ventotene Manifesto, drawn up by Altiero Spinelli and Ernesto Rossi, declared that the 'main problem, which must be mastered before all the others in order to stamp out the illusion of progress, is the definitive abolition of the division of Europe into sovereign nation states' (7). Similar ideas were expressed in other manifestos and articles published at the time.

In France, where the First and Second World Wars were particularly horrendous, the Resistance issued innumerable documents expressing its conviction that the only order capable of ensuring lasting peace in the post-war period was a United States of Europe. For example, the manifesto of the French Liberation Movement, which was published in September 1942 in issue N° 34 of the Resistance mouthpiece 'Combat', said: 'The revolution which we bear within us is the dawn of a new civilisation. This is what worldwide civil war is about. History teaches us that frontiers are continually widening. The United States of Europe – a stage on the road to world union – will soon be a living reality for which we are fighting. Instead of a Europe which is not united but enslaved under the yoke of a power-intoxicated Germany, we and the other peoples will create a united Europe on the basis of liberty, equality, fraternity and the rule of law' (8).

Richard Coudenhove-Kalergi, founder of Paneuropa.

Students in Munich declared: 'The imperialist idea of power, wherever it is found, must be defused for all time. Selfish Prussian militarism must never again come to power. Only broad and generous cooperation among European nations can provide the foundation for a new structure. Every centralised power, such as the Prussian state tried to exercise in Germany and Europe, must be nipped in the bud. The Germany of the future must be federal. Only a healthy, federal political organisation can put new life into exhausted Europe' (9).

The list of documents constitutes the joint heritage of a large part of the non-communist resistance movements. Without directly influencing one another, they all came to the same conclusion about the situation in Europe. The historian Walter Lipgens, who unfortunately died very young, collected the various documents and assembled them into a masterly work on this subject (10). They are the roots of the post-war European movement.

On the shores of Lake Lucerne

The birth of the European movement after the Second World War was marked by two events in September 1946. On September 19, Winston Churchill, British Prime Minister during the war but who had since moved on to the opposition benches, addressed a speech at Zurich University to Europe's youth which caused an exceptional stir. He said: 'We must build a kind of United States of Europe. In this way only will hundreds of millions of toilers be able to regain the simple joys and hopes which make life worth living. The process is simple. All that is needed is the resolve of hundreds of millions of men and women to do right instead of wrong and gain as their reward blessing instead of cursing.... The first step is to form a Council of Europe. If at first all the states of Europe are not willing or able to join the Union, we must nevertheless proceed to assemble and combine those who will and those who can... In all this urgent work France and Germany must take the lead together. Great Britain, the British Commonwealth of Nations, mighty America and, I trust, Soviet Russia – for then, indeed, all would be well – must be friends and sponsors of the new Europe and must champion its right to live and shine.' (11).

Commemorative plaque laid in 1976 at Hertenstein.

At the same time representatives of the various resistance groups met in Hertenstein, on the shores of Lake Lucerne. They were a stone's throw from Rütli, a meadow where, according to legend, Swiss confederates had taken the federation oath 500 years previously. The action programme adopted at the Hertenstein meeting stated: 'A federal European Community is a necessary and essential contribution to world union. Europe will help reconstruction and the creation of a world community of nations by demonstrating that it can settle the question of its own fate by federalism.' (12).

Churchill's speech can be considered as the birth certificate of the post-war European movement, even though he did not intend including Britain in the United States of Europe. Moreover, he cannot really be considered as a federalist. His main objective was the formation of an anti-Soviet bloc. However, the speech had enormous consequences for the nascent European idea.

As for the Hertenstein meeting, it represented the beginnings of organised cooperation between the federalists. Afterwards, groups and associations grew up all over Europe intent on cooperating in order to achieve unification. The most important of these groups were:

1. The European League for Economic Cooperation, founded on May 16, 1946, and headed by van Zeeland;
2. The Movement for a United Europe, founded on January 17, 1947 and chaired by Winston Churchill;
3. The Union of European Federalists, made up of numerous organisations in seventeen European countries; it was founded on December 17, 1946 and brought together in the same organisation socialists, liberals, conservatives and Christian-Democrats; its first Chairman was Hendrik Brugmans;
4. The 'Nouvelles Equipes Internationales' (New International Teams) were founded on June 1, 1947 and were composed of Christian-Democrat members of the French parliament under the chairmanship of Français Bichet, a former minister;
5. The French Council for a United Europe, founded on June 16, 1947 under the chairmanship of Edouard Herriot;
6. The Socialist Movement for the United States of Europe, founded on June 3, 1947;
7. The European Parliamentary Union, founded on July 5, 1947 and led by Coudenhove-Kalergi;

Churchill's Movement for a United Europe and Herriot's French Council for a United Europe were purely national organisations. However, all the other groups aimed to extend the recruitment of members to all the countries of Europe.

British Conservative politician Duncan Sandys, encouraged by his father-in-law, Winston Churchill, created a Coordination Bureau for all these associations in December 1947. They all became members of the Bureau, with the exception of the European Parliamentary Union, and formed the European Movement. In 1952 Count Coudenhove-Kalergi re-founded the Pan-European Union and it became a member of the European Movement. It later broke away during the de Gaulle era. The European Movement was given stimulus by the worsening of the East-West conflict, and the Coordination Committee began preparations for a major conference to synthesize the activities of the various associations. The conference also served as a public demonstration of the political will to unify Europe.

THE MIRACLE OF THE HAGUE

The conference was eventually held in The Hague from May 8 to 10, 1948, five months after the official creation of the European Movement. It proved to be one of the most important events in the history of the Movement, and it sent waves through Europe. The conference organisers were galvanised by the latest political situation: the split between the West and its former ally, the Soviet Union, had just surfaced, leading to general pessimism. Europeans wanted at all costs to preserve their newly-won freedom and democracy. However, the nation states were weak. When 800 politicians representing most political tendencies gathered in The Hague nearly all the democratic European states were represented, along with officials from the recently founded Organisation for the Unity of Europe, artists and scientists.

Winston Churchill was the honorary chairman of the conference. It was divided into a number of working groups to discuss the form which European unity might take and to agree on methods of reaching the goal. Differences of opinion which appeared during this conference were to mirror those which later emerged during the process of European integration.

On the one hand there were the federalists, scattered between the Union of European Federalists and a number of other organisations. They wanted the formation of federation in which the states would transfer their sovereignty to a European Government, a European Parliament and a supreme Court of Justice.

In the other camp were the Unionists, who advocated a looser association in the form of a grouping of states. This tendency was especially clearly seen among the Scandinavian countries and the British.

At later conferences and congresses this divergence was to take on a different form. Constitutionalists placed all their hopes in the creation of a constituent assembly, whereas the Functionalists wanted European unity to be accomplished much more gradually, built upon specialised institutions which would

Opening of The Hague Congress in the Riderzaal, May 8, 1948.

perform at European level the same functions as bodies existing at national level.

The European Movement was always characterised by a dichotomy between the maximalist and minimalist points of view. The maximalists felt that they had to ask for the impossible in order to achieve the possible. The minimalists were afraid that chances of progress might turn sour if they pushed projects which were too ambitious.

The European Movement became a forum for the exchange of views between all the various political and social tendencies. It gave a powerful impetus to the implementation of a policy for European unification. The Movement sought – and often found – new solutions to delicate problems and situations.

The search for a possible compromise began at the first Congress of The Hague. The Congress also made a number of concrete requests, which were summarised in a message addressed to Europeans by Denis de Rougemont.

1. *We want a united Europe, with free circulation of men, ideas and goods within its boundaries.*
2. *We want a Charter of Human Rights, which guarantees freedom of thought, association and expression and the unfettered operation of a political opposition.*
3. *We want a Court of Justice capable of ensuring respect for the Charter by the application of appropriate sanctions.*
4. *We want a European Assembly where the frontline forces of all the nations will be represented.*
5. *And we sincerely commit ourselves to giving our full support, in the home and in public, in our parties, in our churches, in our professional circles and trade unions, to men and governments who strive to carry out this noble task, this supreme chance for peace and investment in a great future for this generation and those which follow it.* (13)

This message gave a clear indication not only of the political aims of the Congress, but also of the institutions which the European Movement wanted to see created. These were:

1. A Charter of Human Rights, the respect of which would be enforced by a Court of Justice;
2. A Council of Europe which would be the forum of European unification and the means of furthering the cause.

COUNCIL OF EUROPE RAPIDLY CREATED

The Congress of The Hague achieved two things. The first was the rapid creation, on May 5, 1949 in London, of the Council of Europe. Then, a year and a half later, on November 4, 1950, the European Convention for the Protection of Human Rights and Fundamental Freedoms was signed. Within the framework of this Convention, a European Court of Human Rights was created. However, the Council of Europe did not fulfil all the hopes of the European Movement, and particularly not those of the Federalists. The fight therefore went on.

The European Movement had, from the outset, aimed to promote the unification of Europe in all fields. It was therefore not only a symbol of the European ideal, but also the movement of all those working towards this goal. It has always attempted to boost the building of Europe, through various congresses, joint activities and political initiatives. During certain periods, it played a particularly active role as a coordinating body, as, for example, during

Meeting of young Germans and French, travelling to Strasbourg, at the border point of Hirschtal/ Pirmasens, November 24, 1950.

the campaign for a European Political Community, which ran from 1952 to 1954, or during the seventies, when it fought for the election of the European Parliament by direct universal suffrage.

From the beginning, the members of the European Movement formed a kind of dual structure. On the one hand there were the national Councils which brought together local groups in favour of European unification and which tried to influence the national policy of their respective state. On the other were multi-national groups allocated specific tasks in building Europe. Over the years the number of groups increased and other associations were born. The Union of European Federalists (UEF), with its national sections and its youth organisation, the Young European Federalists (YEF), has been, since its formation in 1946, one of the spearheads of the European Movement. It has continually taken a maximalist point of view. It has always looked for new paths to European integration and has proposed many ideas to boost the fight for the construction of Europe, even when the political climate has been deeply unfavourable.

The UEF found an ally in the Council of European Municipalities and

Jean Monnet maintains his vigil (here in the European Parliament on March 14, 1968).

Regions (CEMR), active in promoting trans-Europe cooperation at non-metropolitan level. Thousands of twinnings have taken place between European municipalities, creating a basis for the implantation of the European idea in the minds of ordinary people.

Three organisations corresponding to the major political groupings have done much to promote the idea of European integration and unification at national political party levels. They are the New International Teams (NEI), which later became the European Christian Democratic Union (ECDU), the Movement of the European Left and the European Socialist Movement (MGE-MSE), and the Liberal Movement for a United Europe (MLEU).

Scientific aspects of European cooperation were taken up by the European League for Scientific Cooperation, and the Union of Resistance Veterans for a United Europe dedicated itself to promoting the pan-European ideas of the Resistance groups. The European Teachers' Group (ETG) and the Association of European Journalists (AJE) have promoted the idea of European unification in schools and in the press.

Last but not least among the members of the European Movement is the International Federation of Europe Houses (IFEH), an umbrella group for 64 institutions, Centres of Europe and Academies in 16 European countries. These are involved in education in European ideals. More than 100,000 adults each year take part in their seminars and training sessions.

The latest organisation to join the European Movement is the Association of Former Employees of the European Community. These retired workers from the EEC and other European institutions want to continue contributing to the European ideal.

The role of two institutions created within the framework of the European Movement should be highlighted. The Congress in The Hague was responsible for the initiative leading to their creation. The first of these two institutions is the College of Europe in Bruges, the rector of which is Professor Hendrik Brugmans. Thanks to the College, high calibre university graduates have been able to obtain specifically European training after their university studies. The second is the European Cultural Centre in Geneva, of which the writer Denis de Rougemont was director until his death. The Centre furthers the cause of the European Community by organising ventures in the fields of education, science and culture.

The European Movement has never represented all the groups or associations in favour of European unification. The Action Committee for the United States of Europe, for example, never joined its fold. It was founded on October 13, 1955 by Jean Monnet, the first President of the ECSC High Authority. It counted among its members the chairmen of the largest political parties in Europe and trade union leaders from the six EEC member states of the time. The Committee's meetings provided a wealth of proposals for the furthering of European integration. British politicians joined the Committee in the first months of 1969. It was dissolved in 1975, and then re-constituted in Bonn on June 6-7, 1985.

Can the influence the European Movement has exercised and its victories and defeats be quantified? Can its role and the contribution which it has made to European achievements up until now be put in focus?

The European Movement's history is totally intertwined with that of the development of European unity. The European ideal found expression within its bounds: at the conferences which it organised, in the working goups which it set up and in its activities, new paths were explored. Some have shown their

Two Presidents of the European Movement, then Foreign Ministers, Gaston Thorn and Walter Scheel.

value by leading to proposals which contributed to the efforts of the official EEC bodies.

The Movement and its member associations have always been firm advocates of the European ideal, and they have formed the rich substratum on which this ideal has been built. The Movement is the forerunner of a European nation. It has been a critical forum which has helped maintain European unification as a pertinent issue.

In the final analysis, the various accounts given in this book prove that if governments have made progress in the building of Europe it is mainly because there were men and groups pushing them from behind. This is how it will remain.

The European Movement has always expressed popular feeling (Milan European Council, June 1985). On the left: the personalities: Messrs. Spadolini, Pflimlin, Thorn, Tognoli, Bardong and others. On the right: a crowd of people in front of the Dôme.

SELECTED BIBLIOGRAPHY

1. Altiero Spinelli, *La méthode constitutionelle,* in: Bulletin du Centre European de la Culture, 2, May 1958, Genève, p. 12.

2. John Stuart Mill: *Considerations on Representative Government,* 1861.

3. Victor Hugo, *Œuvres complètes,* Volume 31, Actes et Paroles, Edition Rencontre, Mulhouse 1968, p. 288.

4. Denis de Rougemont, *Vingt-huit siècles d'Europe* (Twenty-eight centuries of Europe), Paris, 1961, p. 112.

5. Immanuel Kant, *Die drei Kritiken* (The Three Critiques), Stuttgart, 1956, p. 462.

6. Umberto Campagnolo, *The European Federal State,* Bern, p. 43.

7. Altiero Spinelli and Ernesto Rossi, *Problemi della Federazion Europea,* Rome 1944, p. 21.

8. Walter Lipgens (Ed.), *Documents on the History of European Integration,* Volume 1, Berlin/New York, p. 293.

9. Walter Lipgens, op. cit.

10. Walter Lipgens (Ed.), *Documents on the History of European Integration,*

Volumes 1 – 4, Berlin/New York, 1985, p. 415.

11. S. Patijn, *Landmarks in European Unity*, Leyden, 1970, p. 28 and 34.

12. Henri Brugmans, *L'Idée Européenne 1918-1965*, (The European Idea 1918-1965), Bruges, 1965, p. 267.

13. Edouard Bonnefous, *L'Idée Européenne et sa Réalisation* (The European Idea and its Achievement), Paris, p. 280.

THE FABRIC OF
EUROPE

*

Emile Noël

The European Community is managed by a complex structure of institutions, which have the joint task of governing the EEC and furthering the cause of European integration. The institutional system set up by the Treaties of Rome on 25 March 1957 survived more or less intact until February 1986, when the European 'Single Act' was negotiated and concluded. After its ratification, a number of amendments to the Treaties will be introduced.

THE FOUR INSTITUTIONS

The European Parliament, which has been elected by universal suffrage since 1979, represents the citizens of the various member states. It has an important role to play in the Budget process and in the running of the institutions, especially the European Commission. It plays an active part in the EEC's legislative process.

The Council and the Commission together form the EEC's executive body; and the Council, Commission and Parliament make up the legislative power. The Council is made up of Ministers representing each government. The majority of its decisions can be taken by a qualified majority, through a system of weighted votes. The Commission is made up of independent members. Candidates are put forward by governments for a four-year term and are jointly approved by all the member states. The dialogue between the Commission and the Council forms the major link in the EEC's decision-making chain.

The Court of Justice, composed of thirteen judges appointed jointly by the member states for a term of six years, is responsible for the respect of Community law as laid down in the Treaties and of the legislative acts which they have so far generated.

A Court of Auditors supervises the EEC's accounts and finances to make sure that operations are conducted with propriety. The Economic and Social Committee, composed of members representing the various professional groupings in the EEC, and the European Coal and Steel Community Consultative Committee must be consulted when major legislative decisions are taken.

THE COMMISSION:
CENTRE OF POLICY FORMULATION

The foundations of the economic union of Europe were laid by the Treaties of Rome. The various institutions were then given the task of putting flesh on the bones, and of gradually substituting Community policy for national policy.

The Council has supreme decision-making power over all matters of importance, but it has to act on the basis of proposals from the Commission.

The Commission is an independent body designed to represent common European interest, and has a permanent right and duty to place initiatives before the Council. The European Parliament gives its opinions on Commission proposals as part of the decision-making process, and will have additional powers in this sphere once the Single Act has entered into force.

The Commission, in its role as policy-formulator, must be a spearhead, in the 'avant-garde' of national thinking. Yet it is also a body of government at EEC level, and cannot ignore political and economic realities. It would not be fulfilling its task if it were to simply churn out proposals inevitably destined to be shelved. On the other hand, it must bluntly confront governments with their responsibilities and intervene if ever the viability of the EEC is threatened.

The Commission is structured as a collegiate body in order to ensure that it fulfils its functions in an impartial manner. All its seventeen members participate in the decision-making process, and voting is on a majority basis. The Commissioners are backed up by a fairly large administration staff, over which the Commission has complete control, representing a cross-section of the member states.

COMMISSION PROPOSALS

The EEC legislative process begins with the presentation of a Commission proposal to the Council. In a year it presents anywhere between 500 and 600. Many are mere technical matters, and are rapidly adopted by the Council. The remainder are of a political or economic nature, and it is these which fire discussions in the Council and the Parliament.

Before drawing up a proposal, the Commission normally consults with interested European professional groupings and trade unions. It also makes political contacts within the European Parliament, and in particular with its specialist committees. Preparatory work is carried out by its various services, under the supervision of the Commissioner or Commissioners responsible. Occasionally, national experts are also called in. The dossier thus put together is discussed by the Commission in plenary session. A number of readings may take place, if the importance of the dossier justifies this.

Once a proposal has been presented to the Council, the dialogue begins. Council discussions can only take place on the basis of the proposal put forward by the Commission. When a majority decision is taken, the Council can only adopt the Commission's proposal as it stands, or a proposal which has been amended by the Commission. Unanimity is required for Council amendments to be made to Commission proposals.

THE 'LUXEMBOURG COMPROMISE':
TWISTING THE RULES

The system thought up by the EEC's 'founding fathers' placed the Commission at the centre of the Council's work, although the latter had the last say. One of the essential facets of this system was the use of majority voting in the Council. According to the Treaties, it was to apply to most decisions after the first stages of the transitional period. The foundations of the EEC were therefore seriously shaken when, in 1965/66, the French Government requested that unanimity be required for decisions effecting the key national interests of one or more of the member states, even if the Treaties stipulated that majority voting be used.

The so-called 'Luxembourg Compromise' was a consequence of the discord provoked among member states by the French request. Moreover, in the years to come, the Council began to behave increasingly as if the French suggestion had been accepted with open arms. Unanimity gradually became the rule, with a few rare exceptions for minor decisions, both in preparatory and in ministerial Council sessions. The Community began to come to a halt, even as it expanded from six to nine member states in 1973 and then from nine to ten in 1981.

The knee-jerk reaction against the abuse of the unanimity convention finally came when the EEC began to prepare itself for the entry of Spain and Portugal. In 1984, the Council began voting once again on a majority basis, and the European Single Act gave new impetus to the reverse swing of the pendulum. The Act will substantially widen the range of decisions for which majority voting will apply. The dynamics of the give-and-take interchange conceived by the founding fathers could therefore come back into play.

In-built flexibility of majority voting

The application of a majority voting system does not mean that the minority are left 'out in the cold'. The Commission's proposal serves as the launching pad for Council discussions, and gradually also becomes a focus point for a compromise. In fact, the Commission takes the individual positions of the member states into consideration when drawing up its proposals, and then tries to extrapolate them to a point of convergence.

The European Community is composed of a group of countries of similar economic and political colour. It is therefore in a very different position from large international or world organisations. When a difficulty arises, both the Council and the Commission prefer to try to reach a compromise. As a result, every attempt is made to overcome differences before proceeding to a vote.

Finally, the very fact that a majority voting system exists can discourage governments from adopting extreme or isolated positions. The Commission and member states usually try to align positions to avoid rocking the boat. If the majority voting system is correctly applied it can, paradoxically enough, render unanimous adoption easier and more rapid.

Coherence of EEC policy

The Commission ensures the coherence of EEC policy within the majority voting system. It is a permanent body, and its term of office can only be cut short by a European Parliament vote of censure. It is therefore in a position to define policy and, through its proposals, ensure its continuity. The Council can only vote on proposals introduced by the Commission, and cannot therefore adopt contradictory decisions at whim because of fluctuations in its own composition. It is equally not possible that the Council would impose on a minority member state a measure which would go seriously against its interests. The Commission would have to connive in such a move, which is unthinkable in the correct execution of its functions. Since its creation, the Commission's existence and powers have, therefore, provided a guarantee for the smaller member states, and this is reflected in their affinity to it.

Practical information

The Commission and the Council are a hive of legislative activity, as has already been emphasised. There have been two consequential developments. Firstly, the number of Council sessions has rapidly multiplied. Between fifty and sixty Council meetings are now held each year. These involve either Foreign Affairs Ministers or their counterparts in other fields. Secondly, a large number of specialised committees or working groups have sprung up. They are responsible for preparing the technical background to Ministers' political discussions. Their work is coordinated and supervised by the Committee of Permanent Representatives (Coreper), made up of member states' Ambassadors to the European Community. The Commission is represented in all these bodies, and can make its opinions and arguments known at any point in the discussions.

The Presidency of the Council

Member states acquire the Presidency of the Council on a six-monthly, rotating basis. This means that each member state presides once every six years. The responsibility of the Presidency for organisation of the work and discussion and the choice of priorities has increased considerably as the range of Council activities and the number of meetings has been extended. In the majority of cases there is close organisational cooperation between the Presidency and the Commission.

With the abuse of unanimity voting since 1966, the practice of 'compromise proposed by the Presidency' has emerged. This practice, which finds no basis in the Treaties, has resulted in a monopoly of policy decision-making by the Council when unanimity cannot be achieved on the basis of an original Commission proposal and which the Commission refuses to drop or amend significantly. As a result of this practice the EEC system could easily have deteriorated into nothing more than inter-governmental cooperation. Wider use of majority voting should rectify the situation, with Commission proposals recovering the political significance intended by the founding fathers. This should not prevent the Presidency from keeping its middle-man role and using all its resources to stimulate productive discussion.

On the left: the Berlaymont (centre building), still the provisional headquarters of the Commission in Brussels, and the Charlemagne (left-hand building), where the Council meets in Brussels. On the right: the Palais de l'Europe, Strasbourg, where the European Parliament holds its plenary sessions.

Unanimity voting brought the EEC to the brink of paralysis. This prompted the then French President, Valéry Giscard d'Estaing, to re-launch an old initiative first put forward by General de Gaulle in the sixties and later, in a different context, by Jean Monnet. He proposed that EEC heads of state or government meet regularly to point the Community in the right political direction, to give fresh impetus to EEC activity or to smooth out serious differences. At the same time, Giscard d'Estaing proposed that the democratic balance be preserved by introducing universal suffrage for election of the European Parliament, as stipulated in the Treaty of Rome. Until then, such a move had been blocked by French reservations.

The first elections to the European Parliament took place only five years later, in 1979. However, the European Council, which brings together heads of state and government, foreign ministers and the President and Vice-Presidents of the Commission, began to meet at the beginning of 1975 and gradually became an important part of the EEC machinery. Its existence was not formally recognised until the entry into force of the Single Act.

Looking back over the thirteen years of the existence of the European Council, it has had mixed results. It has no precise regulatory base to operate upon, and its influence therefore is solely due to the personal authority of its members. It has undoubtedly reinforced the inter-governmental cooperation aspect of EEC activity. In addition, temptations arose, for some Ministers, to let slip onto the European Council responsibilities which should have been faced by ordinary Councils. However, these negative aspects have been partially rectified by the refusal of the majority of heads of governments to get bogged down in highly technical discussions, and by the decision to meet only once every six months. This prevents it from interfering in the everyday work of the other institutions. On the positive side, the European Council was very active in overcoming the obstacles to the election by universal suffrage of the European Parliament. Without its intervention the European Monetary System would never have seen the light of day. In 1984 it helped solve the dispute which had split the Community since 1979 by beginning the reform of the Common Agricultural Policy, releasing new 'own resources' for running the Community, soothing the old UK budget sore by reducing London's contributions and, last but not least, making possible the entry of Spain and Portugal to the European Community. The European Council was also the initiator of the

On the left: the EEC Court of Justice in Luxembourg, with a Henry Moore sculpture in the foreground. On the right: the Parliamentary Committees meet in Brussels.

The Summit becomes the European Council (Paris, December 9-10, 1974).

reform of the Treaties in June 1985, and, through its decisions in December 1985, helped prompt the adoption of the Single Act.

THE COMMISSION:
EXECUTIVE BODY OF THE EEC

In the main, decisions taken by the Council lay down essential guidelines for the observance of EEC legislation. For the day-to-day management of EEC policy by the European Commission to be possible, these basic texts have to be adapted to prevailing realities: implementation procedures have to be specified and adopted. The Council can authorise the Commission to adopt and enact application procedures. The latter generally does this with the assistance of committees of government representatives on any given subject (Advisory Committees, Management Committees or Regulatory Committees). Once the Single Act has been adopted, this delegation of powers will become the norm. Several thousands of application procedures are adopted by the Commission each year, some of which (in particular for the day-to-day management of the Common Agricultural Policy) only run for a very short period, such as a few weeks or even only a few days.

The Commission is also responsible for managing the EEC's Budget, and in particular the important joint funds, such as the Agricultural Guidance and Guarantee Fund, the European Regional Development Fund and the European Social Fund. As an illustration of their importance, the 1986 EEC Budget totalled 36 billion Ecus, two-thirds of which went on the Common Agricultural Policy.

EEC LEGISLATION AND
ITS ENFORCEMENT

One of the most original features of the EEC system is that it adopts and enacts regulations which are directly applicable throughout the Community. Unlike

traditional international organisations, whose conclusions are not usually binding and have to be transposed into national law, the EEC institutions have the power to adopt what amount to 'European laws'. They are binding on citizens and firms in the member states, and can be used by them as a legal basis for action in national courts or even in the EEC's Court of Justice.

The legislative activity of the EEC has given birth to European law, which is particularly voluminous in the fields falling under EEC competence. These include the Common Agricultural Policy and its various offshoots, the common trade policy, customs regulations, common technical standards, competition law, and so on. Successive decisions in the EEC's Court of Justice have demonstrated that EEC law has the upper hand over national law in areas which form part of the EEC's sphere of activity. National provisions (laws or governmental decisions) which are incompatible with EEC legislation are rendered inapplicable by an EEC regulation. This situation cannot be altered by subsequent national laws or decisions.

The Commission has an important role to play in the implementation of EEC law and the supervision of its application. It is often considered as a kind of 'Treaty watchdog'.

TREATY WATCHDOGS: THE COMMISSION AND THE COURT OF JUSTICE

One of the basic rules of the EEC is that no member state can take justice into its own hands. The Treaties and resultant regulations must be respected by all, and the non-observance of a regulation by another member state is no justification for everyone else doing likewise. To prevent such a situation arising, the EEC had to equip itself with the means to supervise the member states.

The infringement by a member state of a Treaty regulation may come to the attention of the Commission through the complaint of another member state, or through its own investigations. Once an infringement has been revealed, the Commission opens a corrective procedure and eventually issues a 'reasoned opinion' with which the recalcitrant member state must conform. If it refuses to do so, the Commission brings the case before the EEC's Court of Justice, whose rulings are binding. In upwards of 80% of the cases Court intervention has proved to be unnecessary. Either the member state has rectified the unsatisfactory situation, or, as occasionally happens, it has convinced the Commission that its action is well-founded. The Court, because member states are normally brought to heel once proceedings are opened, only rules on around twenty infringement cases per year.

The supervision procedure at EEC level is backed up by the national courts. An individual can bring a case before the national courts asking them to rule on a dispute relating to the application of EEC law. The courts can then turn to the EEC's Court of Justice to obtain an interpretation of EEC law 'straight from the horse's mouth'. These referrals for a preliminary ruling are becoming more and more commonplace and now amount to more than 100 per year. They can also prompt national governments to change their ways, or to acknowledge that national provisions are not in line with EEC regulations.

The joint action of the Commission and the EEC's Court of Justice can therefore bring to a rapid conclusion an infringement, and also has a dissuasive effect on member states, even in periods of economic difficulty when temptation is high. The global economic impact of Treaty infringements has thus been contained.

After more than thirty years of existence of the European Community, it can be said that its institutional system has stood the test of time. It has survived a number of crises, including one which shook it to its very foundations (abuse of unanimity voting). It has demonstrated its flexibility in adapting to successive enlargements, even if they have not always been trouble-free. The institutional improvements which will be made by the entry into force of the Single Act in 1987 are a further demonstration of the viability of the EEC system.

The Treaties of Rome set concrete objectives (creation of the Common Market, establishment of a number of common policies) corresponding to the economic situation of the fifties. The EEC Single Act does not limit itself, through the return of majority voting, to improving the decision-making machinery of the institutions. It also defines a number of new goals which relate to the needs and challenges of today's society. These include completion of a large internal market, technological development and protection of the environment. The EEC therefore seems to be getting back to its roots, as defined in the Treaties of Paris and Rome. If the institutions fully profit from the opportunities offered them, and if national governments accept without reservation the responsibilities which they made theirs in signing the Treaties, new development possibilities for the EEC will flourish. 'The machinery of Europe' will turn more smoothly and the way will be open for the European people to advance towards an ambitious future.

A BUDGET GEARED
TO THE NEEDS OF
COMMUNITY POLICIES

*

Daniel Strasser

The founding fathers of the European Communities strove to create an independent and strong budget system. These early endeavours have been crucially important to the development of the Communities' finances ever since the European Coal and Steel Community (ECSC) began operating in 1952.

THE FINANCIAL AUTONOMY OF
THE EUROPEAN COMMUNITIES

The expression 'financial autonomy' is not to be found in the Treaties establishing the European Communities, nor in the legislation derived from them. The need and the quest for financial independence grew out of principles inherent in the Treaties: these precepts have resulted in the Communities having more than one independent source of income and have also given them an independent decision-making process, national Parliaments possessing no legislative control over EEC budgets.

The Treaty of Paris, which on 18 April 1951 set up the ECSC, created a simple and flexible system of financial autonomy. Its executive High Authority was empowered to collect a levy on annual coal and steel production for its operational expenses and for research and social reconstruction. One constraint was imposed: the Council of Ministers had to give its approval if this levy was to exceed one percent of turnover.

The High Authority was careful never to breach the one percent mark, although it did go as high as 0.90 percent in 1953-54 and 0.70 percent in 1954-55 and 1955-56. Gradually the ECSC has built up a capital base on which to operate its borrowing and lending activities. (The ECSC had made loans totalling 7.2 billion ecu by the end of 1980 to help modernise the coal and steel industries or to attract new job-creating enterprises to coal and steel regions. For example, in 1978 the ECSC made loans of 80 million ecu to Peugeot-Citroën for a new vehicle plant near Hagondange and the extension of an existing one at Metz, both in the troubled French region of Lorraine. The ECSC made a loan of £2 million in 1981 to the Scottish firm of McKellar Watt, the largest sausage manufacturer in the United Kingdom, so that it could develop its frozen food section). Since 1980 the levy rate on iron and steel has been set at 0.31 percent.

Over the years the European Parliament has gradually been drawn into the exercise of budgetary power, albeit in a limited way, to compensate for the loss of democratic control by national legislatures.

The ECSC 'operational budget' was, in fact, in 1986 only 64 percent directly funded from its own resources (39 percent by levies, 17 percent from interest

payments on its own accumulated funds and eight percent from various other sources). The other 36 percent came from the EEC General Budget. The budgetary system has been atrophied by the ceiling placed on the levy rate and this has, in turn, resulted in an imbalance of policies with social measures taking up 70 percent of expenditure while research, which is of fundamental importance for the future, gets only 14 percent.

The two Treaties of Rome of 25 March 1957 stipulated that the new European Economic Community (EEC) was to have an independent financial system. They did not, however, define what form this was to take, and a system was not put in place until 21 April 1970, when the EEC was given its 'own resources': these took the form of duties on trade from outside the Community (customs duties on the import of industrial goods, and levies on the import of agricultural products) and a contribution of part of Value Added Tax (VAT) collected in each member state.

The EIB borrows for the first time in the Community (in Guilders).

Between 1958 and 1970 the funding system for the EEC and the European Atomic Energy Community (EAEC or Euratom) was far from perfect because the contributions came from annual grants made by member states according to agreed proportions, which had to be approved by national Parliaments as part of their own budgets. However, national legislatures never refused the credits to the EEC. Moreover, given that the EEC budget (which became the unified General Budget of the European Communities) has always been processed by the Council of Ministers by majority voting, it has to be conceded that a passable 'Community spirit' has existed in this field.

The financial independence of the European Community has had significant consequences for the power balance between the various institutions. The Treaty of Luxembourg of 21 April 1970 granted the European Parliament limited powers which made it one of two wings of the budgetary authority. This was followed by the Treaty of Brussels on 22 July 1975, which gave the European Parliament the exclusive right to approve the final EEC accounts of each budgetary year as presented by the European Commission.

DEVELOPMENT OF THE EEC'S BUDGET RESOURCES

The resources placed at the disposal of the Commission for its policies and activities have expanded remarkably. ECSC expenditure increased from 3.3 million ecu in 1952–53 to 439 million ecu in 1986. EEC and Euratom expenditure together rose from 11 million ecu in 1958 to 33.3 billion ecu in 1986. Since 1973, when the first enlargement of the EEC took place, General Budget resources have multiplied eight times in nominal terms and by 2.5 in real terms.

These expanding resources have been largely absorbed by the CAP. Year-on-year expenditure between 1976 and 1979 on farm policy, the Community's prodigal son, grew by as much as 20 to 27 percent. The way the CAP has worked has resulted in so-called 'budgetary imbalances', since a number of member states get far less back from support payments for guaranteed agricultural prices than the size of their VAT contributions to the General Budget. (The United Kingdom, for example, receives between nine and 12 percent of EEC expenditure on the CAP and yet contributes between 18 and 22 percent of the General Budget).

A number of *ad hoc* mechanisms were found in 1981/82, 1983 and 1984 to ease the situation. A more permanent solution was established in the Fontaine-bleau Agreement of June 1984.

The Committee on Budgets at work, under the chairmanship of Jean-Pierre Cot, with on his left Vice-Chairman Richie Ryan, rapporteur David Curry and Vice-Chairwoman Carla Barbarella.

However, the support of farm prices through the CAP's guaranteed funds was not the only policy to grow in importance. An EEC development policy gathered momentum with the creation, in chronological order, of the Social Fund, the CAP Guidance Fund (a social fund for farmers), and the Regional Fund: these have come to be known collectively as the 'Structural Funds'. Their aim is to promote greater 'cohesion', or equality, between member states, a policy which has had only middling success. In 1985 Greece, Ireland, Italy and the United Kingdom, the four least prosperous of the then ten member states, together received 67, 54 and 71 percent of the respective expenditure of the three funds. Because Greece, Ireland and Italy were low contributors to the General Budget, this meant they were net beneficiaries of the budget process. For example, Ireland and Greece have experienced respectively five percent and two percent rises in their GDPs as a direct consequence of inputs from EEC structural funds. However, the expansion of the structural funds has been at the expense of worthwhile contributions to research and technological development, where expenditure has remained at below two percent of the total EEC budget.

This evolution of the EEC's expenditure pattern has not happened without conflict between the two wings of the budgetary authority. Basically, the Council has concentrated its energies on the guaranteed CAP prices, an area of expenditure over which it has absolute say and which has 'compulsory' priority over other budget items. The European Parliament, which has no say over 'compulsory' expenditure, has therefore concentrated its efforts on 'non-compulsory' expenditure. Non-compulsory items constitute 75 percent of the 799 budget items, but only represent 7,400 million ecu, or 22.5 percent, of total General Budget expenditure. The three structural funds, research and development, activities in the technology, industry and energy fields, and aid to non-EEC countries all fall into the sometimes vague category of non-compulsory expenditure comprising what remains once the demands of the CAP have been met. This division of priorities has been the breeding ground for conflicts between the Council and the Parliament: the former has tried to keep a tight rein on non-compulsory expenditure, while the latter has sought to extend the importance of policies beyond agriculture. The Parliament is determined to be taken seriously in deciding Community priorities: it has criticised the budget for being little more than an accounting exercise for the CAP rather than a means of developing other policies necessary for economic integration.

Will President Pflimlin sign or not? Parliament's last word on the budget.

Several institutional, legal and political problems overshadow the budget's future. The institutional budget triangle of Council, Parliament and Commission has generated tension and occasional outright public conflict which have tarnished the EEC's image. Hostility between the Council and the Parliament was particularly fierce on 13 December 1979, 16 December 1982 and 13 December 1984 when the Parliament on each occasion rejected annual draft budgets that had been adopted by the Council. On two occasions (1979 and 1981) individual member states showed their own disapproval of budgets by refusing to hand over their legally required VAT contributions.

The Council of Ministers has twice started proceedings (26 January 1982 and 10 February 1986) in the EEC's Court of Justice to contest the legality of budgets signed into law by the Parliament. The first case was later withdrawn. But the Court ruled on the second: the Council wanted the law on budgetary matters to be laid down clearly and requested that the Court of Justice partially or totally cancel the 1986 budget. On 3 July 1986 the Court annulled the decision taken by the President of the European Parliament on 18 December 1985: the President, former French Prime Minister Pierre Pflimlin, declared that the budget procedure had been completed even though the Council of Ministers said it could not accept a new rate for non-compulsory expenditure voted by the Parliament on 12 December.

Although the Court rendered the budget itself invalid, it did not call into question the validity of payments and commitments already made under it in the course of the first six months of 1986. It had no desire to throw into total chaos the workings of the European Community. And a few days later the Parliament and the Council managed to come to an agreement on the 1986 budget. But a joint Council/Parliament/Commission declaration on 30 June 1982 designed to defuse such tension had proved to be of short-lived effect: some other solution to the problem needs to be found.

A different sort of tension arises between the Council and the Commission, as the latter resists having its power over implementation of the budget

The 1985 budget, dissected by the Court of Auditors.

The budget process, tripartite cooperation: Leo Tindemans (President of the Council), Piet Dankert (President of the Parliament) and Gaston Thorn (President of the Commission) sign the agreement of June 30, 1982.

wrenched away from it. The Commission's battle has only really been successful in relation to the Social Fund and the Integrated Mediterranean Programmes (IMPs), where it retains the full right of implementation.

Friction is also caused by the fact that the Parliament, and not the Commission, is responsible for approving each year's final budget accounts. Up until now the Parliament has never used one of its major powers, dismissal of the Commission for incompetent implementation of the budget. However, on 14 November 1984 it did refuse to approve the accounts for 1982, which amounted to a vote of no confidence in the outgoing Gaston Thorn Commission. (Though the Parliament has the power to dismiss the Commission, in practice this is of little value because it would bring the Community to a halt and the Parliament has no right to appoint a new Commission).

ONE PERCENT LIMIT IMPOSED

With the philosophy of financial autonomy turning somewhat sour, legal uncertainties have arisen, mainly as a result of the Council decision of 21 April 1970 to hold down the call-up of VAT (from each member state to the EEC budget) to one percent of a uniform asessment base. This worked fairly well until 1983 when the Commission had to carry over expenditure from one year to another to meet its obligations. However, this device could not tide the EEC over in either 1984 or in 1985 when member states had to advance extra money, with no guarantee of getting it back. The advances were made on the basis of a series of agreements which found their inspiration not in the Treaty of Rome but rather in an intergovernmental consensus. The budget suddenly changed course from being expenditure-orientated, as it was until the one percent VAT ceiling level was reached, to income-orientated since unanimity was required among the member states for the granting of top-up funds.

Despite a decision taken on 7 May 1985 to raise, from 1 January 1986, the VAT ceiling on 'own resources' from one percent to 1.4 percent, the EEC budget still faces the same difficult problems as arose in 1983. The one percent ceiling had been exceeded for three successive years by the time it was raised. A further increase to 1.6 percent on 1 January 1988, already implicitly agreed by the Council of Ministers, will not do much to alleviate the problems. The funding system for the budget has gradually proved to be inappropriate. There is no doubt that a more flexible system is required. Substantial compulsory spending in the agricultural field is legally required, and particularly at a time when the dollar is weak: each ten percent fall in the value of the dollar costs the

Community an extra one billion ecu each year in agricultural export subsidies.

By 1987 the EEC could again truly be said to be facing a major budget crisis. In a report to member states, the Commission set out a detailed case for more resources, challenging governments to face up to their responsibilities and provide the money to cover their commitments. The Commission said it wanted to switch from the VAT-based system of financing to one linked to the Gross National Product of member states. At the same time the Commission sought to increase resources immediately by one-third and transfer the burden away from the poorer nations of the South towards the richer North.

The Commission expected to spend nine billion ecu more than the Council of Ministers had budgeted for in 1987. The Commission accused the member states of having flunked a challenge. The Community, the Commission said, had 'sunk into a morass of budgetary malpractice needed to conceal or postpone the real financial implications of Community policies.'

At present, the Community budget represents only 2.8 percent of aggregate national budgets and only one percent of the GNP of the EEC's twelve member states together. Consequently, its general impact is limited. If the budget is in difficulty, it is because there has been a lack of clarity in defining political objectives. Member states have to decide whether or not they want a gradual transfer of legislative power, with the necessary financial back-up, from national to Community level; and they have to decide whether they want to work together or through the intermediary of EEC institutions to achieve this. There is no doubt that the Commission is right when it calls for the budget system to be re-thought and its funding base widened. Unless this happens, the EEC's budget will cease to be an effective instrument of Community development.

EUROPE,

A PARLIAMENTARY

DEMOCRACY

*

Hans Nord

Parliamentary democracy has its roots in Europe. But it is not at the origin of the state system in Europe, which is the result rather of the power exercised by princes and potentates who fought wars against one another and formed dynastic bonds. National borders are the outcome of application of the law of the fittest. Within these borders princes built upon their power: in the majority of countries the parliaments of the Middle Ages were the victims of this evolution. It was much later, when the expanding middle classes wanted a share of the power, that parliaments became instruments for limiting feudal power. At the same time, the parliaments increasingly became the political centre of what later came to be known as the 'nation'.

Sovereignty, which was initially the prerogative of princes who were only answerable to God, evolved and subsequently rested in the 'state', where the power belonged in a definitive manner to the people. The state became identified with the people, who periodically elected a representative body to watch over government policy and help make laws. It was at this point that the concepts of the State (a body exercising certain sovereign functions) and the nation (a network of links, partly emotional and sentimental, joining a group of people who feel bound by a common heritage in the form of territory, religion, language, culture and past crises) became rather confused. Their fusion led to the birth of nationalism, which plagued Europe in the conflict-ridden first half of this century.

What is the significance of our European past, which is a common heritage even if the course of events has not been identical, nor run parallel in time, in all European countries? Firstly, it is significant because forward-looking policies, even those aiming for fundamental changes, must also look to the past. Secondly, and most importantly, Europe's history has a bearing on the essential problems which European unification has been facing for almost 35 years now and on the very essence of our system of parliamentary democracy.

One of the essential characteristics of the system of states in Europe has been its resistance to hegemony. European history is peppered with attempts to achieve dominance: Spain, then France and, more recently, Germany attempted to impose their supremacy on Europe by force. All these attempts failed. The main lesson to be learnt from this is that if Europe wants to unite, it must do so with the free consent of the states and the people concerned. But unification will not simply 'grow' without conscious and creative action. Europeans must bury the ghosts of their past. The nation state, which has been the jealous guardian of the 'indivisible sovereignty' inherited from the ancient princes, must voluntarily cede certain tasks to a new European authority. National governments must recognise that the European institutions need

some power, and that consequently rights must be relinquished by national institutions. Moreover, a European parliamentary body exercising true powers has now become indispensable. But are governments, national parliaments and peoples ready for this? Can the nation-state condone its own demise? And can parliamentary democracy, which was achieved at national level only after prolonged and hard struggle, function with success in a diverse Europe which would not be a 'nation' in the sense previously understood by its inhabitants? In this context, it is important to look back at the role of parliaments in the brief but tumultuous history of European integration. Europe must analyse its successes and its failures in order to understand what may reasonably be expected in the future.

DEMOCRACY CLIMBS BACK INTO THE DRIVER'S SEAT

The period between the two world wars was characterised by the development of mass political movements which were opposed to 'bourgeois and decadent' parliamentary democracy. Fascism and National Socialism were at their height. However, after five years of National Socialist terror in Europe, parliamentary democracy came back into fashion. The states of Western Europe, including Italy and Germany, embarked upon the post-war period as parliamentary democracies. Because of the devastating war which had divided Europe, and because of the consequent change in the world balance of power, many people concluded that Europe's only possible future lay in unity. To that end, they tried to nurture a grass-roots movement supporting the ideal. The European Movement, one of the first 'action groups' in the post-war period, was a typical example. In 1948, 800 members of this movement met in the 'Knights' Hall' in The Hague. They included representatives of the worlds of politics and management, business and trade unions, science and the arts. Although they had not been elected by the peoples of Europe, they considered themselves as their mouthpieces and called their meeting the 'Congress of Europe'. They desired to be the true representatives of the peoples of Europe. The conference ended with the unanimous adoption of a recommendation to governments to convene a 'European assembly'.

Divergences appeared from the very beginning in the debates in The Hague, and these took their toll on the subsequent evolution of the initiative. There was disagreement as to whether the Assembly should be made up of national politicians, sent by the respective parliaments, or whether it should represent a wider cross-section of the population. In The Hague the 'national political professionals' won the day, and the first option was adopted. However, some representatives clung to the idea of election to a European Assembly by direct universal suffrage: later EEC Treaties left the way open for this, but it did not come about until 1979.

If the history of 'a European parliament' is examined, it becomes clear that discussion has always been over the same contentious issues: democratic parliamentary power in budget matters and the legislative process; the development of a more distinct identity and the winning of greater legitimacy through direct elections of members of the European Parliament; and the functioning of that Parliament as the driving force behind an integration process leading to a European union in which institutions would have limited yet effective power in fields where member states are not capable of solving problems alone.

These discussions began when the first European experiment, the Council of Europe, declared that a real integration process only had a chance of success if undertaken in a smaller group of countries than that which comprised the Council. The negative attitude towards integration of the United Kingdom made such a development unavoidable. A European Community of Six was born, founded upon Franco-German reconciliation and the establishment of the European Coal and Steel Community as the first institutional building block. The embryonic outlines of the EEC, later to extend action to other fields and membership to a greater number of states, began to develop. A supranational community with its own binding rules, controlled by a Court of Justice whose decisions had to be followed, and a political decision-making process which incorporated both international and constitutional law, was embodied in the ECSC. The 'government' took the form of an independent High Authority, controlled by a parliamentary assembly which could force the former to resign by a vote of no confidence. A Council of (national) Ministers was responsible for ensuring consensus between the member states. Subsequently, this basic structure remained unchanged, but a number of upheavals shook the balance of forces between the different institutions.

Consisting as it did of members of national parliaments, experienced men who knew how to exploit to the full the possibilities offered them by the Treaty, the ECSC Parliament acquitted itself with great distinction.

The invasion of South Korea by the North Korean Army made Western Europe realise that its own defence could only be strengthened by involving the Germans. This was a golden opportunity for those most strongly committed to the European ideal, since participation by the Germans in the defence of Europe could only be at European level, not on a national basis. A European Defence Community was proposed in October 1950 by the French Prime Minister René Pleven after a number of European statesmen – including Churchill – had spoken in favour of a continental army earlier in the summer. The EDC would have created a supra-national European army, with common institutions. Pleven proposed that, within the army, there would be no specifically national unit larger than a battalion: he believed this would reconcile the French people to German rearmament. Such a Defence Community – since defence could not be isolated from general policy – would also be a move towards the creation of a European political community embracing all fields of common interest and requiring joint action. A new Treaty to establish the Defence Community was judged necessary, and the ECSC Parliament was entrusted with the task of drawing it up.

After fierce debate within the Parliament – and also in the Action Committee of the European Movement, led by Paul-Henri Spaak – a draft was produced which was signed in Paris on 27 May, 1952 by France, West Germany, Italy, Belgium, the Netherlands and Luxembourg. But it never got beyond plan stage: in August 1954 the French National Assembly, giving way to communist and nationalist pressures, rejected the project and the Defence Community had to be scrapped.

European integration was given a new lease of life in 1957 when a decision was taken to move along another path, that of gradual economic integration. It was believed that integration in this field would lead member states gently towards European union: the overambitious targets of the early years were set on one side.

The European Parliament inherited the functions of its ECSC forerunner, and became the parliamentary institution for the ECSC, the EEC and EURATOM

together. It had to prepare itself for a long, difficult and often unexciting struggle, which it has nevertheless continued with perseverance. In certain respects, it has been quite successful.

PARLIAMENT AS A CONTROL BODY

The Treaties of Paris and of Rome gave Parliament only one real power: that of dismissing the High Authority, which later became known as the European Commission. Although this was no trifling sanction, everyone knew that such a drastic measure could not be resorted to lightly. Over the years the supranational character of the European Commission became somewhat eroded. The Commission, which was supposed to be a genuine central executive body, was eclipsed by the Council, which meant that Parliament's hold over the Commission became increasingly less relevant. The real power went into the Council's hands...if the word 'power' could really be used in relation to an institution which had ceased taking any decisions. The disastrous habit adopted by the Council of hoping for unanimity, even in cases where the Treaty specified that a majority was sufficient, harmed the decision-making capacities of all the Community institutions and forced the Commission to defer increasingly to the Council's will.

This was why the Parliament decided to campaign to gain greater powers in those fields which had become the exclusive domain of the Council, namely the Budget and EEC legislation. It got its first breakthrough at the beginning of the seventies. A revision of the Treaty gave the EEC its financial independence. It was no longer to be financed by national contributions, but by its 'own resources'. France was deeply in favour of the change. Faced with imminent UK entry, it wanted to secure the funding of the Common Agricultural Policy. However, once the EEC got its 'own resources', the problem of democratic control of expenditure arose. Since control was no longer in the hands of national parliaments, it had to be transferred into a European context. From this point on the European Parliament, which until then had only had an advisory role in budget questions, became, with the Council, part of the budgetary authority. Its competence was certainly limited to 'non-compulsory' expenditure, and it had no control over the income (a percentage of national VAT takings, customs tariffs and agricultural levies), but it obtained the power to amend the Budget and, if need be, to reject it outright. This was an important victory. It has used this power on a number of occasions, with varying degrees of success.

The second area of concern for the Parliament was legislation. The EEC draws up laws which are either directly binding on the public or which oblige member states to make changes in their national legislation. These laws are made in the Council, on the basis of a proposal from the Commission and after consultation with the Parliament. For a number of years now the Parliament has been trying to obtain similar powers in the legislative process to those acquired in relation to the budget. Despite repeated promises made by heads of government, the Parliament has not succeeded. A fundamental obstacle has cropped up, and it concerns the attitude taken by national parliaments towards the process of European integration.

A clear example is provided by Denmark, although it is by no means alone on this issue.

Legislative power is one of the main strengths of parliaments. Many Danes believe this asset should remain national. And, so, many Danish Ministers are

sent to EEC Councils with precise instructions, which come from a powerful parliamentary committee in Copenhagen. The minister therefore has only limited discretion and he must block any Community legislation which runs contrary to the instructions which he has received at national level. He must use his 'right of veto' and cannot accept majority decisions. As a result, national parliamentary democracy is safeguarded.

This runs counter to the Treaties which stipulate, in their original form, that the Council is to take majority decisions in certain areas. In 1965 a crisis broke out in the early Community of Six when the French Government refused to apply the Treaties where majority voting was stipulated. It insisted that no decision could be taken by a majority vote when one member state, for reasons of 'vital national interest', opposed this. The EEC never fully resolved this basic controversy. Meeting in Luxembourg, the immediate crisis was defused when the Six declared that the position adopted by France was unacceptable to its five partners. Nevertheless, the decision-making process evolved in the direction desired by the French. It became accepted practice for the Council to wait until unanimous agreement was reached before acting. Its meetings increasingly came to resemble diplomatic conferences where endless waffling never actually culminated in decisions being taken. This further weakened the positions of the Commission and the Parliament.

This meeting led to the birth of the myth which became known as the 'Luxembourg Compromise'. People began to believe that the Treaties specified unanimity voting as the norm and gave each member state the right of veto. It was an argument used before the entry of the United Kingdom and Denmark in 1973. To those Britons and Danes opposed to EEC membership, it was explained that their fears were groundless, since the veto would protect national sovereignty at crucial times. It therefore became widely believed in the UK and in Denmark that acceptance of membership had been on condition that a national veto could be placed on any decision.

The problem became a burning issue once again in the eighties when Greece, Spain and Portugal were to join the Community, swelling its ranks to twelve. The decision-making procedure, already precarious in the Community of Six, and more so in the Community of Nine, now threatened to come to a complete halt. It had become increasingly evident that more decision-making capacity was required. Smooth running of the Community was essential if economic decline and mass unemployment in the majority of its member states were to be tackled effectively: the Parliament, which from 1979 was elected by direct

On the left: the enlargement of the EEC: hope for parliamentary democracy. The first session of the European Parliament after enlargement (January 1973). On the right: Benelux Ministers Messrs. Werner, Luns and Spaak on the benches of the European Parliament on the eve of the 'Luxembourg Compromise' (January 20, 1966).

universal suffrage, published a study by a group of economic experts in which the reality was set down in figures. The Commission for its part presented a white paper which listed some of the hundreds of decisions necessary for a Europe without internal frontiers. If the EEC wanted to confront the challenges of our time, it had to take a new 'qualitative leap' towards greater integration. In which case, the decision-making process would have to become more efficient and more democratic.

Again, the initiative came from the Parliament. After a number of years of study and discussion, it adopted by a large majority at the beginning of 1984 a 'draft treaty for European union'. This document proposed a revision of the powers of the Council, Commission and Parliament in order to achieve a better balance between the three institutions. It also expressly proclaimed the principle that each institution should complement the other and only be competent in the fields entrusted to it, excluding the domain of national sovereignty.

At the outset, it seemed as if the national parliaments were prepared to endorse the draft submitted by the Parliament. A committee set up by the heads of governments presented proposals which for the most part followed the line taken by Parliament. But when an intergovernmental conference was organised in Luxembourg at the end of 1985, during which details had to be agreed and new texts of the Treaties drawn up, it became clear that the lowest common denominator acceptable to all was very limited, especially since Denmark had placed a reservation which could only be lifted after a referendum of the Danish people.

What were the Danes concerned about? The Luxembourg intergovernmental conference drew up a draft treaty, known as the 'Single European Act', which introduced a number of amendments to the Treaty of Rome. As far as the decision-making process within the Council was concerned, the number of areas where majority voting could be used was increased, particularly in decisions leading to completion of the internal market. As regards democratisation, the Parliament was granted two new powers: its approval will henceforth be required for the entry of new member states to the EEC and for the conclusion of agreements between the EEC as a body with third countries. Moreover, Parliament has increased its influence on the legislative process through a 'cooperation procedure' with the Council. It did not receive true legislative power, but the new process does contain an embryonic hint of 'co-legislation'. When the Council, in accordance with the Act, is to take a majority decision, it will adopt, after a first consultation with the Parliament, a position which the Parliament will also examine at a second reading. A complex transaction will thus be brought into play between the Council and the Parliament, something like the budget procedure. But the Council nevertheless keeps the last word.

This combination of decision by majority in the Council and of increased right of consultation for the Parliament, although very modest, seemed too radical for the majority of members of the Danish Folketing, and grumbling was also heard from Ireland and the UK. Opponents of this procedure felt that national sovereignty would be affected. However, the Danish referendum demonstrated that a narrow majority of the people thought otherwise. The Danes were aware of the fact that a 'no' to the Single Act would mark the beginning of withdrawal from the EEC, and they did not care to take such a risk. After the referendum, the Folketing adopted the Single Act, but made a declaration – greeted elsewhere with disbelief – that the Act left the old

'Luxembourg Compromise' intact and that, as a result, Denmark preserved its right of veto on decisions which did not suit it.

The Single Act is barely beyond the stage of conception, but already it is suffering from some of the same inherent contradictions which plagued its forerunners. However, a general examination of the texts clearly displays the direction in which Europe is going, whether it wants it or not: increased decision-making power for the EEC and more democratic control.

THE BASIC TENETS OF DEMOCRACY

In the eyes of European citizens, a Parliament is, by its very nature, the place where their points of view and their concerns are discussed and decisions taken upon them. It is the meeting place of the entire country, the centre of national debate, the hub of public life. If politics and politicians are sometimes held in rather low esteem, people nevertheless identify with them at critical moments. If this were not the case, Parliament would lose its meaning: it would become an irrelevance and would be incapable of fulfilling its basic tasks.

This leads on to a problem which the European Parliament has faced since its birth. In the beginning, the Assembly had very few powers, or at least very few *real* powers, and it was not directly elected. When it called for more power, the reply was that a Parliament which had not been mandated by the people could not have more power. And when it requested election by direct suffrage, the reply was that there was no point in electing a Parliament which had no power. How could it break this vicious circle?

Some people had no qualms about believing that European integration was not an affair which concerned the man in the street, but was solely a business for states. Sovereign governments, each separately controlled by its parliament, would cooperate and take decisions on matters which were of common interest. A Parliament at European level was therefore not strictly necessary, except to preserve a semblance of democracy and to give parliamentarians the impression that they had a say. Yet the thirty five years history of the European Community clearly demonstrates that such a view is flawed.

The choice has to be made. Either member states remain sovereign; continue to fail to agree with their partners on matters of common interest; the integration process comes to a halt; Europe becomes even more powerless; individual quarrels flourish; and economic, social and cultural disintegration begins. Or the sovereign governments succeed in continuing the integration process and take relevant decisions, by majority vote where necessary. In this latter case, the Council of Ministers, supported by (and profiting from) vast national bureaucracies, will become the centre where decisions are taken, and whose rulings cannot subsequently be reversed at national level. This will undermine national democracy and threaten to make national parliaments irrelevant: if the latter accept this evolution, the age of parliamentary democracy is over. If they refuse to accept this, they will need to counter-react by taking measures to end bureaucratic decision-making at European level. At present, the dilemma is a circular one which contributes nothing to preventing the decline of the European ideal.

In order to solve this quandary, national parliaments and the European Parliament need to consider one another as allies rather than as rivals. The European decision-making process, which is an established reality, should be subject to the same independent parliamentary control as town, regional and

Posters for the 1984 electoral campaign.

national authorities. The different levels, far from encroaching upon one another, complement each other.

However, for democratic control of the quality of European life to be effective, it must not only have parliamentary powers but also policies which have taken on a European dimension. Links which exist between people and their representatives at local, regional and national level should also be forged at European level. Hence the need for European parties and European elections.

Parliament adopted this approach from the very beginning. Its members refused to consider themselves primarily as representatives of their country, but rather as part of a political process. Political colour rather than nationality has been the determining factor. The parliamentarians formed themselves into multinational political groupings, which have strengthened links between parties of similar colour in different member states. This process was accelerated when the first European elections were announced for 1979. Party federations were born at European level which drew up European electoral programmes which were as uniform as possible. This trend gathered momentum at the second elections in 1984.

EUROPE NOT YET VERY 'EUROPEAN'

However, it has to be said that politics are not yet conducted at a European level. The major problems have become European, but politics remain national, as do the issues which people judge to be at stake. In 1979, the level of participation in the European elections was not very high. In 1984, it fell even further. There are a number of reasons for this.

The first is naturally enough the European Parliament's lack of true power, which saps people's interest in voting. But this is not the only reason, for national parliaments also started off with few rights, and had to win the power which they now have. They succeeded because they had popular support.

Secondly, the 'European' elections are not yet truly European. There is still no uniform electoral system, and each member state elects its 'own' representatives as it sees fit. The European Parliament is far from the principle of 'one man, one vote'. In Germany, 750,000 votes are required for one seat, whereas in Luxembourg only 60,000 are required. The date of the elections is not the same in all the member states. And since the member states have been unwilling to apply the uniform electoral system proposed by the Parliament, political relations within it have been falsified. The United Kingdom provides the most striking example, with the Liberal-Social Democratic Alliance obtaining 19.5% of the votes in 1984 without winning a single seat. The psychological effect on the population is even more important. Instead of being a European event which increases awareness of belonging to a Community to which national authorities have delegated certain powers, the European elections have taken on the character of a relatively insignificant national event, interesting first and foremost as a measure of the current balance of forces in national politics.

A third very important factor is the opaque nature of the European decision-making process. The hybrid nature of the Community (half supranational, half international) means that power is exercised in a bureaucratic and intangible way. Conflicts in the EEC are not settled in the normal manner, by the open confrontation of points of view and interests followed by a political decision. They are presented as the opposed interests of different countries. The

'French point of view', the 'British point of view', the 'Dutch point of view' are therefore spoken about, which result in the 'renationalisation' of policies which should be European. The passionate support for and loyalty to individual movements, which are the lifeblood of politics, are not channelled towards the real problems but are used to bolster an 'individual' national position. Reports of a Council meeting are reminiscent of descriptions of an international sporting event: the citizens are mostly told about the heroic stuggle of 'their team' in the match....

The interaction between national and European policies, which should lead to a separate, distinct identity for the latter, therefore seems to be moving in the opposite direction. Europe no longer has an independent and distinct political centre. The centres of political power have remained national, and these centres want to control European policies even although, for structural reasons, they are incapable of this.

This trend has been somewhat aggravated by the fact that European elections have largely severed the umbilical cord between national parliaments and the European Parliament. In the past, each national parliament had a lobby of European parliamentarians. Today, this doubling of office has become very rare, and this reinforces the tendency of national parliaments to associate themselves with the 'renationalisation' of European policy. However, to re-introduce the double office, as some would like, would be too much like tackling the symptoms rather than the cause, which goes much deeper. Apart from the physical impossibility of combining the workload of a national member of parliament and a European parliamentarian, a re-introduction of double office would be a capitulation to renationalisation, termed by some as the 'new realism'. This solution is neither new nor realistic. It is as old as the nation state, and as realistic as the illusion that the problems of the 20th century can be solved with the instruments of the 19th.

What conclusions can be drawn from all of this? Is the idea of parliamentary democracy at European level a mere chimera? It has already been demonstrated that the end of absolute monarchy led to the need for a new link between governments and subjects, and that this vacuum was filled by national and democratic ideas. Does this mean that democracy can only exist in a national framework? Should the observation made by an American scholar, almost one century ago, be taken as correct: 'The democratic state must be a nation state and the state whose population has become national will ineluctably become a democratic state'? Or should we regard this argument simply in the American perspective of 'nation building'?

The national sovereign, democratic and parliamentary state as we know it

The four successive Presidents of the elected European Parliament: Simone Veil, Piet Dankert, Pierre Pflimlin and Sir Henry Plumb.

represents only one stage in European development. It has not always existed. But it has played a vital role in the evolution of Europe. However, today, it has a number of shortcomings. It can no longer fully satisfy fundamental demands which have always been expected of a State, such as guaranteeing the security, freedom and well-being of its citizens. It is already starting to show signs of what the British philosopher Hobbes saw coming more than three centuries ago: what he called the 'Leviathan' was a monstrous beast with an insatiable appetite which, rather than serving free citizens, threatened to reduce them to a state of abject and resigned servitude.

The inability of the nation state to solve the problems of its time set off a process of European integration which was subject to internal and external pressures. This process is continuing, even if Europeans have not yet fully embraced it. And although political thinking remains primarily national, the EEC still has an immense power of attraction. Many countries want to join it and, once they have become members, do not want to leave. There seems to be no alternative.

The real question is not whether the process of economic unification is continuing. That development cannot be reversed. What is important is to know how best to profit from the situation. Will non-European powers come to dominate our market? Or will we prove capable of committing ourselves to the unification process, thus inaugurating a new period in our history? The question is not academic. Our impotence acts as a magnet to others. We are too large to be left entirely to our own devices.

The 35 years which have passed since the creation of the European Coal and Steel Community present a changing image of creativity and European paralysis. The Community is an unfinished symphony. What it needs is a central political authority with which European citizens can identify and on which they are able to exert an influence. As *de facto* integration progresses, the need for this will become more apparent. The EEC institutions will have to move with the tide. The governing bodies of European sovereignty will have to acquire clear features so that their influence on the daily life of the man in the street becomes more tangible. Citizens should regard their European elected

representatives in the same way as they look upon national representatives: the fight for a full-blooded European parliamentary democracy could then be conducted with a real chance of success. This success is not only the prerequisite for true European integration, but also a prerequisite for healthy development of democracy at the national, regional and local levels. Failure would confront member governments with tasks which they could not fulfil, and the resulting discord could even put democracy itself at risk.

The history of the Community demonstrates that perseverance provides the path to success. One victory is no cause for euphoria, since the following day victory may prove to have been an illusion. In the event of defeat, there is no reason to despair: what may seem like a defeat may provide the opportunity of a new offensive. No campaign is lost until the last shot has been fired.

The European Parliament, which has increased from 142 members for six countries 30 years ago to 518 representatives for 12 member states today, has, despite all its setbacks, made progress in three major areas. Firstly, it has increased its powers, although they still remain inadequate. It has set in motion the democratisation of the integration process by the creation of European parties and through elections by direct universal suffrage. Finally, by adopting a draft treaty for European union, it has given the EEC a blueprint which may and should inspire its future evolution.

THE FRONTLINE FORCES
OF EUROPE

*

Roger Louet

THE ECONOMIC AND SOCIAL COMMITTEE AND
THE ECONOMIC AND SOCIAL WORLDS

Although the creation of the European Coal and Steel Community and of the European Economic Community were major political acts, their aims could not be achieved without the real participation of key representatives of economic and social organisations. The founding fathers of the two Communities made allowance for this.

As early as 1958, Walter Hallstein asked delegates from economic and social spheres of work to act, in their areas, as the mouthpiece of European public opinion. They were to present technical points of view and make known the concerns of working people in the member states. Jean Monnet also wanted to make them part of his committee for a United States of Europe.

The first institutional expression of this political desire to associate the economic and social partners with the attainment of the objectives of the Treaty came with the creation of a *Consultative Committee* to the ECSC High Authority. It included representatives of employers, workers and consumers in the coal and steel sectors, and played an important role in the reconstruction and modernisation of these two sectors, which were vital for economic development at the time.

The experiment proved to be successful. Inspired by this, and by the example of similar institutions already existing in a number of member states, the founding fathers of the EEC decided to set up the Economic and Social Committee (ESC). It is an advisory body, composed of representatives of employers' organisations, trade unions, the transport industry, agriculture, small and medium-sized businesses, craftsmen, the professions, consumers and cooperatives. It is a microcosm of production, sales, buying and consumption activities in the European Community. It influences EEC decisions by issuing Opinions on the European Commission's proposals to the EEC's Council of Ministers. EEC legislation which touches on vital economic and social interests is not therefore solely dependent on Council reaction. The permanent discussion which takes place within the ESC enables it to reach a consensus between its members in the general EEC interest.

Although the very muted level of European public opinion is regrettable, it is heartening that the socio-professional groups in the Community which are in the forefront of economic activity are highly motivated and involved in EEC affairs. They form a necessary counterbalance to the sluggish protectionist brake applied by national state administrations on the EEC's decision-making process.

A number of specialist advisory ESC committees have been set up in order to provide the Commission with opinions of experts for the drawing up of some of its more highly technical proposals.

Major projects and infrastructure work funded by the EC or by the EIB: Holyhead port (above) and fish research in Denmark…

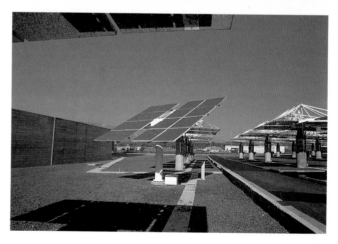

Facing page: Airbus in Toulouse and Ariane in Kourour. Above: North Sea oil.
Below (left): Joint European Tours (JET) in Culham; (right) solar energy.

Satellites and high speed trains.

The fight against water pollution.

The forge of Europe (steel casting).

The major budget choices: agricultural policy or new technology? Following page: the surpluses of the South (olives) and the North (butter).

THE CREATION OF SOCIO-PROFESSIONAL
ORGANISATIONS IN THE EEC

In 1958, when the Treaties of Rome entered into force, they held out the prospect of dynamic evolution of EEC policies in economic and social fields and in agriculture, transport and atomic energy: this was to be achieved by the creation of a single EEC market based upon the free movement of persons, workers, services, goods and capital.

With such evolution in prospect, it made good sense for national professional organisations to marshal themselves as rapidly as possible at European level. They were aware that national structures would be inadequate for making their voice heard in the debates which were slowly getting off the ground at European level.

In addition, it was in the interest of the EEC institutions, and notably the Commission, to find 'allies' for European integration in European socio-professional organisations. It was principally a question of being able to draw upon their experience in the framework of the legislative procedure, which was to be the main underpinning of integration. Also, the EEC, like any modern society, and in particular the pluralist societies of Western Europe, had to guarantee the clarity of its actions and ensure the influence of its organisations. As Jacques Genton, the first Secretary General of the Economic and Social Committee, pointed out, the EEC contributed to economic and social democracy by involving the frontline forces of society in the member states in its activities. Clarity and openness were increased by the 'institutionalising' of these forces at European level.

The Community is made up of institutions which, since their creation, have been preparing, taking and applying decisions. It is now common practice for the economic and social representatives to 'intervene' at each stage of EEC action by giving their viewpoints on how problems can be solved.

The challenge presented to economic and social operators by the prospect of rapid development of EEC policies was partially met within the framework of

The other Assembly has its 25th birthday (ceremony on May 31, 1983).

EEC institutions, especially that of the ESC. The ESC worked closely with autonomous interest groups which evolved at European level representing three different areas:
- the employers;
- the workers;
- farmers, consumers, the craft industry and small and medium-sized businesses.

The European Commission deliberately chose to involve representatives of European, rather than national, organisations in the legislative proposal process. The Commission itself therefore challenged national organisations to unite in specific sectors where EEC policies were evolving rapidly.

The majority of Europe-wide employers' organisations were founded in the period when the customs union was being rapidly completed and some features of the internal market were being implemented. The Union of Industries of the European Community (UNICE) was created in 1958; the Permanent Conference of Chambers of Commerce and Industry in the EEC (EUROCHAMBRES), the Union of Craftsmen in the EEC (UACEE) and the Banking Federation of the EEC were created in 1960; the Savings Bank Group of the European Economic Community came into being in 1963 and the European Centre of Public Enterprises (CEEP) in 1965.

The Common Agricultural Policy was established at the Stresa Conference in 1958. On this occasion also farmers formed an organisation at European level, COPA (Committee of Agricultural Organisations in the European Community). In 1959 agricultural cooperatives formed their own pan-European group, COGECA (General Committee for Agricultural Cooperation in the EEC).

By the early 1960s two European trade union organisations existed uneasily side by side, one with socialist and freethinking leanings (CESL), the other Christian Democrat (OE-CMT). However, they unified in 1973, and created the European Trade Union Confederation (ETUC), which currently represents more than 40% of the 115 million workers in the European Community.

The creation of the ETUC helped to fulfil an EEC aim of creating not only economic union but also simultaneous social union, a principle adopted at the 'summits' of The Hague and Paris (1969 and 1972).

The involvement of consumers' organisations at European level was consolidated by the creation of the Committee of Family Associations in the European Community (COFACE) in 1969 and by that of the European Bureau of Consumers' Unions (BEUC) in 1973. Their formation coincided with the first attempts by the European Commission to develop an EEC consumers' policy.

ACTIVITIES OF THE ECONOMIC AND SOCIAL CONCERNS IN EUROPE

Among the 450 European socio-professional organisations involved in Community affairs, around 25 big employers', workers' and other organisations make a continual direct input into the EEC institutions. They have a say in the EEC decision-making process, thanks to the founding fathers of the Treaty. They are represented in the Economic and Social Committee, in the ECSC Consultative Committee, and in the 50 or so specialist socio-economic advisory committees set up either by the Commission or by the Council of Ministers to help them develop policies and frame legislation.

Their direct field of action is first and foremost concentrated upon the

The ESC in its role as promoter of small and medium-sized enterprises. Here, from right to left, José Maria Zufiaur; the President, Fons Margot; Bill Poeton; Sir John Hoskyns, Diarmid McLaughlin and the Secretary General, Roger Louet.

institutions which participate in the EEC's legislative process, namely the Commission, which makes proposals, the European Parliament, which exercises political influence, and the Council of Ministers. The latter, although it often takes note of ESC Opinions, does not offer the socio-professional groups any possibilities for direct intervention. However, they can influence national ministers through their national organisations and also participate in the Council's meetings.

There are five areas of participation by the economic and social interest groups in EEC activity:

1. *The legislative process*

a) The Economic and Social Committee, which is an advisory body made up of 189 representatives from various sectors, can bend the ear of the Commission, the Council and the European Parliament throughout the procedure.

b) The ESC issues 120 Opinions each year covering all the fields of the EEC's activity.

c) The expertise in the open debates of the ESC allows the EEC institutions (Commission, Council and European Parliament) to evaluate whether a measure is acceptable to, and judged to be necessary by, the economic and social groups. The work of the ESC also allows the institutions to pre-judge which proposals might hit serious or even insoluble problems from the organised interests of our pluralist societies.

d) ESC Opinions are institutional in nature and are therefore distinct from the unilateral positions expressed by other pan-European organisations. They filter the large number of individual interests of the socio-professional groups and re-formulate them into new global positions.

e) The Economic and Social Committee organises conferences on subjects such as EEC enlargement, the role of small and medium-sized businesses, new technology and, in 1987, on the cooperative and mutualist business philosophies and practices. The ESC gives European and national organisations the opportunity to express their opinions on important or essential questions

which concern citizens and socio-professional organisations. It helps increase awareness at European and national level of the need for EEC solutions to major challenges which the European nations can no longer face alone.

f) Some of the proposals of the ESC have been and still are in the foreground of EEC evolution. The following are examples of areas where the ESC has taken initiatives:
- the establishment of a nuclear safety code in Europe;
- highlighting industrial, economic and social questions associated with the introduction of new technologies;
- the development of Citizens' Europe and the theme of the improvement of the quality of life;
- the introduction of new common policies, for example, health care and tourism in Europe;
- examination of the basic principles of reform of the Common Agricultural Policy.

In the field of the EEC's external relations, the ESC has established a permanent dialogue between its members and their counterparts in some 70 member countries of the Lomé Convention. It has also helped to stimulate constructive dialogue on trade relations between the EEC, the United States, Japan and the ASEAN countries.

2. The application and implementation of EEC policies adopted in the framework of EEC Regulations

The principle adopted by the Commission for the creation of advisory committees is that the socio-professional sectors affected by the implementation of the policies must be represented. Implementation of this principle is seen in the participation of organisations representing farmers and their cooperatives, consumers, the food industry, businessmen and workers in the elaboration of Opinions by agricultural advisory committees at the Commission. The socio-economic groups therefore participate in the implementation of the Common Agricultural Policy.

Participation of interested socio-economic organisations also takes place in other sectors. Advisory committees exist for the management of the European Social Fund and the Common Customs Tariff, including customs duties.

UNICE President Carl Gustav Ratjen at the headquarters of the Commission with President Delors.

COPA: defence of a European policy (demonstration in Brussels, 1984, with, among others, Sir Henry Plumb, Baron Heereman and André Herlitska).

Other advisory committees have been established to consider social security of migrant workers, the free movement of workers, agricultural structural policy, fishing and the social security problems of farmers and their families.

3. *Joint administration and management of autonomous EEC bodies*

The EEC has set up a number of autonomous bodies, such as the European Centre for the Development of Vocational Training in Berlin and the European Foundation for the Improvement of Living and Working Conditions in Dublin. Representatives of the social partners, who are among those most interested in the effective operation of these bodies, play a role in their administration and management.

4. *Cooperation between the social partners and EEC institutions*

Cooperation within the framework of the Tripartite European Conference (social partners, Council, Commission) on the major economic and social questions of the EEC (employment, economic growth, balance of trade, monetary stability, development of a 'European social area') did not come to much in the years 1970-77. However, cooperation continued, at least formally, within the Standing Committee on Employment.

A new attempt to improve the social dialogue at European level and to bring the points of view of the partners closer together was launched by the present European Commission President Jacques Delors. It was consolidated in a regular but informal dialogue, which took the name 'Val Duchesse', (after the meeting place) between the Commission, the Union of Industries of the European Community (UNICE) and the European Trade Union Confederation (ETUC).

5. Sectoral cooperation between the social partners

In this related field, where the objective is the establishment of collective framework conventions in particular sectors, the process began with agriculture. COPA drew up with the Professional Organisation of Agricultural Workers (EFA) a framework agreement on the harmonisation of the number of working hours and certain working conditions in specialised agricultural professions.

Another example was the agreement between ESC employer and worker members in the road transport sector on the content of a framework Directive, drawn up by the ESC, on the working conditions of drivers of heavy lorries. The bulk of the ESC framework Directive was adopted by the EEC.

DIRECT ACTION BY
EUROPEAN ORGANISATIONS

Apart from the institutional links of the socio-economic partners with the EEC, in the shape of advisory bodies, participation and dialogue, the socio-professional organisations all have bilateral links with the EEC. The form these take depends largely on the circumstances and on the enterprise of those concerned.

At one end of the scale, small local associations make representations on a once-only basis on a point which directly concerns them. At the other, there is the systematic and well-organised intervention by COPA in the agricultural price-setting discussions during several months each year at the Commission, the Economic and Social Committee, the European Parliament, the Council of Ministers and often the European Council. Between these two extremes, European organisations take part directly at various stages. The most important of these is the preparation stage, when the general slant of a Commission proposal can be influenced. Intervention either takes place at the technical level

COPA heads, including François Guillaume, demonstrating in front of the Council of Ministers in 1983.

Steel industry in crisis: workers' demonstration in Metz, 1984.

of the Commission's General Directorates, Directorates and Divisions, or at the political level of Commissioners and their *chefs de cabinet*. Attention is then focussed on the European Parliament and the Economic and Social Committee at the later, and more precise, stage of the elaboration of EEC Regulations and Directives. The organisations can turn back to the Commission if the Parliament and/or the ESC call for any amendments to the original project. The European organisations also try to prompt the Council to take account of their requests: they target national ministers who, in their roles as political personalities, are sensitive to the entreaties of the European organisations because large numbers of voters are affected at national and European level.

THE INFLUENCE OF
EUROPEAN ECONOMIC AND SOCIAL FORCES –
AN EEC ACHIEVEMENT

The EEC raised and maintained the interest of the social and economic groups in the construction of Europe by offering them a wide range of opportunities for intervention and action. The EEC opened up its decision-making process to the economic and social reality of European industrial society, which is now going through the transition into a post-industrial society which will be characterised by the preponderance of information technologies and services and increased leisure time.

When the different groups – employers, workers, consumers, social workers – expound their ideas in the Economic and Social Committee, or in other European cooperation and dialogue bodies, they feel that their views, representing large segments of society, are taken into consideration. The fact that

they are ready to talk and to make compromises with other sectors on EEC policies demonstrates that they are gradually becoming aware of the need for a European dimension in their activities.

Their personal success when they make progress on one or other of the ideas or concerns of the Community, and also their disappointment when they return from Brussels empty-handed, prompts dialogue and reflection within their national bodies.

Their daily presence in the EEC arena makes a contribution to increased awareness in the Community of grass-roots problems. The joint action of the socio-professional groups and their representatives, institutionalised in the ESC, prompts the conclusion that they represent a 'third force' in Europe. Alongside the Commission, which is the proposal centre, and the European Parliament, which represents the European people as a whole, the Economic and Social Committee is the force which ensures the expert participation in the EEC of specialised groups in our societies.

CAPITAL,

HEADQUARTERS,

METROPOLIS...

*

Jean A. Pirlot

George Podiebrad, King of Bohemia, wearily raised his eyebrows and said with a sigh:

– 'All the Princes whom we wished to bring together are to a man demanding that the Assembly be sited on their territory. Yet it is impossible to give satisfaction at the same time to the Duke of Burgundy, the Duke of Bavaria, the King of Poland, the King of Hungary and his Lordship of Venice....'

– 'We must join forces to resist the Turks. Is this matter of life or death not enough for problems of precedence and prestige to be momentarily silenced?' asked Antoine Marini, trying to conceal his impatience.

– 'You are well travelled, Master Marini,' said the King. 'You have had the occasion to remark the extent to which Christianity has been torn apart, weakened and decimated, stripped of its radiance and of all its past splendour. The vanity of our Princes has much to account for in this decadence'.

– 'Could we perhaps suggest that the Assembly sit for five years in one town, and then move on for five years in another?' asked Marini.

– 'Now there is a sound proposal, Master Marini! I admire your art of reasonable compromise. If King Louis of France agrees to lead our coalition, a ray of hope may finally be ours for the taking.'

Hradcany castle, Prague (engraving, XVIIth century).

The enterprising negotiator from Grenoble and the Hussite leader and vanquisher king of Bavaria were to pick one another's wits for many a day yet in the year 1463 in the Castle of Hradcany, Prague. Probably for the first time in the history of Europe, a plan for a union was proposed to governments for their appraisal. Five centuries later, the problem of which town should have the honour of being the Institutional headquarters is still not resolved....

SCHEME FOR UNIVERSAL PEACE

The Abbot Charles-Irénée Castel de Saint-Pierre was a free-thinker. He took advantage of the long winter evenings in 1706-1707 to draw up the 'Traité de Paix Perpétuelle' (Treaty of Permanent Peace), the implementation of which would lead to a 'Permanent Union of all sovereigns'.

The Abbot did not doubt that disputes would still arise. These would be resolved by a permanent arbitration council, in which would sit one representative of each sovereign, each with one vote. But where should the council be situated?

– 'In a Free City, which will become Peace City!' asserted the Abbot Saint-Pierre.

The Abbot attached precise political significance to the word 'free'. Charles-Irénée Castel de Saint-Pierre had been a member of the 'Académie

française', but was expelled from this learned assembly when he made derogatory remarks about King Louis XIV.

The Abbot very craftily focussed the debate on to the choice of 'Peace City'. According to the Treaty, this had to be a 'free' city. By 'free', the Abbot understood 'not under the control of a sovereign'. Its very freedom would keep the objective of the Treaty intact, since the permanent council would not be under the influence of a Prince and fall foul of his ambitions.

The King of Prussia welcomed the Treaty of the Abbot of Saint-Pierre with much less benevolence than the King of Bohemia greeted the ideas of Antoine Marini. His Majesty wrote sardonically to Voltaire: 'The plan is very practical. It only requires the consent of Europe and a few other such minions'.

Was, then, the Abbot of Saint-Pierre a mere utopian? Hardly more so than his fanciful contemporaries who called for the abolition of slavery or the independence of the English colonies in North America and their formation into a powerful federation. The Abbot was not perturbed. He wrote: 'I believe that European arbitration may only grow up very gradually, by infinitesimal stages, perhaps over a period of two hundred years. Today it is only a question of taking the coalition's first stage, by organising a congress, in the Hague or elsewhere'.

THE HAGUE

The Congress of The Hague finally took place more than two centuries later in 1948. The location was chosen by a process of elimination. In London, the Labour Government had no wish to host an event sponsored by the Conservative Winston Churchill. It would have looked too much as if France was monopolising the event for its own ends if held in Paris. During the controversial post-war exile of Belgium's King Léopold III, the choice of Brussels would have given rise to political problems. There was no question of the Congress being held in Berlin or in Bonn. Athens, with the threat of civil war just around the corner, would not have provided the right atmosphere. In Rome, the wounds of the past were too fresh to speak of the future. This left Luxembourg, but it did not have the hotel facilities for eight hundred

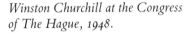

Winston Churchill at the Congress of The Hague, 1948.

Strasbourg (aerial view).

participants, not counting the administrative staff.

Participants in The Hague drew up a general outline of the form which European unification could take, but they did not touch on the question of a capital. Spirits were running so high that the question would have seemed out of place, almost trivial.

The Spanish writer Salvador de Madariaga, who chaired the Cultural Committee at The Hague Congress, received a long ovation when he declared: 'Europe must be brought into existence. And it will exist once the Spanish speak of 'Our Lady of Chartres', the British talk about Krakow as familiarly as London, the Italians of Copenhagen as they would speak of Rome, and the Germans speak fondly of Bruges, and all shudder in horror at the thought of any of these treasures being destroyed'.

One year later, the Statute of the Council of Europe was signed in Westminster. Article 11 of this Statute stipulates that Strasbourg is the permanent headquarters of the Council of Europe. The story goes that Strasbourg was proposed by Gladwyn Jebb (the future Lord Gladwyn), who had passed what he said was a pleasant 'study' trip there during his youth. This neatly provided the solution to the problem posed by Antoine Marini five hundred years earlier.

STRASBOURG

Minister Paul Reynaud gave a rather unenthusiastic first French reaction to the choice of Strasbourg. Was this not a way to keep the Council of Europe from the eyes and ears of the press? 'A meeting in Strasbourg cannot possibly have the same impact as a meeting in Paris...', he declared.

However, Europe has such a vast and rich history that each part has its share of renown. If we dig far enough back into the history of Strasbourg, we unearth the Oaths exchanged between Charles the Bald and Louis the German in front of their troops in the year 842 to seal their pact against their brother Lothair.

Strasbourg was only a 'free' town – in the sense intended by the Abbot of Saint-Pierre – between the Treaty of Westphalia in 1648 and its annexation by Louis XIV in 1681.

But can a town which has been fought over so often, destroyed by the

Alamans, occupied by the Huns, reconquered, French, then German, then French again, be anything other than deeply, intensely free? The inhabitants of Strasbourg have wanted to live their own lives, and preserve something of their culture, regardless of the ruler of the moment. The cathedral is a monument to the skill of the town's architects, with its subtle changes of style, which somehow respect an overall equilibrium.

THE INSIGNIA OF
MANKIND

Strasbourg calmly passed through the Reformation at the beginning of the sixteenth century and the Revolution of the eighteenth, unscarred by the hatred and violence which tore apart so many other cities.

Strasbourg's European role was taken on with the same quiet determination, as if the citizens of the town had made their own the motto on the admirable tapestry by Jean Lurçat in the blue dining room of the 'Palais de l'Europe': 'The hilt of his sword was emblazoned with the insignia of mankind'.

The industrial development of Strasbourg is still in full swing, from breweries to petro-chemical factories. The port has moved from the banks of the Ill to those of the Rhine. Airport traffic is growing all the time. Most importantly, the dynamism of the Strasbourg authorities has proven Paul Reynaud wrong: the world does not pass Strasbourg by.

The 'Palais de l'Europe', built by the architect Henry Bernard, has ample space not only for the 518 Members of Parliament, but also for hundreds of international journalists who have reported speeches ranging from that of the President of the United States to those of the late Italian MEP Altiero Spinelli calling for European union.

LUXEMBOURG'S CHANCE
COMES

In 1951, when the European Coal and Steel Community was created, five of the six signatory governments agreed on Brussels as the headquarters. But the Belgian Minister had to turn down the honour, since the Belgian Parliament had been promised that the Belgian nomination would be...Liège.

In all innocence, and in an attempt to save face for his colleagues, Joseph Bech nominated the capital of his country, Luxembourg, as the seat of the ECSC.

The question fired lively discussion in Luxembourg for a number of years. The Grand Duchy had had its fill of foreign domination. It had passed through the hands of the Burgundians, the Spanish, the French, the Spanish again, the Austrians, then the French again and the Germans from time to time.... In the course of just five centuries, all this had been just a bit much! It is understandable that some Luxembourgeois were not therefore overjoyed at the prospect of being simultaneously occupied by five countries!

Yet some voices were raised in favour of the idea. Why not transform Luxembourg into some sort of 'European district'? After all, the country was well used to having a weird and wonderful status. The Congress of Vienna had made it both the personal property of King Guillaume the First of the Netherlands and a member of the German 'Deutscherbund'. It had also belonged to the 'Zollverein' customs union with Prussia in 1842.

KIRCHBERG

Luxembourg has, in fact, been able to strike the right balance. Bech was not given permission to propose the capital of the Grand Duchy as the headquarters of the Common Market – the ECSC was quite enough. The north-east of the town, the market garden area of the Kirchberg plateau, was gradually built over with ultra-modern offices. A series of gracious and slender bridges spanning the deep ravines which dissect Luxembourg keep the Kirchberg in touch with the heart of the city.

Luxembourg does not have the resources which enabled the French state to give vast funds to Strasbourg. Some local resentment was caused by the investments made in buildings which could be used by the European Institutions. Why build a European Court of Justice when the Luxembourgois judges had been calling for new Law Courts for so many years? And where was the money found for a European school, when the children of Luxembourg had to struggle on in cramped conditions?

Nevertheless, in the tradition of the country, Luxembourg has invested its money prudently. A number of European organisations, such as the European Communities Statistical Office, the Court of Justice, the European Investment Bank, the Office for Official Publications of the European Communities and the Court of Auditors have been persuaded by this real estate investment to set up permanent office in Luxembourg. At the same time, the Luxembourg Government has succeeded in creating a major financial centre by attracting an ever-larger number of banks.

BRUSSELS

When the Treaty of Rome setting up the European Economic Community was signed, the Belgian Government did not want to lose a second opportunity. At this stage rather more importance was attached to the question, and Brussels was proposed as the new administrative centre. Europe already had two capitals, and some felt that these were quite enough. Consequently, the Executive Commission of the EEC was instructed to state on its headed notepaper that the Brussels address was only 'temporary'.

Since then, the executive bodies of the ECSC, Euratom and the EEC have been amalgamated into a single 'European Commission', and the Berlaymont has gradually expanded over 100,000 square metres. Yet the situation remains the same. The words 'temporary address' are still there.

The Union of Industries of the European Community (UNICE), the

Aerial views: Luxembourg (on the left) and Brussels.

On the left: the omnipresence of television in Europe. On the right: the press as the mouthpiece of public opinion.

European Trade Union Confederation (ETUC), the Committee of Agricultural Organisations in the European Community (COPA) and the European Bureau of Consumers' Unions (BEUC) are only a few of the well-known names among the hundreds of associations which have set up shop in Brussels to follow and try to influence the proposals made by the European Commission.

Indeed, since the beginning of the fifties, Belgium has conducted a very discreet welcoming policy for international non-governmental organisations. Belgian constitutional and linguistic problems have acted somewhat as a brake, but the trend has been established. At the beginning of the eighties Brussels renewed its effort to attract the European headquarters of international organisations. They brought in their wake a mass of lawyers specialised in international and European law.

THE CAPITALS OF EUROPE

Perhaps Europe will never have a single capital or headquarters. It already has three centres of activity, and indeed each town in Europe could be a viable candidate. Europe's strength lies in its diversity.

The fascinating development of new technology has resulted in rapid and reliable telecommunications between all the administrative and political units. An answer has been found to the problem of storing innumerable files and data. The human factor is the only area where evolution has been slow.

Why should the European Community want to create a political and administrative megalopolis, a paper ghetto? The example of neither Washington D.C. nor Brasilia are worthy of imitation.

Europe has a great deal of work ahead of it, in fields as varied as aeronautics, health care, basic research and defence. The organisations which must develop or be created cannot be allowed to suffocate in one crammed town.

The European University is in Florence, the European Centre for Vocational Training Studies in Berlin, the College of Europe in Bruges, the European Foundation for the Improvement of Living and Working Conditions in Dublin and the European Cultural Foundation in Amsterdam. Europe's central bank governors meet in Basle, its researchers study nuclear energy at Geel (Belgium), Ispra (Italy), Petten (Netherlands) and Karlsruhe (Germany). The list could go on. Europe should take pride in having made both official and private organisations feel at home throughout its lands.

CITIZENS' EUROPE

*

Pietro Adonnino

The European Economic Community constitutes the first step on the road to the creation of a United States of Europe. The completion of the project is a fundamental necessity for the people of the Old World. However, the further unity progresses, the greater the obstacles which surge in its path.

These difficulties are clearly seen in the continuous debate over what the priorities of the unification process should be: should economic or political integration come first? And yet in practice these two elements are intrinsically linked, and it is difficult to imagine how they could be dissociated.

The EEC will go down as a unique project in the annals of history. For this reason alone, it is crucially important to be resolute and to shun disillusion.

One of the essential conditions for success of the unification project is support by the peoples of Europe. The results of European Commission surveys carried out on this subject would seem to confirm that this condition has been met, although to a greater or lesser extent from country to country. Unfortunately, this is to paint too rosy a picture. Citizens certainly support the EEC's ideals, but not always with the necessary conviction.

Each member state draws up its national policy with respect to its own public opinion. However, the latter often demonstrates collective reflexes which are damaging to the unification process.

These reflexes need to be replaced by a clearer vision of reality. People must come to perceive the Community as acting in the name of all and in the general interest, and that some sacrifices are required in pursuit of this ideal.

At the Fontainebleau European Summit in June 1984, the heads of state and government decided to set up a Special Committee for a Citizens' Europe,

Two British stamps inspired on European themes.

Customs? No, thanks! Members of Parliament (from right to left) Dieter Rogalla, P.A.M. Cornelissen, Elmar Brok and Rüdiger Hitzigrath.

Family name: Europe....

made up of representatives of the various governments.

The Committee was created to advise the European Council on decisions likely to safeguard citizens' interests or the support and commitment of citizens for the European ideal. In order to avoid ambiguity and interference with the activities of other EEC bodies, the Committee, which I had the honour of chairing, decided at its first meeting to set itself a deadline of one year to reach conclusions.

One of the aims the Committee set itself was to demonstrate to the citizens of the various member states that, despite the complexity and the diversity of the proposals made, it was possible to reach quickly a unanimous decision within the EEC, provided that everyone worked in a Community spirit.

The Committee's work method essentially consisted of making a judgement on the political worth of proposals. Each proposal was first evaluated for its value and Community interest. Solutions were then sought for the individual problems which one or other member state faced with the proposal.

It goes without saying that the Committee had close links with the European Parliament: the Committee's objective was to defend citizens' interests, and the Parliament is the key forum for the expression of the opinions and wishes of the EEC's citizens.

Priority was given to proposals either because they were indivisible from the principles and the import of the European ideal, or because they would have an effect on everyday life.

Forty proposals were finally presented to the European Councils of March 1985 in Brussels and June 1985 in Milan, and were all unanimously adopted.

The European Council gave the European Commission and the Council of Ministers the task of introducing the legal measures necessary for the implementation at EEC level of the proposals which had been approved. Unfortunately, their fulfilment has fallen behind schedule, and it is desirable that steps be taken to speed up the process.

Among the proposals presented, those which concerned teaching were of especial importance, for it is a field which affects the citizens in all the member states. It was suggested that schools and technical colleges should be encouraged to introduce more intensive language teaching, and that the integration process of the European nations should be among the subjects taught.

The Committee made a number of proposals on cultural matters, and more particularly on media, and especially television, policy.

One subject which the Committee could not neglect was that of the fundamental rights of citizens in the member states of the EEC. It presented a proposal tackling two aspects: harmonisation of voting procedures for the election of the European Parliament, and the granting of the right to vote to citizens residing in a member state other than their own at the time when national elections are held.

A common passport.

One of the proposals concerned the extension of the right to petition as a protection measure which can be used where the citizen feels he has been a victim of power abuse. It was also suggested that the right of residence of EEC nationals in the member state of their choice should be dissociated from the question of work.

The Committee paid special attention to problems arising from one of the main objectives of the Treaty of Rome, namely the free movement of persons, goods and services. Another proposal along the same lines was for the mutual recognition of diplomas and other professional qualifications, so that citizens can actually exercise their right to free establishment. At the same time, some

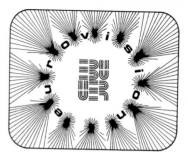

Eurovision, 50 years of radio and television without frontiers thanks to the EBU/UER (European Broadcasting Union).

A common symbol: the European flag is raised in front of the Berlaymont on European Day 1986 (from left to right, Ambassador Rutten, Jacques Delors, Pierre Pflimlin, Carlo Ripa di Meana).

policy directions were defined on the question of EEC organisation of tourism.

Young people are not only citizens of today, but also the seed of tomorrow's society. The Committee's convictions on this point led it to make proposals designed to promote international exchanges between young Europeans. Sport for the young was another priority, and both the spectators and active participants were taken into account. A number of other proposals dealt with the status of volunteer workers from the European Community in the Third

European campaign against xenophobia and racism.

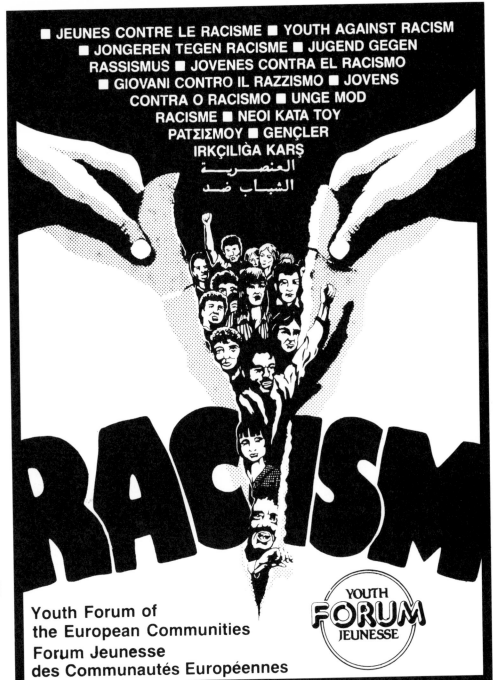

- JEUNES CONTRE LE RACISME ■ YOUTH AGAINST RACISM ■ JONGEREN TEGEN RACISME ■ JUGEND GEGEN RASSISMUS ■ JOVENES CONTRA EL RACISMO ■ GIOVANI CONTRO IL RAZZISMO ■ JOVENS CONTRA O RACISMO ■ UNGE MOD RACISME ■ NEOI KATA TOY PATΣIΣMOY ■ GENÇLER IRKÇILIĠA KARŞ العنصرية الشباب ضد

RACISM

Youth Forum of the European Communities Forum Jeunesse des Communautés Européennes

YOUTH FORUM JEUNESSE

European Years as part of an attempt to create a 'community' feeling: 1986-Safety, 1987-Environment.

EUROPEAN ROAD SAFETY YEAR
1986

World. Sectors such as health care, social security and prevention of the use of drugs were also included in the Committee's proposals.

Finally, the Committee suggested that European citizens could also show their commitment to Europe and their common identity by symbolic acts, such as removal of national border signs, raising of the EEC flag, listening to the Community anthem or using stamps indicating some aspect of belonging to the EEC.

As a result of the Committee's proposals, the flag of the European Community was raised, for the first time, outside the Commission's headquarters in Brussels in late 1986 alongside national flags to the ringing out of the European anthem.

EUROPE,
THE HOPE OF
THE THIRD WORLD?

*

Katharina Focke

Will the title of this chapter ever signify more than a pious wish on the part of the European Community and a straw clutched at by the Third World? Let us review the situation.

The issue of Third World development is addressed by the Treaty of Rome that founded the Community. In its preamble it states that one of the aims of the Treaty should be to strengthen the bonds between Europe and overseas countries and to ensure the development of their prosperity, in accordance with the principles of the United Nations Charter. Chapter four of the Treaty of Rome stipulates that an association be set up between overseas countries and member states of the European Community.

THE END OF AN ERA

In 1957-58, colonialism was breathing its last. Four member states possessed colonies, and the EEC believed it had an obligation to them even after they achieved independence. This principle was embodied in a number of treaties. In 1963 the Yaoundé Convention was signed between the EEC and 19 independent African states. It was followed in 1969 by the second Yaoundé Convention, and in 1971 by the Arusha Convention which dealt with the former British colonies of Kenya, Uganda and Tanzania, in anticipation of British membership of the EEC. Since then, three other treaties, known respectively as Lomé I, II and III, have been signed between the EEC and 66 African, Caribbean and Pacific (ACP) countries.

The colonial past of the member states influenced early development cooperation on a limited regional basis in that it was focussed mainly on the African continent with a steadily increasing number of countries. The first bare bones of this cooperation were the setting of customs quotas. Gradually trade preferences were established and finally a development fund. EEC development activity started up in the Mediterranean region also, with a series of protocols and declarations of intent signalling cooperation between the European Community and, successively, Algeria, Morocco and Tunisia.

In 1971 the Commission issued a memorandum concerning common policy on cooperation with developing countries. It tried for the first time to put down on paper its concept of EEC relations with the Third World. In its introduction, the memorandum pointed out that the majority of these countries had already established active bilateral cooperation agreements with individual member states, and that 'they only see the EEC as a customs and agricultural organisation which may present a threat to the development of their trade and which, at any rate, does not offer any prospect of direct cooperation which could help them solve their development problems'.

At the outset, therefore, developing countries had no faith in the abilities of the EEC. On the contrary, they had a 'frankly negative image of the Community'. The EEC strove to change this image, essentially by taking customs and trade measures designed to show that the Community was naturally extrovert.

Shortly before the memorandum was issued, the Generalised System of Preferences for finished and semi-finished products, giving certain goods preferential access to European markets, came into being. This system was applied to *all* developing countries. Food aid was already in operation, with the first programme dating back to 1968.

The memorandum demonstrates clearly that the first enlargement of the EEC opened up the old argument as to whether the Community should concentrate its development policy on certain selected countries or make a general effort. It also bears witness to the Commission's desire to settle this question once and for all. The memorandum justified the bias operating until then, stating that it was a natural consequence of the 'existence of privileged ties as a result of historical and geographical circumstances' and of the EEC's limited means. It also pointed out, however, that the EEC had begun to extend its area of cooperation to other developing countries in Asia and Latin America and that the EEC had begun to participate in world-scale operations, in accordance with the objectives of the United Nations Commission for Trade and Development (UNCTAD).

The final declaration of the EEC summit in Paris, in October 1972, stated that the Community was aware of the continuing problems of global under-development and stressed its desire to increase its share of development aid to and cooperation with the poorest countries in the context of a world policy. It also stated that it would pay particular attention to the needs of countries towards which it felt a special obligation for historical and geographical reasons, and because of commitments which had already been made.

A compromise was reached between those who believed in limiting cooperation to certain regions and those who favoured a global effort. At the same time, the *political* foundations for supra-national cooperation with all

On the left: the streets of Lomé decked with flags. On the right: local press publishes a special issue on the event.

Mr. Eyadema, President of Togo, welcomes Messrs. Barry (President of the EEC's Council of Ministers), Thorn (President of the European Commission) and Naimaliu (President of the ACP Council of Ministers), for the signature of the IIIrd Lomé Convention.

developing countries were laid. A high-level working group, known as the Development Council, was set up, composed of representatives from the Commission and from member states. This group started work on fixing the 'principles and objectives of cooperation policy on development at world level'.

When the first oil crisis occurred in 1973, the EEC became more aware of its interdependence with the developing world, and took initiatives to step up the North-South dialogue. In 1977 it was decided that a special fund should be created for those developing countries hit most severely by the oil crisis. Global North-South negotiations also got underway at that time, but broke down in 1980 at the United Nations preparatory conference, and the subsequent Cancun summit Conference on North-South affairs failed to revive them.

During the first half of the seventies, development cooperation received new impetus. What results did it yield?

PROVISIONAL CONCLUSION:
DISAPPOINTMENT

In principle the Lomé Convention is a real achievement. And though it has proved to be too restrictive in the areas of trade and funding, it has partly met the expectations of its partners. However on some levels it has been a real disappointment. In Africa, particularly, its efforts have been a bit like putting a sticking plaster on a broken leg: it has not been able to keep pace with the ever-growing problems.

The Lomé Convention will only be a success when:
– there is closer coordination with the bilateral development programmes of member states so that methods and objectives can be harmonised;
– there are international agreements on trade policy, on raw materials and the handling of the Third World debt;
– special efforts in line with the recommendations of the United Nations Special Conference on Africa have been undertaken;
– more funds have been released for development and there is better coordination of their use.

Aid to developing countries has many forces, including technical assistance, food aid and emergency aid.

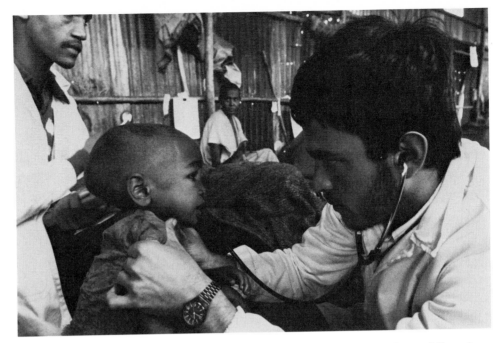

In cooperation with other regions of the world, too, results have fallen short of what could have been achieved in view of early perceptions that the community's special political attributes qualified it well for region-to-region links. Cooperation with the EEC has not met the expectations of numerous developing countries which have been affected by the worsening of East-West relations during the eighties. The cooperation agreement with the Association of South East Asian Nations (ASEAN) has yet to be convincingly implemented. And the joint agreement with the Central American countries and that with the CONTADORA states has still to be brought to life. Furthermore, the cooperation agreements with the coastal countries of the southern and eastern Mediterranean have also to be re-negotiated, and the need to link it to a regional Mediterranean policy also remains to be accomplished. Though steps have been taken towards regional cooperation, the scent of compromise between the wishes of the Commission and the European Parliament on the one hand and the concessions which member states are willing to make, on the other, lingers everywhere. The agreements as they currently exist are just enough to keep the flames of hope from being entirely extinguished.

And what has befallen the plans for global development? The Generalised System of Preferences probably still is the most important instrument for a comprehensive policy on cooperation and development. Yet the position which the Community adopts, its commitment, its influence on conferences such as UNCTAD and the GATT (General Agreement on Tariffs and Trade) are becoming increasingly decisive. However, the UNCTAD Conference held in Belgrade seriously disappointed the Third World countries. Europe did not use its influence as the world's leading trading partner to spur the United States into action. The results of the next UNCTAD and GATT conferences are not yet to be predicted, but there is reason to fear that the EEC will give way to the temptation to ignore the interests of developing countries in favour of concentrating its attention on its own trade relations with Japan and the United States. In short, protectionist tendencies are gathering force in the European Community while old trading practices, especially in areas such as textiles and agricultural products, prevent many Third World countries from gaining a

stronger foothold on the world market. Member states' export policies are often blinded by self-interest in flagrant disregard for the flowery declarations of intent on development cooperation.

As far as food aid is concerned, will the current reforms succeed in turning this into a truly effective instrument for development? Or will the EEC fail to progress beyond the stage of emergency food aid and limited, blow-by-blow compromises that try to link its own agricultural interests with the principles of development policy? For the moment these questions remain unanswered.

A VOICE IN THE WILDERNESS

If the EEC's budgets for the years 1977 and 1986 are compared, it can be seen that the proportion of resources for development aid for the countries outside the Lomé Convention has increased from 20 to more than 200 million Ecus. This is partly due to pressure from the European Parliament: however, notwithstanding the increases, the EEC's slim wallet has rendered its efforts almost imperceptible. The money has been divided up between a plethora of bilateral projects.

In the seventies, the Commission drew up the first four-year plan for development aid (worth 730 million ecu) at world level. This plan did not survive the EEC's budget quarrels and the zeal with which the Finance Ministers went about making savings. It should be noted that EEC expenditure on development currently represents only about 12% of the sum total of development aid paid out by the individual member states. Furthermore, the majority of member states are far from reaching the 0.7% of GNP set as a target by the United Nations, either through EEC aid or through their own bilateral agreements. A second memorandum from the European Commission in favour of increased and improved development cooperation remains a dead letter. And repeated appeals from the European Parliament for a qualitative improvement in development aid as well as a substantial increase in funds have also been ignored.

Many of the good intentions of the seventies have not been translated into

action, especially concerning the lightening of the debt burden of developing countries. The Community has never paid sufficient attention to this problem, and joint action to resolve it has been too rare. Over the last decade the Commission has been demanding that more state aid be granted and under more favourable terms, so that the countries receiving aid do not suffer from a too rapid increase in their indebtedness. The Commission has also stressed the importance of coordinating multilaterial measures designed to relieve the debt burden. In 1982, in its second memorandum, it again proposed that the member states define a common position for Europe to adopt within major financial organisations, such as the International Monetary Fund (IMF) and the World Bank. The Parliament, too, persistently requested that joint action be taken. But, despite all these pleas, the member states are still far from united in this field.

The Commission is not present at IMF conferences and is unable to exercise influence on coordination sessions which precede them because, unlike the practice within UN organisations, it does not even have observer status. Thus the developing countries have so far had no reason to hope for much help from Europe with the re-absorption of their debt, although the EEC should be ideally placed to define a global development policy, covering in one big package the reduction of debt, the improvement of trade conditions and an increase in aid. At present only Finance Ministers, who are most concerned with national interest, have a say in these matters.

The situation is no better on the question of raw materials. Apart from the proposal to extend to the poorest developing countries the Lomé Convention's STABEX Regulations (which bring a measure of stability to export earnings), the EEC has not taken any concrete initiatives to improve the existing agreements or conclude new ones. Ideological discussions on free market versus interventionist philosophies have so far prevented solutions to the problem of raw materials. Meanwhile, as an annual warning, the Parliament inserts into the budget a remark on the 'Common Fund for raw materials'. It has almost become a ritual!

For more than fifteen years now, the Commission and the European Parliament have been calling for more coordination between the EEC and the member states on the question of development cooperation. Furthermore, they have constantly stressed the need for coordination between development activities and other business conducted by the Community. They have had very little success. And yet this is the crux of the matter. If only Europe had the political will, it could make a real contribution to the development of countries which, despite their constant disappointments, still hope that Europe will come to their aid.

In this respect, part of the text of the Commission's first memorandum in 1971 has not lost its pertinence. It declared that the Community and its member states must strive to act with greater coherence. This need, it stated, had been stressed by the European Parliament. Greater coherence was required, for instance, between economic policy within the EEC (in agriculture, industry, social matters, and so on) on the one hand, and development policy on the other. Since that time, the creation of a European Monetary System and the institutionalisation of foreign policy cooperation have increased the need for such coherence. The growing burdens which both the European Community and developing countries have to bear are similar — the economic crisis, havoc on financial markets, unemployment, threats to the environment, the East-West arms race and a number of regional conflicts. One has to agree with the

second Commission memorandum, published in 1982. This gave the opinion that political measures taken by the Community on its own behalf have a greater influence on Third World countries than do measures dealing specifically with development. The Community's Third World partners, the Commission continued, consider it to be fully responsible for the attitudes which it adopts: the Commission is, in their eyes, the natural forum for coordination and cooperation between the policies and the points of views of the various member states. Unfortunately, the member states themselves do not see the Community that way. The European Parliament has so far not been able to change this situation, despite all its efforts to redefine the EEC's role in the relaunch of the North–South dialogue.

What conclusion can be reached, thirty years after the signature of the Treaty of Rome? Many of the hopes of the Third World rest upon what the Community *could* and *should* do if it decided to use its potential. Before this can take place, however, Europe needs to be fully aware of the interdependence between developing countries and itself. It needs to recognise that there is a community of interests in cooperation from region to region, in defusing conflict and in setting up a North–South dialogue which leads to an international system based upon peace and justice. Some of the basic requirements for success already exist in the form of the Lomé Convention, agreements with the Latin American countries and in the Generalised System of Preferences, but these are not enough. Much remains to be done if Europe wants to avoid stamping out once and for all the hope invested in it by the Third World.

EUROPE,

AS SEEN BY THE REST

OF THE WORLD

*

Robert Triffin

The overwhelming majority of the close on 5 billion inhabitants of the world have absolutely no mental image of Europe. Only a tiny elite minority are aware of the influence which Europe can have on their everyday life and their future. Having lived for more than forty years in the United States, I have had numerous occasions to remark the very small place given to Europe in the perception and preoccupations of the average American, in particular in comparison to the attention given to domestic policy and the Soviet Union, and in particular to that given to sport and cartoon books.

Secondly, this elite has a multifaceted image of Europe, varying with time and space.

Up until the First World War, there was no disputing that Europe was and had been for centuries the cultural, economic and political centre of the world. This is clearly no longer the case in a world which has become oligarchic and in which most of the influence has passed from Europe to the United States.

From a cultural point of view, *American English* has become very much a world language, easily outstripping all its closest rivals (British English, Spanish and French). It is even creeping into other national languages, and *franglais* is one example of this.

The American elite is certainly aware of the almost exclusive role played by Europe in its cultural heritage of the arts and the sciences. However, it is also aware that current-day growth in this heritage is no longer dependent upon Europe, as it still was in, for example, the thirties and forties, when Europe suffered a massive 'brain drain'. This trend seems to be reversing and the United States now exports more intellectual power than it imports . The rest of the world is flooded with many more American books and articles – either in English or in translation – than the United States is with foreign books and articles.

Europe has also capitulated to the United States on the education front. Up until the First or even the Second World War the elite of other continents came for education in European universities and even primary and secondary schools. This is clearly no longer the case today. Foreigners are not at all attracted by primary and secondary schools in the United States, but the intellectual elite finish off their education in American, rather than European, universities.

The two World Wars drained the former economic and, more especially, financial and monetary predominance of Europe and passed power in these areas over to the United States.

In fact, from a strictly economic point of view, Europe's phenomenal growth since the last war, strongly stimulated by the Marshall Plan, the

To travel in Europe (centre pile), you need deeper pockets than to visit the United States (left-hand pile) or the Soviet Union (right-hand pile).

removal of customs barriers and other moves towards European integration, has far outstripped that of the United States. It has therefore been able to make good all or part of the gap which opened up from 1913 onwards.

However, the dollar has become generally accepted as the main 'parallel currency' (a currency other than the national one used or held in a particular country), and this has led to excessive United States influence in financial and monetary affairs. It has held on to this influence despite the suspension of dollar convertibility and very large fluctuations in both directions of the paper dollar against the other major national currencies. The wave of foreign investment in the United States was first viewed with amazement, and then became an accepted fact. Foreign investment increased tenfold between 1970 ($110 billion) and 1985 ($1210 billion) and was clearly the main factor in the inflation explosion which took place at world level during this period.

The United States is therefore now the focal point for the attention at one time accorded to Europe by governments, local authorities, banks, firms and individuals wishing to invest or borrow outside of their own country. The United States has inherited the terrifying responsibilities of leadership of the world economy imposed by such economic and financial hegemony.

The EIB borrows for the first time in a third country (in Dollars).

The way in which the US shouldered its responsibilities varied to a large extent in the period 1913-1985.

The *isolationism* of the inter-war period has ceded to growing *interventionism*. The source of inspiration for this and the consequences of it have radically changed in the course of the four decades following World War Two.

For almost twenty years the United States assumed its role of 'superpower' with complete confidence in its capacity to shoulder the major part of the burden of construction of a better world, working hand in hand with all the countries of the 'free' or 'non-communist' world. It tackled this with a generosity and success never before seen. The Marshall Plan and aid to the Third World were linked to joint efforts to liberalise world trade and step up regional cooperation, particularly in Europe, where the final objective was the economic and political integration of the member states. Jean Monnet, founder of the Action Committee for the United States of Europe, was without any doubt the European statesman to whom the U.S. government listened to the most intently.

No one tried to contest the military supremacy of the United States, which was accepted by almost all the countries in the world. It was particularly evident in Western Europe with NATO, which was seen as an essential safeguard against the aspirations of the other superpower, the Soviet Union.

The Vietnam War, which was a disaster in every sense of the term, dealt a severe blow to this esteem, both in the United States and in the rest of the world.

Such a defeat was incomprehensible in the United States. It was all too easy to accuse the lack of cooperation between allies, and particularly General de Gaulle and his Phnom Penh speech, as being responsible. Similarly, the responsibility for the temporary suspension of dollar convertibility in August 1971 was placed firmly on the shoulders of the Europeans, and more particularly those of de Gaulle. To come up to the present, does not the spectacle of the Europeans dragging their feet over the fight against communism in Central America and against international terrorism explain why the United States felt it necessary unilaterally to take the military decisions necessary to defend the free world?

Moreover, is not the refusal of Europe to accept fully its commercial and

economic responsibilities largely to blame for the massive US budget and balance of payments deficits?

Fortunately, the flow of foreign investment has helped the United States to face up to this situation, although at the price of abandoning its role as the world's banker. US capital exports nosedived from $119 billion in 1982 to $20 billion in 1984 and $38 billion in 1985, or from 94% of the rest of the world's capital imports to 16% and 25% respectively.

This evolution is bound to upset the comparative image of Europe and the United States both within Europe and in other countries.

The world's best informed leaders are less afraid of a return of the United States to *isolationism*, in any event highly unlikely, than an aggravation of its *unilateralism*. Such a trend is already taking shape in Central America. In this area the United States has rejected the competence of the International Court of The Hague to deal with the matter and turned down the peace proposals of the Contadora Group of the Presidents of various countries. In certain highly ambiguous declarations, the White House recommends that international law be revised in order to legalize military measures beyond national frontiers so that 'terrorists' will be deprived of sanctuary in any corner of the globe.

These same leaders would like Europe to reinforce its influence on the foreign and military policy of the United States and firmly re-assert its commitment to the 'Harmel Doctrine', which aims to slow the frenzied rearmament race and to reduce the risk that today's atmosphere of cold war, which is already inflicting burns in some countries, does not result in collective suicide. They are well aware of the fact that the chances of a return to the brief *détente* of the Nixon era depend as much on the attitude of the communist countries as on that of the United States, but they are much more optimistic in this respect than the American negotiators. The repeated declarations by Mikhail Gorbachev, and in particular at the last Party Presidium in January 1987, have had considerable impact and may realise the worst fears of the American Administration and certain circles of NATO by *unhinging* the Atlantic Alliance.

There is no doubt that the failure of the 'Salt 2' Treaty can be directly attributed to certain eminent American personalities, such as Henry Fowler and Eugene Rostow, and their arguments that the national product of the NATO countries, which is three times that of the Warsaw Pact countries, was bound to ensure the success of the United States in the arms race. Why, then, negotiate the bounds of a race which would deprive the United States of its major advantage?

The same argument can be used to conclude that Gorbachev's declarations are possibly or even probably sincere. The main problem would then be for him to impose his proposals upon the Soviet administration and the military. If he is sincere about political and military détente, it would be highly regrettable were the systematic scepticism of the 'hawks' of the Atlantic Alliance to bring about the failure of his efforts.

In any event, it should be noted that both communist China and the Soviet Union have recently accepted the European Community as a body in trade negotiations rather than condemning it, as in the past, as an instrument of NATO.

In conclusion, the vision of Europe held by the rest of the world in the future will depend first and foremost on its response to these questions and hopes.

In the economic sphere, will it be able to give the Third World countries the compensation which they were seeking for the drop in their capital imports

Messrs. Reagan and Gorbachev meet in Reykjavik. Staunch Europeans protest: why does Europe not participate in the major events of the late twentieth century?

Trade war between Japan and Europe: EEC external affairs Commissioner Willy De Clerq hands a bottle of European cognac and a bottle of whisky to Japanese Minister for Foreign Trade, Mr. Kuranari, at the Berlaymont.

from the United States and increasing US protectionism against their exports? More importantly, will the EEC succeed in reforming the international monetary and financial system, or at least offer the European Monetary System, based upon the ECU, as an alternative to excessive and disastrous hegemony based upon a fluctuating dollar? The current system has reached the absurd point whereby the world's poorest countries, with the smallest capital reserves, are spending half of their savings, which would be better used on their own economic recovery, investment and employment, fuelling the US internal and external deficits.

If the EEC is to act in this field, it will first have to complete its *economic and monetary union*, so often promised by heads of state and government, and introduce the *political union* which goes hand in hand with this. Far from destroying so-called national sovereignty, which has long been a myth, such a union is indispensable if Europe is to escape from its current status as a *quasi-protectorate* of the United States. To do this, it must first demonstrate its capacity to re-negotiate the defence aims of the Atlantic Alliance by much wider introduction of conventional weapons rather than banking upon the nuclear and chemical option, suicidal for Europe and probably for the rest of the world. The fact that the economic cost of the nuclear option is becoming insupportable on both sides of the Iron Curtain should make it possible to negotiate their reduction once and for all, instead of continually stockpiling them in the senseless race to overarm, which only increases general insecurity.

Ecu coins, minted by the Belgian Treasury at the suggestion of Mark Eyskens, Finance Minister, on the occasion of the 30th anniversary of the Treaty of Rome.

Bring in
the Europeans

*

Jacques-René Rabier

'*Are there any true Europeans?*', Salvador de Madariaga mused a quarter of a century ago. There are, he continued, three ways of looking at the question. From the least demanding perspective, it can be noted that we belong to the same continent and have a common cultural history. Secondly, we can try to demonstrate that the people born in Europe form a 'definitive and distinctive family' of mankind. Finally – and this is the most contentious approach – we can investigate whether and to what extent the 'Europeans' thrown together by history and geography count 'a sufficient number of people who are aware of belonging to a family…to form the core of European conscience and opinion' (1).

It is the third option put forward by the distinguished Spanish historian which will be explored here, using as a basis data collected over the past fifteen years by a unique opinion poll known as the 'Euro-barometer'. (Created in 1974, 'Euro-barometer' is carried out every six months, using cross sections of the adult population in each member state of the European Community. It was inspired by a proposal from the European Commission, acting on a European Parliament resolution.)

The reply to de Madariaga's question is far from straightforward. The answers given to four questions posed by Euro-barometer between 1984 and 1986 can possibly help in answering de Madariaga:
– To what extent do people consider themselves to be 'citizens of Europe'?
– What is their attitude towards the ideas of European unification and the creation of a United States of Europe?
– Is membership of one's country in the European Community viewed positively or negatively?
– Do the different nationalities trust one another, and if so, to what extent?

European 'citizens':
still a rare race

'*Do you ever think of yourself not only as a citizen of (your country), but also as a citizen of Europe? Often, sometimes, or never?*'

Slightly more than half of all 'Europeans' (for convenience sake, individuals who took part in opinion polls in the EEC member states will henceforth be designated as Europeans) stated that they 'often' (19%) or, sometimes, (36%) considered themselves as citizens of Europe. Replies in the affirmative were more frequent in Luxembourg, France and Germany than in the other member states. They were very rare in Ireland and the United Kingdom (2).

It has to be understood what is meant by 'sometimes'. There are grounds for believing that those who answer in such a way feel more a vague attachment to a European identity than a clear sense of belonging to a 'community'.

However, two other points merit emphasis:

Citizens' Europe, culture and economy, ordinary people and the elite (Spanish and Belgian royal couples at the opening of Europalia Spain, Brussels, 1986).

– Greece, Spain and, to a lesser extent, Portugal, which make up the newest members of the EEC, are among the most conscientious Europeans.

– Generally speaking, the 'opinion leaders', or those sections of opinion which are more aware and more 'involved' than their counterparts, are much more inclined to consider themselves as citizens of Europe than the rest of the population.

(In the 'Euro-Barometer', replies to two questions, dealing respectively with a person's tendency to discuss politics and to impress his viewpoints upon others, can be used to place that person on a 'leadership scale'. The answers to remaining questions can then be analysed in light of the person's 'degree of intellectual involvement').

EUROPEAN UNIFICATION: TIME-HONOURED MYTH OR POLITICAL OBJECTIVE?

A number of questions are asked to evaluate attitudes to Europe over a period of time. Two of these, dealing respectively with the movement for 'unification in Western Europe' and the 'formation of a United States of Europe', are referred to below.

European unification

'In general, are you for or against efforts being made to unify Western Europe? Are you very much for or only to some extent? If against, are you only to some extent against or very much against?'

This question gauges the general attitude towards the European Community, in its various forms, ranging from simple inter-governmental cooperation, as seen in the Council of Europe, to integration of national political systems into a European political community. The question does not therefore deal with a precise objective. It is rather an attempt to quantify attitudes to movement in a certain direction significant for the future of Europe.

The overwhelming majority of Europeans are in favour of European unification, with 33% strongly in favour and 44% generally in favour. The Luxembourgeois, Germans and Italians have always been the most enthusiastic, and are now joined or surpassed by the Spaniards and the Portuguese (3).

There has been little fluctuation on this point over the years, but positive replies have fallen slightly compared with 1973, suggesting that the attempts at European unification are less credible among younger, more 'aware' sectors of society. This trend is general, with the exception of the United Kingdom, where political cooperation wins more support than the idea of firm commitment to a European federation.

The 'United States of Europe'

'Some people talk of the idea of forming a 'United States of Europe', putting together the member countries of the European Community. This means a kind of political union like that between the fifty states of the USA, or the ten provinces that form Canada. Does this idea of forming a United States of Europe someday, including you (your country) seem a good or bad idea to you?'
'Whether you like the idea or not, do you think that a United States of Europe is likely to come about, and if so, when — the next ten to fifteen, twenty to thirty years from now, in several generations or never?'

Clearly, the expression 'United States of Europe' is metaphorically connected with the USA, an image which some find hard to swallow. On the other hand, it also has a certain mythical value, and provides a powerful ideological slogan for the advocates of European integration.

The declarations made by two British leaders at a forty-year interval provide a clear demonstration of the two poles:
– Winston Churchill (Zurich, 1946): 'We must build a kind of United States of Europe.... If at first all the States of Europe are not willing to join the Union, we must nevertheless proceed to assemble and combine those who will and those who can'.
– Margaret Thatcher (The Times, December 1, 1984): 'I do not believe that

A crowd's only significance is its source of inspiration. (March of steel workers in Paris, April 1984).

The Court in session.

The Presidents follow on: Mrs. Thatcher gives a report on the European Council in London to the European Parliament in Strasbourg (December 1986). The next President of the Council, Belgium's Leo Tindemans, listens behind her.

The Parliament, an excellent forum for statesmen: François Mitterrand (May 24, 1984),
Ronald Reagan (May 8, 1985); Anwar Sadat (February 10, 1981);
Juan Carlos I (May 14, 1986).

Several hundred million television viewers for the ECC (European Community Championship).

Sail for Europe, a pioneer in the training of Pan-Europe teams.

On Wall Street, rates hit the ceiling…

Aid to developing countries has many forms, including food aid…

On the ceiling of the Sixtine Chapel, Michelangelo's Adam no longer manages to touch God's creative finger. Man becomes autonomous.

Interest in the European concept is more marked among citizens with a good education and a socio-political commitment, who can be classified as 'opinion leaders'. Here, surrounding Anne-Marie Renger, Vice-President of the Bundestag, Messrs. Scheel, President of the Federal Republic of Germany (on her right), Pflimlin, President of the European Parliament and Thorn, President of the European Commission (both on her left), along with members of the presidium of the German Council of the European Movement.

we shall ever have a United States of Europe in the same way that there is a United States of America. The whole history of Europe is too different'.

Yet the attraction for Europeans of this idea is undisputable. In six out of the twelve member states, the absolute majority of those questioned considered it a 'good idea'. The respective percentages are 71% in Italy, 56% in France, 55% in Luxembourg, 53% in Spain and Germany and 52% in Belgium. A relative majority was also recorded in the Netherlands, Greece and Portugal, although there was a 35% 'undecided' rate in the latter. Views are divided in Ireland, but tend towards acceptance of the idea. The only countries with a majority against the idea are the United Kingdom and Denmark (4).

Does this then offer some cheer to the advocates of a European Federation? This would be too hasty a conclusion.

The replies to the second question – 'How long do you think this will take?' – throw a damper on the enthusiasm.

Among those who believe that the United States of Europe will one day become a reality, only one-third believe that it will happen in the next ten to fifteen years. Two-thirds think that twenty to thirty years, or even several generations, will be necessary for its realisation.

Furthermore, if the results for the six original member states are examined over a long time span, it would appear that the completion of the United States of Europe is getting pushed further and further back in peoples' imaginations. In other words, the myth, as defined by Georges Sorel, persists: 'The image of a fictive (unreal) future which expresses the sentiments of a collectivity.' But as time goes by, its attainment is postponed ever deeper into the future (5).

The myth is the 'instigator of action', to quote Sorel once again. Yet Europe has demonstrated how a lack or insufficiency of action can weaken the political potential of the myth. The European Community is a historical entity which was founded in 1951 and endowed with new powers in 1957 and in 1987. It started out with six member states, grew to nine, then ten and then twelve. For some, it represents the forerunner of the United States of Europe, for others, it remains a simple way of managing, after a fashion, what are seen as mutual economic interests.

THE EUROPEAN COMMUNITY:
(JUST ENOUGH OF) A 'GOOD THING'

'Generally speaking, do you think that (your country's) membership of the European Community (Common Market) is a good thing, a bad thing, or neither good nor bad?'

This gives some idea as to how people rate the usefulness of the European Community. Answers are more strongly influenced by the advantages gleaned from membership than by a person's attitude to European unification.

The replies registered since 1973 have fluctuated slightly according to the economic and political situation, but on the whole they have been consistently favourable, except in the United Kingdom. In Spring 1986 (last available results), 60%–80% of people in ten of the twelve member states considered that membership of the EEC was 'a good thing'. The percentage was 83% in the Netherlands, 81% in Luxembourg, 74% in Italy and 69% in France. The Greeks were less enthusiastic, but a majority still held the EEC in esteem (44%, compared to 16% against and 26% undecided). In the United Kingdom, where opposition to the Community was very strong in 1977-83, the tide has now turned and a majority now think that the country has profited from EEC membership. Denmark is rather a special case. Opinion had, since 1974, always been divided into three more or less equal groups: those for, those against and those unsure. Then came the referendum in February 1986 on the issue of European Union, which seemed to jolt more people into the EEC camp. For the first time since the EEC entry referendum in 1972, the percentage of those in favour of the EEC rose to 51%. However, it is too early to say whether this trend will be consolidated (6).

To sum up, Europeans are accustomed to living side by side with the EEC. It is impossible to weed out from those who think the EEC is a 'good thing' the percentage who really feel that the interests of the European people and their destiny are now as one. It is highly telling that advocates of European unification prefer the phrase 'European Community', whereas those against or the undecided prefer to speak of the 'Common Market'(7).

The twinning of destinies implies that the partners trust one another. Is this true of the EEC member states?

The Belgian farmer has discovered that he is European and that he understands the Common Agricultural Policy (demonstration in Brussels, March 1971).

MUTUAL TRUST

'Now, I would like to ask about how much you would trust people from different countries. For each country, please say whether, in your opinion, they are in general very trustworthy, fairly trustworthy, not particularly trustworthy, or not at all trustworthy?'

To 'have trust' in someone means that we are confident that that person will act with our best interests at heart in difficult circumstances. On the contrary, to distrust someone means that we consider them to be unreliable in times of need. To be considered by others as 'trustworthy' signifies that we will not be suspected *a priori* of bad intentions.

The above question has been put to people in all the EEC member states on a number of occasions since 1970. All twelve member states were covered for the first time in Spring 1986. Members of the public were asked about their reaction to the other member states, and to Switzerland, Turkey, the United States, Japan, China and the Soviet Union (8).

Logically enough, peoples' awareness of each country depends on its size. Higher rates of reply were obtained for the larger countries, namely the United Kingdom, Germany, France, Spain and Italy. Lower rates were registered for Belgium, Greece, Ireland, Portugal, Denmark and, bringing up the rear, Luxembourg. There is therefore a high positive correlation between the prominence attached to a country by outsiders and its demographical size.

To be known is one thing, but to be considered trustworthy is quite another. It would even appear, according to the results for the EEC member states, that the relationship between the two variables is negative. The more a country is known, the less it is trusted. The 'leading' countries of past and present inspire, if not mistrust, at least wariness.

The Danish, Dutch, Luxembourgeois and the Belgians are considered the most trustworthy.

They are followed by the Germans and then, rather further down the scale, the Irish, French and the British.

The four Mediterranean countries, Spain, Greece, Portugal and, at the bottom of the ratings, Italy, bring up the rear.

The trust ratings can be compared with those calculated in November 1976 for the nine member states of the time.

The prominence of the different countries in people's minds did not greatly vary between 1976 and 1986. Given that prominence is dependent on demographic factors, this is not surprising. Sharp variation, at least in the short term, is highly unlikely.

The trust factor has also remained fairly stable, with a slight upward trend (particularly in the case of Italy), and the range of factors among the member states has diminished.

Ten years would seem to be too short a period for any significant fluctuation in these complex relationships, which are the result of general cultural heritage and personal experience.

Significant changes are seen in comparing data over a longer period of time. The most striking has been the increase in mutual trust between the Germans and the French whose past mutual hostility was a major reason for the creation of the EEC. In 1970 French people still regarded the Germans with suspicion, and in Germany, too, the French were treated with a certain wariness. In 1986 mutual trust is abundant. The French and the Germans both now trust each other more, for example, than they trust the British.

Nationalist feeling can sometimes be lethal: here is the crowd of spectators a few seconds before the struggle between English and Italian supporters at the Heysel stadium (Brussels, May 1985).

Too few third countries have been included in the poll for any general conclusions to be drawn. The United States and the Soviet Union loom largest in Europeans' imagination. Switzerland, geographically and culturally close to three of the EEC member states, also figures. The Japanese and the Chinese are much too distant. Little appears to be known about the Turks, apart from through the Crusades, the threats of the Ottoman empire to Europe in centuries gone by and today's immigrant workers in Europe.

On the trust scale, the Swiss are 'above all suspicion'. On average, they are considered to be the most trustworthy nation. (But no new assessment has been made since the Rhine was poisoned by Swiss chemical companies). Europeans trust the Americans a lot less than the Swiss, but slightly more than...the Japanese. However, Greece and Spain do not reflect the general trend, and the majority of people questioned expressed their 'wariness' of the Americans. The Chinese are held in fairly high esteem in Denmark, the United Kingdom, the Netherlands, Greece and Spain, but mistrust reigns elsewhere. The Russians are distrusted throughout the EEC, with the exception of Greece, which occasionally seems to prefer the Soviet Union to the United States. But Europeans (excluding Denmark) reserve their worst ratings for Turkey, candidate for EEC membership and NATO's bulwark in south-eastern Europe.

Are these attitudes changing? Evolution is taking place, but very slowly. Little difference can be seen between the replies in 1976 and 1986.

In terms of prominence, there is virtually no change, apart from a slight increase in uncertainty about the Chinese. Comparison is therefore possible between the Swiss, the Americans, the Chinese and the Russians.

There has been no decrease in the trust which Europe places in the Swiss or the Americans, but perception of the Russians and, more especially, of the Chinese has changed. The Russians are regarded with much less suspicion, due, it would seem to Gorbachev's efforts to draw back the Iron Curtain (without, however, opening up the frontiers) and give the country's leaders a younger image. Much more spectacular progress has been made in the case of China. In 1976 the Chinese were bordering on the same low ratings as the Russians. Today they are almost on the point of stepping into the black, which cannot be said of the Russians.

IN CONCLUSION

To get back to de Madariaga's question: *'Are there any true Europeans, are there enough people aware of belonging to a family to form the core of European conscience and opinion'?* The answer is somewhat mixed.

1. The European Community is an objective reality. It consists of a 'market' which is more or less 'common' and a number of permanent institutions whose task it is to promote political cooperation and dialogue. Its citizens (or at least their governments) and leaders of all kinds (political, professional, trade union) are aware of this. Public support is not lacking, at least when the issue is clearly stated and not dramatised. This has been demonstrated by the UK referendum in 1975, the Danish referendum in 1986, and the electoral successes of Filipe Gonzalez in Spain and of Mario Soares in Portugal a few weeks after the entry of their two countries to the EEC. On the other hand, the election of the European Parliament (1979 and 1984) has not been greeted with a great deal

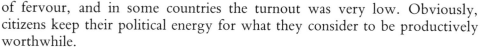

of fervour, and in some countries the turnout was very low. Obviously, citizens keep their political energy for what they consider to be productively worthwhile.

2. The creation of a politically integrated European Community, able to act as one voice in the external arena, to regulate where necessary internal trade and to define autonomous areas of activities for the member states and for regional and local authorities, remains a myth. Granted, it is a powerful myth, deeply anchored in the culture of the majority of Western European states, but not in all. It is an attractive idea for one European in two, provided that neither the implications nor its attainment come too close to the bone. 'It makes good sense', they say, but 'it's certainly not around the corner'.

3. There are all kinds of difficulties; this is not the place to draw up an exhaustive list. Resistance of governments, national authorities and political parties and the lack of complete commitment to the European ideal among citizens are just some of the major obstacles.

Although the construction of Europe has begun, and no-one or almost no-one would think of tearing down what has already been achieved, very few voices are heard urging people further in its direction.

United Europe has its advocates, but it does not yet have enough citizens. European public opinion clearly exists, but awareness of European citizenship, or the desire to have it, is evidently lacking.

For these militants of European federalism, European Union is a political objective worthy of full-time effort. (Demonstrations in Brussels in March 1985 (on the left) and in Milan in June 1984 (on the right), on the occasion of the Summit of Heads of State and Government.

SELECTED BIBLIOGRAPHY

1. Salvador de Madariaga: '*Mais y a-t-il donc des Européens?*' (Are there any true Europeans?) in Humanities and European Integration, College of Europe (Bruges) and A.W. Sythoff (Leyden), 1960, pp 11-17.
2. See Euro-barometer n° 24, December 1985, pp 53-55
3. See Euro-barometer n° 25, June 1986, pp 50-54
4. See Euro-barometer n° 24 December 1985, pp 95-101
5. See Euro-barometer n° 24, December 1985, pp 101-103
6. See Euro-barometer n° 25, June 1986, pp 55-59
7. See Euro-barometer n° 21, May 1984, pp 32-34.
See Euro-barometer n° 24, December 1985, pp 55-59
8. See Euro-barometer n° 25, June 1986, pp 26-48

WHAT MAKES
EUROPEANS TICK

*

Jan Kerkhofs

The search for happiness has always been a feature of human cultures. The quest for this philosopher's stone has taken various forms. It is expressed in the bravery of heroes, by military conquest, by the desire to succeed in life, as in the *Ethica Nicomachea* of Aristotle, or by the hope of happiness after death. But it would seem that the quest for individual happiness has never been conducted with as much intensity as in current-day Europe. There can be no doubt that Denis de Rougemont hit the nail on the head when he declared, in his book *Aventure Occidentale de l'Homme*, that respect for the individual, the concept born along with Christianity, has been a sort of *leitmotiv* running through history, leading up to the modern-day 'European spirit'. However, at the beginning it was an elitist concept, and has only entered into collective consciousness in recent centuries. It is clear that self and its desire for fulfilment have taken over from romanticism and existentialism as the forces of motivation of our society. Sacrifices to exotic gods are no longer made, and man has become his own god.

The European Value Systems Study Group carried out, between 1981 and 1986, a study on the scale of values among Europeans. The study, which provided a representative picture of the opinions of 240 million Europeans, confirms this thesis, although it provides a finer interpretation of it. Unlike other cultures where the *group* occupies a central position, in the West *individual* freedom has become the generator of the development of the civilisation process. There are numerous illustrations of this phenomenon, ranging from Saint Paul's *Letter to the Galatians* to the *Vorlesungen über die Philosophie der Geschichte* of G.W.F. Hegel, and Michelangelo, who expressed this sentiment in his own special way when he painted the ceiling of the Sistine Chapel – Adam is reaching out towards the creative hand of God, but his finger does not quite touch Him. Man's vocation is to be self-determining. It is in trying to achieve his freedom that man achieves happiness. This is the dream which lies behind all man's voyages into the unknown.

However, there will always be a more or less open conflict between this freedom and another value, that is expressed in the revolt of slaves, in peasant uprisings, in the French Revolution or in the many faces of socialism. This second value is *equality*. It is seen in modern society in the continually growing interest in human rights in general, and for women's rights in particular.

Research has shown that these two values constitute the essential driving force of human development, but that priority is nevertheless given to freedom.

Other recent studies suggest that freedom now tends more and more towards individualism, and even towards narcissism. It is seen, for example, in the importance attached to health, the body image, sport and music. As a result, the third catchword of the French Revolution, *fraternity* or *solidarity*,

would seem to be losing a great deal of ground.

However, the scale of this egocentricity should not be over-estimated. Having a family is still an integral part of the drive for happiness for the majority of Europeans. A successful relationship with a member of the opposite sex (and two children) has a great deal of importance. Three Europeans in four find that marriage is not an antiquated institution. The family would seem to be the only possible justification for sacrificing one's life. When people are asked to list according to priority seven political values, which include technology, ecology and work, the family always takes first place. This tendency is even much more marked in the north than in the south of Europe. But a great deal of importance is nonetheless attached to personal values. The youngest age groups are no longer willing to sacrifice their happiness for a failed relationship. They prefer to divorce and to relaunch the quest for happiness with another partner. Tolerance is increasing in this area, particularly since the state now offers more security to individuals, children and old people, and also because women, who now have access to higher education and to the work market, depend less and less on their husband or on his family. The emancipation of women has increased their chances of finding personal fulfilment.

The coexistence of individuals necessitates, however, a reliable social and ethnic framework. Studies have shown that Europeans seem to feel a reasonable degree of confidence in this framework. Trust rather than distrust is felt in all the big institutions, with an (ambiguous) preference for the police and the army and slight suspicion of the press and trade unions. In comparison with the North Americans, the Europeans demonstrate more scepticism. Could this be partially due to Europe's experience of totalitarian regimes? Or is it the result of their distrust of large-scale structures and their preference for their village, town or region over the bigger entities of the state or Europe? The

Although our society is considered as permissive, honesty remains a key value and the foundation of a family is considered as a necessary condition of happiness (Jerome Bosch - Le jardin des délices - Allegory of Luxury (inscription) - Madrid - Prado Museum).

collective European consciousness has clearly been deeply marked by the stigma of numerous wars. Surveys have revealed an overwhelming desire for peace. Interest in ecology is also growing rapidly. These two elements seem to suggest widespread dread and awareness of the vulnerability of Western Europe, which is now perceived as small, both physically and in terms of power. Successive studies have revealed strong concern, bordering on schizophrenia, as to how peace and security can be combined and how progress and science can be reconciled.

Awareness of Europe's vulnerability makes Europeans politically very cautious. The democratic system in Europe is appreciated, but the importance of politics is not over-estimated. In this area, the majority of Europeans try above all to avoid extremes. They plant themselves firmly in the centre. The Germanic countries are slightly right of centre, and the Latin countries slightly left. The majority prefer gradual reform, and reject revolution or restoration. People are against state control and for participation. In relation to other non-Western cultures, the current-day European seeks 'well-balanced dynamism'. It is almost as if he wants to integrate as many values as possible into the system, in order to create a subtle balance in which forces play off one another.

A personal ethical system underlies the social framework. In his work *Les valeurs du temps présent* (The Values of the Present – 1983), J. Stoetzel analyses in a very pertinent manner the hierarchy of values in Europe. He maintains that the Judaeo-Christian Ten Commandments have not lost their normative value for the majority of Europeans, even if the younger generation are much more permissive than their parents, particularly as regards sexuality. Although the firm tie which exists between ethics and religion is tending to loosen, the moral foundations of society do not seem to be crumbling as a result. Honesty is the value which is placed above all others. If parents are asked to draw up a list of 17 qualities which they would like to instil into their children, honesty is always included. In a world increasingly built upon scientific and technical truths, this preference is both symptomatic and vital.

In many major cultures one religion or one ideology holds sway over individual and collective ethics. Europe is distinguished by the fact that Christianity, although important, is not the only cornerstone of European ethics. Moreover, the after-effects of the Reformation, which led to a divide between Catholics and Protestants, have been pushed into the background. Religion and faith have become a much more personal affair, although Christianity still exercises a strong effect on European culture. Nine out of ten Europeans profess to being Christian. Three-quarters believe in God, whereas two out of three say they are 'religious' and do not believe that death is absolute. However, the Church has lost a great deal of its influence, particularly among young people. Yet many still attach themselves to a religion, mainly to put their minds at rest: no other institution has supplanted the Church in this field.

The collective consciousness of Europeans is much more varied and complex than this brief schema may suggest. Each European is a personal synthesis of a wide range of influences. This is the expression of the desire to build a highly personalised world. The ways in which each European sees the world and his ambitions are individually coloured by the influence of innumerable factors, including the heritage of the Celts, the Germans, the Greeks and the Romans, the ways of thought of the Catholics and the Protestants, the believers and the rationalists and by aesthetic and emotional factors. All this rests upon a

backcloth of traditions, certain of which date back to ancient times. Some imbue an entire nation, whereas some are uniquely regional. Age also plays a role in the formation of personal values. After fifty, people become more inward-looking and more sceptical. It is precisely because they have come under so many influences that Europeans are so intensely confronted with freedom and, at least potentially, with a sense of responsibility. Swamped by so much determinism, but also with a wide range of possibilities, the European sets out on a quest for individual happiness more aware than ever of his fundamental solitude. He continues to be a sort of Xerxes, obliged to forge his path on his own. But he is characterised by the fact that he continues to believe that beyond the horizon he will find something even more fascinating.

EUROPE: AN OPPORTUNITY FOR WOMEN

WOMEN: AN OPPORTUNITY

FOR EUROPE

*

Jean A. Pirlot

165 million women in the Community now benefit from a large number of social advantages which have been made possible by the progress towards European unification. This little-known aspect of the EEC merits reflection.

When the Treaty of Rome was being drawn up, the French negotiators unexpectedly insisted that an article, 119, should be inserted which stipulated: 'Each Member State shall ensure ... the application of the principle that men and women should receive equal pay for equal work'.

The negotiators' consciences were not pricked by the time-honoured slogan 'Liberty-Equality-Fraternity'. The French motive was international competition. Italy had a large, under-paid female workforce which, if the free circulation of goods within the EEC were to become a reality, would have given it a clear competitive edge. So, 119 was not inspired by any real desire to liberate women.

For many years no EEC laws were adopted to implement Article 119. But women became less and less tolerant of the fact that their pay was not on a par with the value of their work. An example of this was provided by the women's strike at the Belgian arms factory 'F.N. de Herstal' and demonstrations in the streets of Liège for equal pay rates.

The decisive push in the right direction was given by the EEC's Court of Justice in a ruling which has since become famous. Belgium again came under fire when a Belgian air hostess took her case to the Court. It ruled that even in the absence of precise legislation the principle of equality must be respected.

There was a remarkable surge of activity at this time, as feminist organisations were irritated and in some ways galvanised by the inertia of governments. They stepped up their activities, and the oldest and more traditional women's organisations took up the fight. There was a mushrooming of committees, sections and 'women's affairs' working groups within trade unions, political parties and professional organisations.

Many of these bodies rapidly came up against the strong resistance, or at least the indifference, of governments. The Court of Justice ruling pointed them in the direction of a more fruitful field of action: the European Community. The European Commission had followed events closely and, at the invitation of feminist organisations, it set up an information service on women's affairs.

Naturally enough, it became a network service stimulating contacts between the organisations. The EEC magazine 'Women in Europe' collects information from all the member states and distributes them in all the EEC's official languages. National chairwomen and local organisers can thus compare developments in the various member states, find people to write to, strike up contacts, trade experiences and propose strategies.

The first big battle that these women and their associations won was on the occasion of the first direct election of the European Parliament. A campaign was conducted in all the member states to promote women candidates. The result was remarkable: with 17% of women Members, the European Parliament has a higher representation of women than any national parliament.

Meanwhile, the European Commission had begun work on two Equal Opportunities Action Programmes. The first centred upon the legal instruments necessary for women to enjoy their rights fully. The second (1986-1990) emphasised the need for 'positive discrimination' to redress the balance with men, even in times of economic crisis. Activities include additional professional training specifically for women in some companies and other administrative systems in order to encourage their movement up the professional ladder.

The full effect of these policies, which grew up during the Women's Decade (1975-1985), has yet to make itself felt, but the results have already been gratifying.

Women still bear the brunt of unemployment. There are still no women among the members of the European Commission. Women are still under-represented in the Economic and Social Committee, in the Court of Justice and in the Parliament itself. But unprecedented change has been set in motion thanks to the construction of Europe, change which without a doubt the authors of the Treaty of Rome did not *really* have in mind.

EUROPE

AND ITS CHILDREN:

THE PROSPECTS

✳

Jan Dereymaeker

'For the generation born between 1958 and 1967, Europe is either an established fact or an ideal. The established fact consists of the will and desire to unify Europe. The majority of young people either were not alive during the great debates on the ideas of European construction, or they were too young to participate in them. The European institutions and their achievements are realities which no one calls into question. However, this is not enough to rally the enthusiasm of young Europeans....' (The Young Europeans, EC Commission, Dec. 1982).

When television developed in the fifties and sixties, psychologists and educational specialists published erudite works predicting the advent of a generation of children enslaved by the small screen. These writings are today slowly gathering dust in obscure corners of libraries. People are no longer obsessed by the consequences of television. Their interests lie in widening the choice of programmes and improving their quality. A parallel can be drawn with what is happening today between young people in Europe and the Community. The young are totally indifferent to that Community which lives in a closed circuit between Brussels, Luxembourg and Strasbourg, and which no longer inspires interest in the European ideal when competing with other major issues of our time and the evolution of the world community.

And yet today's generation has not come up with anything new. Its ideals – peace, human rights, freedom, social justice, equality of opportunity - were those which inspired the advocates of a united Europe thirty years ago, for which clear evidence is to be found in this very book. Unfortunately, it has become difficult or even impossible to perceive these ideals in present-day Europe, in a Community where the only subject of conversation is agricultural surpluses and where each government tries to grab the biggest slice of the cake.

This chapter will be dedicated to reflections on what the future of Europe should be. We will be guided in our quest for an ideal Europe by our young people, through the views expressed by their representatives in the Youth Forum of the European Communities. They present an idealised image of the Europe of the future, born from various currents of thought among young people in all member states of the Community.

FROM POWERLESSNESS TO AUTONOMY, FROM 'NON-EUROPE' (1) TO A UNITED POLITICAL COMMUNITY

The circumstances of the upbringing of Europe's young people have made them conscious of the world around them. The youth of today consider themselves first and foremost as citizens of the world. The continual flow of

images brought to them by the media have made them aware of international problems. Hunger and poverty in the Third World have become everyday realities for them. They are subject daily to highly disturbing truths: the frenzied arms race, overproduction, the abundance of useless or frivolous consumer goods, deterioration of the natural world, the growing foreign debt of the Third World, the interference of the two super-powers in the internal affairs of small countries for example Afghanistan and Nicaragua the innumerable forms of repression used in countries such as South Africa, Chile, Ethiopia and Vietnam, the terrifying butchery in Lebanon and the Gulf war.

How can young people be expected to understand and accept that Europe has no coherent and credible policy to propose concerning these world-scale problems? Divided by narrow considerations of national interest and by the desire to hang on to illusions of national sovereignty, the Community has shown its inertia and its powerlessness to bend the framework which the two superpowers have put in place, the system of two blocs and the North-South divide. 'Non-Europe' is a sad reality. It has disappointed the hopes of the Third World, which thought that it had found a partner for its development. It has also disappointed the expectations of its youth, who believed the European Community would play an active role in the construction of a new world order from which hunger and exploitation would be banished forever.

When it was created, the Community's justification for its existence was that it could guarantee a peaceful future to the nations of Europe. Horizons have since widened and the credibility of Europe in the future will depend upon the way in which, or whether, it tackles today's major planetary problems. This is the way in which the youth of today sees the European adventure.

At the level of paper principles, everything necessary for a European political revival already exists. There can be no doubt that the Lomé agreements, which attempt to institutionalise the North-South dialogue, are a commitment which is very different from the attitude taken elsewhere towards the Third World. However, the relatively narrow economic framework of these agreements has to be regretted. In fact, many of Asia's and Africa's least developed countries, along with all the states of Latin America, are excluded from the Lomé Conventions whose scope urgently needs widening.

The economic and human potential of Europe has a key role to play in the development of Third World countries. The ECU could be used to support European attempts to approach these problems in a new way. The European

Ivor Richard, a former European Commissioner responsible for social affairs and employment, is surrounded by a delegation from the Youth Forum sporting T-shirts with the slogan 'Give us a future'.

currency could provide an alternative to the omnipotence of the Dollar in the world economy.

It still remains to be seen whether the member states will decide to put the Communities' assets to use. Will the member states have the resolve to take up the challenge? Young Europeans want solidarity which they see as essential to bring the underprivileged people of the Third World out of the abyss of poverty.

'NO FUTURE?'

In the 'swinging sixties' Europe harvested the first fruits of economic cooperation: there was nothing to suggest that the coming generations would have to face an economic, social and cultural crisis as profound as that which struck in the 70s and 80s.

It was approximately ten years after the unrest of May 1968 that the walls of our cities began to be plastered with the gloomy slogan 'No future'. Governments were called to deal with their most difficult problem ever, youth unemployment. Calls were heard for an original and specifically European solution to a problem.

But Europe did not respond to the hopes of its youth, although European policy certainly had a number of positive characteristics: the European Social Fund has helped millions of Europeans, and in particular young people. But national governments refused to relinquish their old ideas for reducing unemployment. They organised additional training programmes for adolescents who had become saturated with schooling, but were unable to offer them a real chance of a job at the end. EC funds sweetened the pill but did not alleviate the disease. It was no longer possible to solve a structural problem such as youth unemployment by applying economic recovery measures at national levels, since those of the different countries cancelled one another out. Only coordinated economic and social policies, along with other original and courageous measures, can offer hope. These measures should include the redistribution of available jobs, which would require solidarity between workers and the unemployed.

The fight against drug abuse, unemployment and racism are the priorities of the Youth Forum of the European Community.

'TOUCHE PAS A MON POTE!' (HANDS OFF MY MATE!)

This slogan, which accompanied the symbol of an outward-facing palm of the hand, blossomed across wide areas of mainland Europe in the mid-eighties. It was inspired by young people's vision of the future of European society. It represented an insistence on the equality of the children of a multi-racial Europe – the Alis, Joëlles, Mohammeds, Antonios, Seans, Susans, Johanns and Fatimas living in the same areas and sharing schools in London, Berlin, Brussels, Amsterdam or Paris. When the European institutions signed a Joint Declaration against Racism and Xenophobia in Strasbourg in June 1986, they took a clear stance for a multi-cultural Europe open to all ethnic groups. They firmly committed themselves to fighting against any discrimination on the grounds of race, colour, language, religion or beliefs. Young Europeans also resolved to give equal political, social and cultural rights to the thirteen million immigrants: these rights include free movement within the Community, the principle of equal pay for equal work and respect for each people's culture and customs. Real discrimination still exists in Europe. It is particularly hard to bear for the children of immigrants who have been living in a country for two

For a noble and unambiguous cause, young people mobilise with enthusiasm. The badges held by these young girls show an upheld hand on which is written the slogan 'Touche pas à mon pote' (Hands off my mate).

or three generations. This discrimination continues to jeopardise their future. Whatever the colour of their skin or the origin of their passport, the new generations expect the Community to work with them to end this discrimination and create a new, multiracial Europe.

'EUROPE? NO, THANKS!'

Seveso, Chernobyl, acid rain, poisoning of our major rivers, pollution of the Mediterranean and the North Sea; the list of environmental disasters is a long one. There seems to be no border capable of stopping the advance of ecological catastrophes.

Both in Europe and in the Third World, industry has greedily exploited natural resources, and continues to do so with brutal acceleration. As a result, its development model has been seriously called into question by a growing number of young people. They expect the Community to intervene. Not only against the direct consequences of catastrophes on scales which extend beyond national borders, but also to play a major preventative and regulatory role so that there are limits to the damage suffered by the natural environment as a consequence of the different norms and whims of production and marketing from country to country.

It is not merely a question of protecting consumers of naturally fermented beers against imports of brews from a neighbouring country on the grounds that they may be contaminated with chemicals. One must get to the crux of the matter and introduce regulations for all the important sectors of our manufacturing industry. Problem areas include the energy sector (conventional or nuclear), the agro-food industry, whose current production methods threaten to exhaust the soil, and matters such as the disposal of nuclear waste. Attention needs also be paid to the havoc which may be wreaked by extensive built-up areas, the threat of desertification looming over southern Europe, and the question of threats by transport systems to the natural environment. Experience has shown that the member states have always preferred to keep their own territory clean while surreptitiously dumping their waste across or outside their borders. Why are so many nuclear power stations built on borders if they are really as safe as the 'experts' would have us believe? A Community approach is essential to find solutions to these problems.

Europe: the name of a democracy which has yet to reach adulthood

In the previous pages, some of the preoccupations of young people regarding European society and the Community in which they live, or in which they would like to live, have been described.

Young people are well aware of the current crises within the EEC. They harbour no illusions that the future will necessarily be rosy. However, when we look for adequate answers to the major issues of our time, we inevitably come to the same conclusions: democratisation of institutions, European union and participation of the citizen in European unification.

When, after 25 years of existence, the Community feels a growing need to carry out in-depth reforms, governments still reject bold proposals put forward by the European Parliament and prefer to follow a minimalist strategy. The Single Act of December 1985 is a typical child of the system of unanimous voting, a system which can only produce decisions corresponding to the lowest common denominator of the different national positions.

The tense situation in Europe and in the world is leading to a rebirth of nationalist sentiment which the Single Act is not managing to stifle. What political or democratic justification can be offered for a system as authoritarian and uncontrollable as that exercised within the Council of Ministers, a system within which all of Europe can be dictated to by a minority (the veto of a single member state can block the whole process) and which frequently prevents the elaboration of a European policy?

Too narrow a path to European unification

One reason why institutional reform has proved so difficult is that it has depended too much on politicians to be really successful. The European Parliament's initiative did not receive enough public support.

If we really want to increase the powers of the EEC and introduce more democratic control of EEC administration, we first have to aim at greater involvement of ordinary people, and especially young people, in the unification process. For this to happen, the concerns shared by a large part of the population must first be honestly reflected in the policies of the European Community, which are currently excessively dominated by agriculture. Secondly, the democratic rights of Parliament and of European citizens must be given room for fuller expression.

The identity of European states is rooted strongly in history. On the other hand, the historical and cultural foundations of the European Community are not yet well established. They do not provide an identity and a 'raison d'être' for Europe.

There have been a number of attempts to take the Community beyond 'shopkeepers' Europe', including notably the Tindemans Report, the Spinelli Report and the work of the Adonnino Committee on 'Citizens' Europe'. The European Movement and other federalist organisations have made a large contribution to awareness of the problems connected with the unification of Europe. But is all this energy not too often spent on convincing the converted rather than on winning over the vast majority of ordinary people who have no interest in Europe?

The EEC has worked a great deal on its public image, creating flags, symbols, anthems and even sporting events (regattas, bicycle races, tennis tournaments).

However, young people in Europe wonder whether the development of this image is not merely a front erected to hide the weaknesses of the construction, a front which repels people from the European ideal rather than attracting them to it!

CITIZENS OF EUROPE, UNITE!

We need to listen to the founders of the Community, to the politicians and leaders who have written this book, to those who sit today around the negotiating table. When these men were young, they exchanged ideas with contemporaries from other countries, they sang, danced, walked and swam together. They laughed together, drew up projects and explored the cultural, social and political realities within which each lived.

Today we see the opposite. Non-governmental participation is now clearly lacking in the construction of Europe. And yet it is at this level that the deep heartbeat of Europe is to be found, the heartbeat of citizens and their everyday personal experiences. And not at the level of a Europe filled with the didactic thinking and propaganda of officials living in their ivory towers, who besiege the media so that they can dole out to us 'The European Truth'. We must build a Europe of 'aware and organised' adults and young people, with a special emphasis on young people who tend to be more flexible and interested in discovering the culture of different nations. Europe must invest in them.

The widening gap between the 'managers' of Europe and the man in the street must be closed. Non-governmental European organisations are not a superfluous luxury, mere background material on the European stage or an embarrassing note in the democratic choir. On the contrary, their rich diversity makes them the voice of people's Europe, a school of European cooperation which has its eyes open to the realities of life. They are the foundation which could give Europe, thirty years after its creation, fresh inspiration and fresh hope for the dream of the founding fathers.

In 1989 Europeans are to elect their Parliament for the third time. This is an opportunity to take a step towards the ideal. It will also be the 200th anniversary of the French Revolution. The time will be ripe for the coming of a European Revolution, a peaceful revolution, which would set the Parliament up as a Constituent Assembly to create the framework of a United States of Europe. Today this is just a dream. In the Year 2000, will it be a reality for Europe's grandchildren?

'I giovani incontrano l'Europa' (Young people reach out to Europe): this young Italian girl demonstrates in June 1984 on the Dôme square in Milan with 100,000 other people during the Summit of the Heads of State and Government which was to study the project of European Union put forward by the European Parliament.

NOTE

1. M. Albert, R.J. Ball, *Progress towards Recovery of the European Economy in the Eighties*, European Parliament, August 31, 1983.

Europe: an overview

THE TREATIES OF ROME

30 YEARS LATER

*

HOW THE ACTORS AND 'PRIVILEGED WITNESSES'
OF THE EUROPEAN CONSTRUCTION
PERCEIVE, AFTER ALL THOSE YEARS,
THE WORK ACHIEVED

We have asked some twenty actors and former actors on the European scene the same 4 questions:

I. Would you call, so far, the making of Europe a success or a semi-failure?

II. What or who is the reason why Europe has not become a full reality yet?

III. What should have been done instead or differently?

IV. What now needs to be done above all?

Heinrich AIGNER
° 1924, Member of the Bundestag (1957-80), Member of the European Parliament since 1961. Chairman of the Budgetary Control Committee.

I. When an edifice is still being built, it is not really appropriate to judge whether it is a success or not. History is not created by guesswork, but by men's work, will and creativity.

And yet an assessment can be made of the achievements up until now through comparison of the two Europes, separated by a wall, by barbed wire and by minefields. In free Europe the dynamics of peace have stood the test of time and have drawn in 400 million human beings (EEC and EFTA) who are willing to cooperate in a wide range of fields. Frontiers are conceived in a new light, as old ideas are rejected in favour of a new openness. The concept of the Maginot line is now no more than a joke.

The countries of Central and Western Europe have, from the same starting point, arrived at diametrically opposed positions, with increased compartmentalisation of the two sides. In the East, the hegemonic aspirations of the Soviet Union gave rise to total isolation, increasingly bitter conflict and an exacerbation of feelings of hostility and hatred. Both sides had to overcome the wounds of two world wars. East Germany, Hungary, Czechoslovakia and Poland lost the peace and lost their freedom: justice and reconciliation for them have proven to be nothing more than a wild dream.
Europeans should not forget these facts when they judge the success and the trials of European integration.

II. To put it in a nutshell, Europe is suffering from a lack of will, based upon self-confidence, from lack of awareness of a historical destiny.

Each day, the authority of the nation states is seen to be frittering away in an alarming fashion. The state will only be able to recover its authority through the parallel development of European power. This is an essential point, for the ultimate justification of any state must rest upon its capacity to guarantee its nationals security, order and the conditions necessary for harmonious development.

The responsibility for the member states' failures can be pinned on:
– political parties which still seem to be incapable of concentrating on anything apart from their own national image and of going beyond it towards a Europe which awaits on the horizon.

– governments which think that they alone are capable of guaranteeing and defending their legitimate national interests.

– bureaucrats who insist on receiving a 'piece' of European power in compensation for the transfer or 'loss' of any sovereignty to European institutions. This is why the EEC still lacks an efficient decision-making infrastructure. It has to make do with the mere sum of national policies.

– those who do not recognise the need for an unequivocal majority in the fields of security and foreign policy if the EEC is to stand up to the formidable expansionism of the Soviet Union at a time when the EEC appears unable to agree.

– the media which by-passes the real problems of European unification in favour of the quest for sensationalism.

III. There is no one path to European integration. All are worth following.

It would perhaps have been preferable to begin with political union of France and Germany. The bitter memories of the self-mutilation which Europe practised until 1945, the legacy of Hitler and of Stalin and the ardent commitment to Europe of a Germany which underwent rapid reconstruction would have provided powerful incentives for the construction of a new European order, particularly since the two traditional enemies, France and Germany, would have been the advocates. Motivation would have been much stronger than in the Economic Community of today. The latter is condemned day after day to escape the innumerable traps of compromise between national interests, while struggling with cumbersome decision-making processes.

However, this is to forget that political union between France and Germany was scarcely possible in the fifties and sixties, and that if it had been it would have been at the price of French political hegemony. In such a situation, the rest of Europe would have reacted to counter this, and European construction would probably not have come about any faster. On the contrary, it is likely that sides would have been taken and new rivalries would have stirred in the breast of free Europe. Europe cannot be built by fanciful projects. It will only be born after a sustained effort to strengthen gradually the European reconciliation process. Nor will Europe be created from purely intellectual concepts; sentiment will also have a role to play. A great deal of time is required to change the way in which a nation feels about things, particularly when its future history rests upon irrevocable decisions.

IV. 1. Accelerated introduction of political cooperation, culminating in the election of a European President.

2. Continued development of the European Monetary Fund and organisation at European level of an autonomous central bank system.

3. Progress towards the objective of removal of all customs checks by 1992.

4. Much more intensive teaching of foreign languages, from the nursery school to university level.

5. Development of specifically European information bases, independent of existing national structures.

Christian DE LA MALÈNE
°1920, Senator of Paris, former French Minister, Member of the EP from 1959 to 1961 and then again from 1962, President of the Group of European Progressive Democrats.

1. Europe is everywhere, in all areas, from the most fundamental problems to highly detailed regulations. Little by little, joint obligations have appeared as a network of European laws has been laid down. This process has been a fairly constant one, creeping forward without member states being fully aware of it.
But what has this entity, which seems imposing, meant in reality? Has cooperation resulted in positions which are respected? Are the regulations and the laws observed when they pose problems? People are for Europe and its regulations when these appear to be beneficial, and forget them when they get in the way.

II. It is rather futile to suggest that officials, policies, governments and administrations are responsible, as if they could fundamentally go against the wishes of their people. The European Community is an 'investment' for the European nations, but they do not all appreciate the timeliness and importance of the adventure in the same manner. These differences of appreciation inevitably hold back those nations which would accept greater investment in the European ideal. Must the EEC,

in order to progress more quickly, drop those who refuse to commit themselves more fully? This is an option which should never be discarded, but it has severe limitations.

III. The European nation cannot be 'decreed'. We can only work towards its birth. Linguistic barriers weigh heavily on this effort, and it is an error to believe that institutional mechanisms can by themselves overcome lack of general will.

IV. The main task facing Europe is to recover the notion of solidarity. It has suffered huge setbacks since the beginning of the European enterprise, and it is imperative that these should be overcome. No progress will be made in the European Community if the EEC serves to make the rich richer to the detriment of those who are less well-off. Any organisation of nations or people which does not make the necessary material tranfers will either collapse or face paralysis. Europe's failure on this issue is very dangerous and may even prove to be fatal.

Maurice FAURE
° 1922, negotiator and signatory of the Treaties of Rome; on three occasions French permanent representative to the Community; French senator.

1. A failure, to the extent that the EEC remains, forty years after its foundation, an institution for good neighbourly relations and not an attempt to create a common government.

II. It is very diluted. The construc-

tion of Europe required a change of habits, mentalities and structures. It came up against the force of inertia in national administrations and the lack of clear and coherent political will among governments which could have countered the former.

III. Probably at the beginning, when the idea was new and fired people's imaginations, we could have done more. People were more open to the idea than today. Unfortunately, the failure of the EDC dealt a very severe blow to European enthusiasm. And governments have since been employing the give and take tactic, never succeeding in deciding between national and Community solutions.

IV. Almost everything has been tried and almost everything has failed. Awareness of the seriousness of the crisis in European union must be aroused. We are indeed still at the stage of nation states.

I feel that Finance Minsters could tackle with more courage the question of increasing monetary solidarity and use of the Ecu. It constitutes a difficult but tempting short-cut to the single market and political liberalisation. It is our last chance.

Etienne HIRSCH
° 1901, one of the editors of the Schuman Declaration of May 9, 1950, President of the Commission of the European Atomic Energy Community (1959-1962), President of the European Federalist Movement (1962-1975).

I. *It is a success.* Thanks to the movement set in motion by the Schuman Declaration, relations between France and Germany have been fundamentally transformed. Since the creation of the European Communities, conflicts such as those of 1870, 1914 or 1939 have become inconceivable. *It is also a failure* since, 36 years on, we are still far from the objective of European Federation stipulated in the Declaration.

II. With the initiative for European construction coming from France, it is sad to have to admit the responsibility of the French Government for rejecting the project for a European Defence Community, followed by the responsibility of General de Gaulle for the so-called Luxembourg compromise. This gave member states the right to a veto, which the governments eagerly grabbed in a free-for-all which rendered the EEC powerless.

III. It should have been made clear to public opinion that, in this day and age, national sovereignty is not possible in areas such as monetary matters, foreign policy and defence. The support of the public should have been won to overcome the resistance of ossified political and administrative structures.

IV. Decision-making structures must be set up. The Commission must be transformed into a true *federal government,* the decisions of which are controlled by the European Parliament and a Chamber of States which would replace the

Council of Ministers. Only then can the EEC regain its international role and face up to the challenges of the modern world.

Pierre LARDINOIS
° 1924, Member of the European Parliament (1963-67), French Minister of Agriculture (1967-72), Member of the European Commission responsible for Common Agricultural Policy (1973-77), and since 1977 Chairman of the Rabobank.

I. I feel that it is neither a success nor a failure. The Community has been successful in that it has been responsible for increasing wellbeing within its boundaries and holds a great deal of attraction for third countries. On the other hand, it has not succeeded in the thirty years since its creation in attaining a

level of cohesion which will guarantee the freedom and prosperity of Europe in the years to come.

II. The Treaty of Rome is based on a generally liberal market concept. During the sixties, the welfare state grew up and national authorities took over a central position, pushing market forces into the background.

III. There have been two very clear breaks in the process of European unification, namely the Luxembourg Agreement of 1966 and the oil crisis in 1973. On both occasions exceptional opportunities were wasted since leaders chose the wrong

solutions and allowed national interests to prevail over EEC interests.
IV. Europe must now make every effort to set up a truly liberal internal market by adopting an approach which takes account of the need for the free play of market forces if the social and economic problems facing a Europe are to be solved.

Yves LePortz
° 1920, Vice-Chairman of the European Investment Bank (1962-70), Chairman of the EIB (1970-84), Chairman of the Committee of Stock Exchange Transactions in Paris since 1984.

I. A success, I would say, certainly as far as the EIB is concerned: well established on the world's financial markets, its lending activities have shown a continued growth, especially marked in the last ten years, at a time when, may I underline, the European Community was struggling with severe economic difficulties.
The EIB focuses on practical objectives which allow measurement of the degree of success it has achieved: in terms of capital investment financed, jobs created and, in relation to the considerable investments in the energy field, the number of tons of oil imports saved from outside the Community. In financing capital investment to stimulate economic development in the Community, the EIB has adopted as its guideline Robert Schuman's words: 'Europe will not be built in a day, nor to an overall design; it will be built through practical achievements that first establish a sense of common purpose.'
II. The EIB has benefitted a great deal from the way it was set up. The effective functioning of the EIB has been possible because of the continued and unanimous support of the member states. The EIB has never suffered from the vagaries of politics in the Council of Ministers. Other strong points are its solid financial structure (Community budgetary problems do not play a role)

and the fact that financing decisions are based exclusively on the Bank's professional expertise in project appraisal (projects may not be imposed for political reasons). Last but not least, as foreseen in the EIB's Statute, which forms an integral part on the Treaty of Rome, the governing bodies of the Bank decide, with few exceptions, on the basis of majority votes.
III. One can always do more or, at least, try to do more. Whether the EIB could also have done more is arguable. It was created by the Treaty of Rome as a bank to which specific tasks were assigned.
The definition of the Bank's tasks in the Treaty of Rome allows for considerable flexibility, and within these parameters the Bank responds to existing Community needs. Regional development remains a pressing concern; energy investment became a priority after the oil crises of the seventies; and financial support for industrial modernisation, in particular the introduction of advanced technology to increase the competitiveness of European industry, will be one of the EIB's major tasks for the eighties and beyond.
In the execution of its tasks, however, the EIB does more than support Community economic policy objectives in the areas specifically assigned to it. For example, when financing a project, the Bank promotes awareness of the environmental consequences and the Bank's staff will use moral suasion to convince

the project promoter to choose the least polluting solution available.
IV. As an immediate priority: the establishment of a true internal market, which is long overdue. In their domain, the Bank's governing bodies have already underlined the significance of international competitive bidding for efficient project implementation and for the establishment of one true European Market. More important perhaps, further steps must be taken to liberalise capital movements in the Community, to strengthen the European Monetary System and to move further towards monetary integration.
Here, too, the EIB makes a contribution. Without assuming or aspiring to a monetary role, it stimulates, as the world's largest borrower and lender in ECUs, the use of the ECU. The increasing convergence of national economic policies in recent years is a positive development. In many countries the inflation rate has been brought down to the level of the early sixties. We must be careful not to miss, as we did at that time, the opportunities for progress in financial and monetary matters which present themselves now.

Johannes (Hans) Linthorst
Homan†
°(1903-86) negotiator of the EEC and EURATOM Treaties, Dutch permanent representative to the European Community (1958-62), Member of the ECSC High Authority (1962-67).

I. The cornerstone of the Treaties of Paris and Rome, namely a large-scale barrier-free economy with political and legal development on the same level, has not been achieved. The Common Market has only been completed on a very small scale. The economic policies of the member states have not been integrated in a satisfactory manner. As a result, EEC law has not developed to its full extent, although a clear jurisprudence has been established by the Court of Justice.

II. There is practically no member state which, at one point or another, has not been responsible for stagnation in the building of Europe, either because it set itself priorities incompatible with those of the Community or because of reticence in some way or other. France was responsible for the 1966 attempt to reduce the EEC to a classical intergovernmental alliance, which was just what the three Treaties wanted to avoid. In fact, the Treaties sought to organise the power hierarchy in the same way as the nation state, in which each level of government administration – local, regional and national – has its own bodies and its own responsibilities. The EEC Treaties aimed to create a fourth level; the supranational, where the Commission and the Council would each have their specific tasks: they need recognition that they represent something different and something new.

III. It was clear even in the EEC transitional period (1958-1969) that success was highly unlikely, and this for two reasons. Firstly, following a number of conflicts between the member states, two of the areas of action specified in Article 2 of the EEC Treaty, namely the Common Market and coordination, lost a great deal of their unifying force. Intergovernmental progress took precedence over the supranational slant. France launched carefully thought-out attacks on supranationality, weakening the principle yet further.

Moreover, when France insisted, at the signature of the Luxembourg Protocol, that Council decisions be taken by unanimity, it removed any value of EEC mandate from the proposals which the Commission submitted to the Council.

Three stages can be identified in this weakening process during the transitional period. In 1963 a German proposal marked the beginning of the slide towards the strict striking of a balance between what was given and what was received. This principle was a god-send for supporters of short-term concepts and of the status quo. The objectives of the Treaty, namely long-term planning and dynamic modernisation of infrastructure, were thus abandoned. The second stage came in 1966, when the French demands that the Council take only unanimous decisions began to look suspiciously like self-interested exaction: use of this negotiating tactic had been specifically warned against in the 'Principles' section of the Spaak Report as early as 1956. Finally, in December 1969, at the summit of heads of state and government, the member states accepted most of the Commission's proposals in its October 1969 report on 'Economic Union and Enlargement', but passed over without comment those parts suggesting how the disastrous consequences of the Luxembourg Protocol could be corrected. The member states thus contributed to the belief of candidate countries that the provisions of the Treaty of Rome specifying majority voting no longer applied. This considerably slowed down the enlargement process.

IV. The attempt – even though severely limited – to correct shortcomings which began in 1986 should be fully backed. In the meantime, all pro-unity forces must continue to work and fight for the acceptance of the Community ideal as a guiding force. It is now clear that member states' promises in this field have remained dead letters, and that all our hopes for European Union must be placed in the Commission and the Parliament.

Joseph M. A. H. Luns
° 1911, Dutch Foreign Affairs Minister (1952-71), former NATO Secretary General.

I. The greatest disappointment of my political career has been the inability of the Common Market to fulfil the intentions of the signatory countries of the Treaty of Rome. These consisted in developing a new political entity which would gradually be transformed into European union. It is highly regrettable that these objectives have remained a dead letter and that, after so many years, the European Community has no supranational authority and has never got beyond the stage of an association of sovereign countries.

II. France must shoulder a great deal of the blame for this stagnation. There are a number of examples of its negative attitude towards the Community. France was responsible for introducing the use of the veto in all areas, even the least important ones. The supranational authority of the Commission has gradually been eroded. The European Defence Community was rejected by the French Parliament. These are just a few examples in a long list.

III. The provisions and the spirit of the Treaty should have been observed to the letter and the continual and excessive use of the veto by cer-

tain governments should never have been accepted.

IV. I believe that the Community's first priority should be to strictly limit the use of the veto and to honour the strict intentions of the Luxembourg compromise, which stipulated that a veto should only be brought into play for questions affecting a country's vital national interests.

Sicco MANSHOLT
°1908, Dutch Minister of Agriculture 1945-58, Vice-President and then President of the European Commission (1958-1973), designer of the Common Agricultural Policy.

I. Neither one, nor the other. It is still too early to answer this question. History will give the answer. At the end of the bloody war which began as a civil war at European level, we said 'Never again!'. It is understandable that we were impatient to see Europe politically united in a few decades. And the method of beginning with economic integration in order to oblige nations to cooperate on the political front was considered logical. It had our full-hearted support. But it has since become clear that the development of a political process is not always simple and logical. Numerous other factors, which were underestimated at the outset, influenced the course of evolution. We must accept that these factors exist and act in consequence.

II. It is too easy to say that this or that politician is responsible for this stagnation. It is too simple to say that if General de Gaulle, a man whom I still consider a great European, had not forced the Community to take decisions by unanimity voting when he was President of France, then all would be different. In fact, the reasons for failure are to be found in a conflict between two points of view which are far from being resolved; on the one hand, the desire to re-trench in familiar natio-

nal sovereignty and, on the other, the even more urgent need to take common action to tackle the major problems of our time, which cannot be solved in the framework of restricted national frontiers. The first point of view is an expression of fear of a supranational authority, and of the fact that national civil servants, the diplomatic corps and national parliaments do not want to give up their power to European bodies. Only necessity is likely to change their minds.

III. The Treaties of Rome, which were the flowering of political will, gave us the means to accomplish an important part of our aspirations. However, we have not exploited them to the full. In my opinion, one of the main reasons for current shortcomings is the very fact that we did not exploit to the full these possibilities – clearly laid down in the Treaties. The use of the unanimity principle in the Council of Ministers has robbed Europe of a number of excellent opportunities of taking a strong lead. It is almost as if the EEC wants to render itself powerless, thus making it incapable of tackling problems which form part of our joint responsibility.

IV. By clear awareness of the nature of the flaws and by relentlessly seeking to act on a joint front. We face important responsibilities which we must shoulder together. For example, a solution must be found to the increasingly serious threats facing the environment. Europe must ac-

cept its responsibility for the poverty and hunger which billions of human beings in the world suffer; it must have the courage to face up to its responsibilities in the fields of peace and security, responsibilities which cannot be abdicated to the two super-powers. Finally, if the nations of Europe want to continue playing a role of any importance in the world, they must find a joint answer to the immediate challenge of technology. It is therefore essential that the European Commission uses its powers more widely in order to give itself the means to fulfil the decision-making and executive tasks which have been settled on it. In conclusion, the amount of politics which goes into discussion and action must be increased, and pure administration reduced. Two conditions must, obviously enough, be met for this to be achieved: the Council must take majority decisions and the Parliament must be invested with real legislative power!

Marceline OREJA AGUIRRE
° 1935, Spanish Foreign Affairs Minister (1976-80), negotiator for Spain's accession to the Community, Secretary General of the Council of Europe since 1984.

I. Europe is clearly a success. I do not share the Euro-pessimism shown by some people. Without being blindly optimistic, we can be justly proud of the achievements of the past 40 years. We have advanced greatly since the disastrous situation in Europe at the end of the Second World War.

In 1945 Europe was swept with desolation. Quite apart from the millions of deaths and massive destruction which left Europe drained, the deep essence of the European spirit had been corroded by Nazi barbarism.

Faced with the ruins of Europe, reconstruction was imperative. But there was no desire to make Germa-

ny pay, as after the First World War. Europeans wanted to re-build together. The founding fathers of Europe, with their visionary genius, understood that there would be no lasting peace until close cooperation and solidarity links had been forged between all the European nations. Peace in Europe is now an accepted fact. But it should not be forgotten that during its entire history our continent had never before known forty years without a major conflict. The EEC has therefore achieved something which can be an object lesson for all cooperation enterprises. The peace which we enjoy in Europe today does not find its roots in military power but in a joint desire to build the future together. This is both its force and its value.

Of course, we are not yet at the final objective, which is European union. The obstacles placed in our path by national self-centredness are still numerous. But what matters above all is that no one seriously questions the desire to unite. The development of the European Community has had failures and weaknesses, but no one wants to move back in time; few people want to stop the movement. It is therefore up to us to act so that Europe progresses as rapidly as possible and each day meets Europeans' expectations to an ever greater extent.

II. Europe is not an autonomous entity. Its progress or setbacks are the result of the political will of the European actors. These are first and foremost national governments. Political will is increasingly seen to be wearing thin, and the European commitment of our governments no longer seems to carried by the wave of enthusiasm seen in the fifties and sixties. What is the reason for this? I think it is to be found in the economic and social crisis which Europe has been living through since the mid-seventies. National self-centredness and short-sighted policies are always exacerbated by a crisis. In a difficult situation governments find it hard to resist protectionist

temptations and introspection, even though these are diametrically opposed to the principles of cooperation and solidarity which are supposed to lie at the root of European construction. Our leaders, and more especially public opinion, are not sufficiently aware of the fact that union and cooperation will give them a chance to solve the problems of unemployment, monetary instability and budget deficits.

III. I think that the EEC's great weakness is its lack of individual identity on the international stage. The EEC is not yet a fully-fledged actor in international affairs. Europe's destiny is often played out in negotiations in which it either does not participate or does not participate sufficiently. Europe's security, and in particular the East-West dialogue for which our continent is both the testing ground and the field for manoeuvres, is more often than not negotiated between the superpowers without Europe really having a say. At the economic summits of the industrialised countries, where Western leaders meet every year, the EEC plays understudy to the roles played by certain of its member states.

The EEC will become a respected partner and one which is listened to when it affirms its own identity. For many nations of the world the EEC constitutes a hope and an alternative to the almost impossible choice between the two superpowers. Europeans must respond to these expec-

tations by fully honouring their own commitments and responsibilities.

IV. I believe that the key priority for Europe now is the same as in the past and as it will be in the future: to strengthen and enlarge the application of democracy and respect of human rights. Apart from the economic, commercial and scientific stakes, the EEC is above all a political project, a plan for a new type of society whose foundations are pluralist democracy and respect for human rights and laws. The plan for a new type of society comprises the following fundamental values: humanism, diversity and universality. The most ambitious objective which the builders of Europe can set themselves is to meet European citizens' expectations for freedom to develop fully in a free society. Promoting the protection of human rights in Europe consists essentially of reinforcing the legal apparatus guaranteeing civil and political rights recognised by the European Convention for the Protection of Human Rights and Fundamental Freedoms. To achieve this, procedures for bringing cases before monitoring bodies must be tightened up, with particular attention paid to shortening the delays, and the range of guaranteed rights must be widened. Non-judicial means for the protection of human rights (such as the ombudsmen) should be extended and new legal instruments negotiated (such as the draft convention against torture). Finally, education and information should be broadened in order to create a 'human rights' awareness among European citizens.

If human rights are to be respected in the widest sense of the term in modern-day society, challenges of a new and different nature must be met. These challenges include terrorism and violence, drugs and dropouts, inequality of the sexes and intolerance, computerisation and mass means of communication, research and genetic engineering. All these challenges may be at the base of potentially serious attacks on the digni-

ty or the integrity of human beings. If the EEC is to remain faithful to itself and to its principles, it is imperative that it take up these challenges.

But, most importantly, the EEC must do something to halt the disease which is sapping the foundations of our democratic societies: unemployment and in particular youth unemployment. It would be very dangerous to accept unemployment as part and parcel of our social fabric and as a constituent part of the post-industrial civilisation in which we are living. The drama of unemployment is only given voice by statistical data. But behind these figures lie despair and distress that cannot be quantified. Unemployment is a cancer which gradually destroys the individual and society. It sets up discrimination between those who have work and those who either do not or who have precarious or underpaid work, thus piling up the risk that Europe's social fabric will be torn apart. Drugs, violence, racism and xenophobia are in part the by-products of unemployment. Europe must find some sort of remedy to unemployment if human rights are to be fully respected and democracy reinforced.

John PINDER
° 1924, Chairman of the Federal Trust, Chairman of the European Federalist Union (EFU), Vice-Chairman of the European Movement in Britain, Professor at the College of Europe in Bruges.

I. The burial of the Franco-German animosity is a historic achievement, and the EC has also enabled Europeans to carry through the second industrial revolution. But the EC as it stands today does not meet the challenge of the third industrial revolution or of superpower predominance. Nor will Europe meet these challenges without economic and monetary union and a European defence community. In short, we can claim important achievements but

we cannot speak of real success until we have established a European federation.

II. What do we mean by 'European construction'? Let us call a spade a spade, and say plainly that we mean a European federation, which may differ from existing federations but must have a common money, economic policy and defence force, a big enough budget to pay for them, and a European parliamentary democracy to control all this power. The federalists are responsible for securing acceptance of this idea. Rather than blame the obvious targets such as de Gaulle, Britain and so on for preventing its realisation, I think we federalists must blame ourselves for our failure so far to convince our compatriots that we must build this construction on the achievements of the Community's founding fathers. British federalists must bear the heaviest blame for failing to rekindle the flame of federalist enthusiasm which swept our country in 1939-40, but was extinguished after the rejection of Churchill's offer of union with France.

III. The European defence community could have been established in the 1950s and the economic and monetary union in the 1970s. This would have radically improved the world security and monetary systems, and Europe's place in them, just as the customs union made the EC the trading equal of the US in a reformed world trading system. We Europeans should have had the courage to do these things.

IV. The EC should be converted into a European Union. While this need not embody everything in the European Parliament's Draft Treaty, it must provide for monetary union, an adequate budget, and codecision between the European Parliament and a Council in which majority voting is the rule. We should at the same time intensify the cooperation of EC countries in security and foreign policy in preparation for the further step of a defence community which will complete the European federation. History will judge us harshly if we fail to complete the work of the founding fathers in these ways.

Walter SCHEEL
° 1919, Member of the Bundestag (1953-74) and of the European Parliament, Foreign Affairs Minister (1969-74) and President of the Federal Republic of Germany (1974-78).

I. There have certainly been setbacks and disappointments for all those convinced of the need to strive for the difficult goal of European unification.

Nevertheless, the victories weigh heavier in the balance than the failures. The most striking, and often forgotten, achievements are that there has now been peace in Europe since 1945, that war is no longer a conceivable political option in Western Europe, and that the member states of the EEC now take joint decisions in certain important political spheres.

II/III. The unification process could have been more dynamic if the EEC's decision-making structures had been made more democratic and more efficient. Up until now, EEC policy has mainly been defined in isolation by the EEC's Council of Ministers. This has meant not only that it has escaped Parliament's democratic control, but is inaccessible to the citizens of Europe. The Community has therefore been deprived

of vital parliamentary democracy in a Community which now affects everyday life.

At the same time, national governments need to honour the objectives which they set themselves. Many decisions taken by the Council of Ministers have remained dead letters or have come up against obstruction in national bureaucracies. This opposition must be overcome. The establishment of a more efficient decision-making process, with the use of majority voting in the Council, as defined in the European Single Act, could help this process.

IV. Any further moves towards integration should keep in sight the end objective of European (political) union. The next step must therefore be to implement the reforms decided at Luxembourg. These reforms do not go far enough, but they do represent a timorous step in the right direction.

The internal market must be completed before 1992. Its creation is important for it will set up a community without frontiers which will perceptibly change the lives of ordinary Europeans.

The European states must adopt joint policy stances more frequently. Europe must establish a common external policy if it wants to bring influence to bear on international politics.

European political cooperation has been a positive experience, but has not yet been sufficiently translated into homogeneous decisions on foreign policy.

The improvements in European political cooperation written into the 'Acts of European Unification' are to be welcomed. They will oblige members states to consult other members of the Community before taking a definite stance on any matter of foreign policy. This is a considerable achievement. However, a common foreign policy should be the objective.

A further stage would be the acceptance by national parliaments of the European Parliament's draft treaty

on the creation of European Union. On the basis of this agreement, and through cooperation with the various national parliaments, the European Parliament could then rework its proposals. Finally, a second draft treaty could be submitted to the national parliaments for ratification. It would only be allowed to enter into force after ratification by a specified number of member states. It is important that this new draft treaty be ready in time to be presented as the main theme of the third round of European elections.

Dirk SPIERENBURG
°1909, Vice-President of the ECSC High Authority (1952-62), Permanent Representative of the Netherlands to the EEC (1963-1970).

I. The European Community has been a success in the sense that the initial common market in coal and steel, the subsequent customs union and the Common Agricultural Policy have, despite all their defects, allowed the Community to make an important contribution to the prosperous and peaceful development of the entire western world in the last thirty years.

From the political point of view, the Community, and in particular the ECSC, contributed to the Federal Republic of Germany's decision to join the Western camp. The Community has reinforced the cohesion of Western Europe and its capacity to sur-

vive and flourish. It has also been open to the entry of other European countries and has developed a new style of relations with the developing countries.

On the other hand, the European Community has not created a true common market and it has not made progress beyond economic integration to political union. From this point of view, it has failed.

II. Generally speaking, national governments are responsible for the stagnation in the construction of Europe. Governments neglected to lay the foundation of a joint economic and monetary policy when the economic situation was good. Too much energy was invested in endless controversy over the entry of new members. However, the serious defects in the decision-making process are the main culprit in preventing the Community from carrying out the task which was entrusted to it by the Treaties and from taking the political decisions necessary for the establishment of a common economic and monetary policy.

France must shoulder a special responsibility for this stagnation, following its refusal in 1965 to respect the institutional clauses of the Treaty of Rome. There is no doubt that the so-called Luxembourg compromise, which rendered unanimity necessary in the Council and monopolised decision-making power in the Council to the detriment of the Commission, paralysed the development of the Community.

III. We should have accepted the proposals that the Hallstein Commission made to the Council on March 31, 1965 which provided for the completion of the common market, a more definitive funding of the Common Agricultural Policy, and budgetary powers for the European Parliament.

We should have accepted in 1973 the guidelines for economic and monetary union laid down by the Werner Report.

IV. What must Europe's priorities be now?

1. The first priorities must be completion of the common market, reform of the Common Agricultural Policy and introduction of other common policies provided for in the Treaty.

2. The Community must have a stable and guaranteed funding system.

3. The current monetary system must be reinforced and negotiations opened on the entry into the second phase of the Giscard-Schmidt plan, which provided for the creation of a European Monetary Fund, which would have made the ECU a reserve currency and a full settlement currency. Those who cannot or will not partipate in negotiations to this end should not place obstacles in the path of those who want to do so.

4. Finally, there must be an all-round strategy involving the EEC and its member states in order to ensure that Europe fully participates in the current technological revival in the world.

5. These objectives form an entity and for their attainment the institutions must play the important role for which they were conceived.
In particular, the Council must fulfil its functions in a more efficient manner. It must take basic policy decisions and must confine the implementation of these policies to the Commission and not to groups of national experts. It must also return to use of the majority voting system in accordance with the conditions stipulated in the Treaty.

Altiero SPINELLI†
1907-86, Italian Resistance fighter, European federalist thinker, Member of the European Commission (1967-76) and of the European Parliament (1979-86); author of the draft Treaty of European Union.

1. No-one can deny the advantages which our peoples have gleaned from the achievements of the European Community and the para-Community structures of Political Cooperation and the European Monetary System. However the EEC's instruments of action, namely the institutions, have gradually seized up as new common policies have become necessary in areas such as the economy, foreign policy, security and the environment and as the need has arisen to revise existing common policies and integrate them into a much broader and more complex political whole.
Despite the growing need for closer union between the countries and the peoples of Europe, based upon Community and para-Community institutions, progress seems to be increasingly difficult as time wears on.

II/III. The reasons for this paralysis are clear. The Commission does not have sufficient political authority to exercise the planning and execution role which is its by right. It has to give way increasingly to the authority of the Council.
The European Parliament does not have the power to execute the legislative role which it should logically assume, and it can therefore do no more than protest against the inaction or feeble action of the Council. The Council, which is the decision-making body, is by its very nature constrained to negotiate between twelve different national points of view, each rigidly conceived in the framework of a strictly national procedure. Modest, stop-gap and disjointed results are the best which can be expected from such a situation. In crisis periods, the Council's decision-making capacity dwindles away, since national policies inevitably tend to diverge and the Council is unable to draw up common policies on a scale to match the problems.

IV. If our countries do not pool their efforts and their resources, they will become economic, political and military outcasts and will consequently be at the mercy of whichever imperialist system proves to be the strongest. If they unite in an organisation which allows them to preserve their respective national identities (in other words along a federalist model), and which they therefore can respect, the advantages of joint action in areas where this is possible will be numerous and significant. The European nations must face up to the facts. European construction cannot be put on its feet on the basis of inter-governmental diplomatic work. It must be built upon democratic European foundations.
The directly elected European Parliament has demonstrated that it is capable of the mediation and compromises necessary for the establishment of a viable, realistic plan for European Union.
The time has come to grant the European Parliament the role which belongs to it by right as the only body legitimately representing the European peoples. It is the constituent body for European Union.
The European peoples must be asked whether they want to take such a step. They must be asked whether they actually want to proceed towards European Union and whether

they consider that the only democratic path to this goal is to grant the next European Parliament, which will be elected in June 1989, the mandate to draw up a new Constitution for European Union.
The Governments of the member states must organise a policy referendum before the European elections in order to involve ordinary people in the construction of European Union.

Leo TINDEMANS
°1922, Secretary General of the European Christian Democrat Union (1965-73), Member of the Monnet Committee (1960-75), Belgian Prime Minister (1974-78), Member of the first elected European Parliament (1979-81), Belgian Foreign Affairs Minister since 1981.

I. The question is often asked, and not only by the 'Euro-pessimists'. Those who lived through the fifties and sixties with unshakeable faith in European unification are undoubtedly disappointed. European Union has not been accomplished, despite the promises, the official statements and a number of reports. The second phase of the monetary system has not been reached. Joint measures against the economic crisis and unemployment have proved to be impossible. In a word, there is an impressive list of reasons for disillusion. However, without wanting to cultivate a historical contradiction, the progress made since 1950 is considerable.
Barely forty years ago we came out of the most recent and the most bloody of the European civil wars. Europe was in ruins, and there was a great deal of bitterness between the victors and the vanquished. We can now see how far European reconcilation has come.
The European Community still has a spark of dynamism. European Political Cooperation found its legal basis in the Single Act, approved in Luxembourg in December 1985.

Moreover, the force of attraction exercised by the EEC cannot be denied. However, we also have to admit that some member states wanted to go further and more quickly, but that they have come up against a great many obstacles. Why is the internal market still not completed? Why do national, not to say nationalist, reactions still dominate our ways of thinking?
We can say that the achievements are a success. But what will the future be built upon?
II. It is too early to examine our consciences or to name names. Let us leave that to history.
III. When I re-read the biography of Robert Schuman, and I recall, once again, the prudence and caution required of him for the launch of his plan, in 1950, I perceive more clearly the difficulties facing European integration. Perhaps the objective of unification should have been stated more clearly, and all the new member states carefully questioned as to whether this was what they had in mind. In my opinion, the EEC is in need of a compass, for I occasionally feel that at present Europeans do not know where they want to go or what they want.
IV. First, we must carry out what was agreed upon at Luxembourg. In other words, the European Single Act must be applied, and within the specified time limit, namely 1992. Next, and if possible at the same time, we must improve the European Monetary System. Economic

and monetary union form an integral part of a true European union. Political cooperation should also be improved, so that the EEC can have a common foreign policy, at least for the four major issues of our time, namely:
1. Relations with the United States;
2. The North-South dialogue;
3. The situation in the Mediterranean;
4. Security.
The third task concerns building citizens' Europe. When it comes down to it, European union is for the ordinary citizens and not for the pleasure of certain politicians. Finally, the EEC institutions should be reinforced so that their operation can be improved. In a word, everything possible should be done to complete European Union. The promise to do this was made by the heads of state and government in 1972, and the deadline set then was 1986. We are now in 1987. Should we not also take a long look at the credibility and political will of our European leaders?

Pierre URI
° 1911, French co-editor of the Schuman Declaration of May 9, 1950, Reporter to the Spaak Committee, Head of the ECSC.

I. How can one of the great revolutions of our century be termed a failure? Can we imagine this continent without European construction, despite all its flaws, which has transformed bloody rivalries into friendships between nations? The enlargement of the market, a zone of relative monetary stability and a new style of cooperation with developing countries are all major advances. But, paradoxically, the EEC exists more for the rest of the world than for its own citizens. Inflexible and complicated discussions have taken over from clear vision and firm will. Little wonder that public opinion has become discouraged.
II. The responsibility is shared. The

ECSC, directed by Jean Monnet, carefully chose to avoid any geographical distribution among its employees. It took the best, and the result was, at least for a period, a perfect balance between national origins. Prior attribution of jobs makes any rational organisation impossible, since the different General Directorates must be of comparable sizes. It makes it obligatory for the Commissioner, the General Directors and the Directors to be of different nationalities, which prevents the most competent Directors from winning a post of Director General. The most competent leave, whereas others accept promotion to posts for which they are not capable. The reintroduction of the practice of unanimous voting by de Gaulle and then by Margaret Thatcher has led to clumsy and complicated compromises rather than simple and clear solutions. The European Council, which was intended as a body for launching new initiatives, has been tranformed into a court of appeal. This prevents the institutions of the Community from assuming their true responsibilities and in the final analysis prevents them from functioning properly.

III. There is a clear imbalance between the dismantling of destructive barriers, such as the removal of obstacles at frontiers, and the building of constructive designs, for which imagination has been lacking. The only common policy, agriculture, betrays the Treaty of Rome, which states that satisfactory income for farmers should be combined with satisfactory prices for consumers. The bigger farmers are the more they are able to profit from the price support system, although they are the least in need of it.

Since the oil crisis, the member states have committed errors in the fight against inflation: they have fought the resultant oil price rise by treating it as a problem of surplus demand. They have only stopped inflation by allowing unemployment to grow and have only increa-

sed competitiveness by reducing wages, thus reproducing the prewar policies which transformed the recession into a tragedy. As a result, instead of boosting one another's growth, member states act to impair one another.

IV. Removal of the budget obstacle. Even after removal of customs duties and levies, which cannot be charged to a single member state since it is impossible to know where the final users of goods might be situated, the calculation of net balances between each member state's contributions to and receipts from the EEC budget makes no sense. In a common market it is impossible to know who has benefited from specific expenditure which anyway might not be tied to the place where the money was paid. Instead of unjustifiable repayments to certain member countries, the EEC should take into account the differences in per capita income in each country. The most favoured regions would pay more, through the application of different rates of EEC VAT. The expenditure of the Social and Regional Funds should be increased to give more to the poorer areas. The Common Agricultural Policy must be rebalanced and priorities concentrated on Europe's industries of the future. Defence policies must be rationalised. Faster progress must be made towards European union to give the EEC more impact in the world of the future.

Simone VEIL
°1927, French Minister (1974-79), Member of the EP since 1979, President of the first elected EP (1979-82), President of the Liberal and Democratic Group in the EP since 1984.

I. The very fact that the question can be couched in such terms shows the gap which has opened up between attitudes now and those at the end of the Second World War. Although our countries were still in ruins and people were exhausted by all the death and suffering, they succeeded in the fifties in creating the ECSC and launching the idea of a united Europe. The Peace Treaty, unlike that at the end of the First World War, did not try to make Germany pay for its past, but to lay the groundwork for a prosperous future in an atmosphere of reconciliation.

Much more than a necessity, Europe was then an act of faith. Given that our countries have been at peace for more than forty years, and that conflict between them now seems inconceivable, Europe is certainly a success.

Similarly, in the space of thirty years, the Common Agricultural Policy has generally attained its objectives; the free movement of persons and goods has become a reality; and the existence of the Community, with notably the EMS and trade policy, obliges all of the governments to define their own economic and social policy in accordance with joint decisions.

Why, then, is the Community the source of so much disenchantment today, and why does it seem to have come to a halt?

The most pressing and the most inspiring objectives have been attained: peace and prosperity. Europe is now faced with a new challenge: that of its role in a world in which the military domination of the United States and the Soviet Union reigns and in which new economic powers are making their presence felt, particularly around the Pacific.

On top of these external threats, the Community is also having to cope with internal crises. On the one hand, national egoistic behaviour is making progress in the construction of Europe increasingly difficult and, on the other, the ambiguity seen by some concerning Europe's role in the world gives rise to doubts as to the permanence and the firmness of certain countries' attachment to the Atlantic Alliance.

A strong Europe built on sheer force of will is the only credible answer to these dangers.

II. I feel that it is better to look at *what* is responsible for this stagnation, for it is not a question of individuals, or even of countries as such, but of objective factors and our political systems. People who declare themselves very 'European' throw their convictions to the wind when faced with an EEC decision concerning their country or electorate.

There are very few exceptions to this contradiction between the public speeches and the real facts, and both 'EEC-ism' and nationalism can be used for the purposes of domestic policy. Why, then, is there this systematic preference for the national to the Community?

The first reason is that the strengthening of the Community, and in particular of the powers of the Commission and the Parliament, is necessarily at the expense of the national institutions. Governments are obliged to take account of common decisions in national policies.

Civil servants are the most affected by these transfers of power, and therefore do their utmost to delay the consequences.

Economic and social operators, such as company heads, executives and the professions, do not use Europe as their reference and only push for progress when this will give rise to immediate material benefits. Indeed, they block all progress in Europe which may go against their corporative interests.

Generally speaking, the stagnation

in the construction of Europe is due to the very short-term view of all those who are more or less directly concerned. They are very anxious not to give up anything of immediate personal self-interest and they thus block any possibility of compromise, which is essential for the healthy operation of the EEC and for it to make progress. On the other hand, a more couragous and less demagogic view of our medium- and long-term interests would open our eyes to the fact that the only solutions which offer any real prospect of a future are European.

III. It is not certain that a different path could have been taken, for the projects which gave priority to political Europe all fell through. The failure of the EDC represented, in this respect, the loss of a key chance. But the opposition at the time, in France particularly, to this type of initiative was undoubtedly too strong.

It is difficult to know what the consequences would have been of the ratification of the draft Treaty, for the French were too deeply divided on this question. Similarly, the delay in the entry of the United Kingdom meant that it finally joined on the eve of the oil crisis, when conditions were much less favourable. An institutional thrust would certainly have allowed considerable progress in the construction of Europe. In this respect, the 'Luxembourg Compromise' and the general abuse of unanimity decision-making

have blocked a vast number of proposals essential for the implementation of the principles of the Treaty of Rome and the pursuit of its objectives.

However, although efforts should be continued to bring about real institutional reform, advance using the lowest common denominator should not be discarded, for experience has shown that up until now it has been the only way of making progress against implacable opposition. It is possible that the 'maximalists' who refused the Fouchet Plan are also responsible for wasting time.

IV. I believe that Europe should set itself as priorities those things which are objectively attainable. Consequently, everything which makes it possible to complete the internal market is a priority; and this involves, first and foremost, as an indispensable condition, return to the practice of majority voting for decision-making. Secondly, the use of the ECU should be developed to turn it into a truly European currency. Finally, if we really want to form a powerful economic force which can compete with the United States and Japan, a European industrial area must be created. The CAP has overcome a challenge which at the outset appeared to be highly complex and difficult. An equally ambitious target should also be set for the 21st century for advanced European technology.

There cannot be a common industrial policy along the same lines as the pooling of coal and steel or the CAP, but the strategies which up until now have been exclusively national must henceforth take on a European dimension. If such an approach, denounced by some in the name of liberalism, is not adopted, Europe will continue to deprive itself of the assets of a large internal market.

Removal of barriers and harmonisation of legislation is not enough. There are methods of intervention which could support EEC companies

and push policy in directions judged essential for national interests: the MITI in Japan and the military credits in the United States are striking examples of this.

Otto von Habsburg
° 1912, Chairman of the Pan-European Union, West German Member of the European Parliament since 1979.

I. The construction of Europe must be placed in its historical context before trying to judge it. Many of my contemporaries make the mistake of placing it in the much narrower context of their own lifetime. History has taught us that major acts should never be judged in the framework of a single generation.
If the process of European unification is placed in a wide enough historical framework, it becomes clear that a lot of water will flow under the bridge before it is actually completed. However, it is also obvious that the venture is far from being a failure. The word 'success' can be used for the progress that has been made in 41 years, particularly if this progress is measured against the way in which other integration processes have evolved. The formation of the United States of America, for example, which was a much simpler business than that of unifying Europe, took more than one hundred years to complete.
II. The only reason for Europe not making the progress which many have dreamed about is a lack of political will. Europe is very strong on the economic front. More progress has been made on the psychological front than we dared hope for. When I was young, the French considered the Germans as traditional enemies, and vice versa. Each young man of my generation was convinced that he would have to fight at least once in his lifetime against some other European nation. When I was young, the barbed wire along the banks of the Rhine certainly made us sober, but it was regarded as a

necessary evil. Young people are incredulous if told these things now. The evil spirit of traditional rivalry has disappeared from their world. Yet whereas it is easy to sign Treaties and create institutions, it is infinitely more difficult to change the mentality of nations with a long history. And this is just what the Community has succeeded in doing in laying the foundations of future progress.
To emphasize it once again, if the construction of Europe had benefited from greater political will, it would already be at a much higher stage of political integration. It would have been possible to overcome the reticence and the resistance of national bureaucracies. They constitute the last obstacles on the road to European union.
III. Historical reality should never be forgotten. To take an example, it is easy to claim that the European Community would have done better to begin with political integration, since politics holds the key which opens all doors. Schuman rightly said that it was wrong to place the supply corps (namely the economy) in the front line when the assault troops (politics) were stationed behind. But at the time, it was quite simply impossible to envisage any other path. It should not be forgotten that European integration began at a time when the wounds of the Second World War were far from being healed.
IV. The imperative now is to stimu-

late political will. An essential condition of this is the abandonment of the use of unanimity voting by the Council of Ministers. It is also essential that the foundations of a common security and external relations policy be laid as quickly as possible. We know that we can expect no initiative in this direction from the Council. The Commission and the Parliament must be the driving forces of a united Europe. These two bodies must henceforth fully assume their responsibilities in this area.

Pierre Werner
°1913, Minister from 1953, Prime Minister of Luxembourg (1959-1974 and 1979-1984), author of the EEC report on Economic and Monetary Union (1970).

I. Since the European Economic Community actually does exist, operates and has expanded, we can hardly term the construction of Europe a failure. On the other hand, success, although impressive on the economic front, is far from complete and will only be complete with the advent of economic and monetary union. Institutionally speaking, political construction is badly out of balance and only makes advances with difficulty after periodic failures. However there have been successes, such as the election of the European Parliament by direct universal suffrage.

The Community has also succeeded in finding an original formula for its economic and financial relations with a large number of Third World countries (African, Caribbean and Pacific States) through the Yaoundé and Lomé agreements.

Even if the content of the Luxembourg Act signed in December 1985 by all the national governments is unsatisfactory on a number of counts, it at least confirms the willingness of the 12 Member States to consolidate integration.

II. Responsibility for stagnation in the building of Europe is divided, to varying extents, between all the member states. The slump in political will which has been evident since 1973 stems from an inadequate reaction to the oil crisis and to economic and monetary crises.

The fact that the younger generations are less marked by the events of the pre-war and wartime periods has also played an undeniable role in this stagnation, as has the development of a society of abundance in Europe.

III. One of the weakest points of the Community is the cumbersome nature of its decision-making machinery, especially since the so-called Luxembourg Compromise in 1966. Centralisation and coordination of EEC responsibilities at a high ministerial level in national governments would have resulted in more systematic and responsible negotiations within the EEC's Council of Ministers.

Georges Pompidou regarded such an option as the first step on the path to a confederal or federal executive power.

Moreover, we should have had the courage at the beginning of 1973 to enter into the second phase of economic and monetary union, the principle of which was decided at the Summit of The Hague in December 1969.

IV. The priorities are completion of the internal market by removal of all remaining barriers and dismantling of protectionism; the development of the EMS by wider use of the ECU and the creation of a true European Monetary Fund; the setting up of a more binding procedure for the harmonisation of economic, financial and energy policies; the organisation of European research in high technology; and democratic and balanced division of powers between the European Parliament, the Council and the Commission.

The strengthening of cooperation in the field of international politics seems to me to be a continuing priority which should not exclude security and defence problems.

Landmarks in the
European integration process

*

September 5, 1944 Belgium, the Netherlands and Luxembourg set up Benelux, an economic union.

September 19, 1946 Winston Churchill, in a speech in Zurich, calls for the creation of a 'sort of United States of Europe'.

September 21, 1946 Conference of European Federalists in Hertenstein.

June 5, 1947 US General George Marshall offers the European countries an aid programme, on the condition that they form some sort of union.

March 17, 1948 France, the UK and the Benelux countries sign the Treaty of Brussels, the forerunner of the Western European Union.

April 16, 1948 16 European nations set up the OEEC, the framework organisation for Marshall aid.

May 8-10, 1948 Congress of the European Movement in The Hague proposes the creation of a Council of Europe.

April 4, 1949 Creation of NATO.

May 5, 1949 Ten European countries sign the Statute of the Council of Europe.

May 9, 1950 Robert Schuman proposes pooling production and consumption of coal and steel within a European organisation.

April 18, 1951 Treaty of Paris establishing the European Coal and Steel Community (ECSC).

May 7, 1952 Proposal for the creation of a European Defence Community (EDC).

August 10, 1952 High Authority of ECSC established with Jean Monnet as its President.

September 10, 1952 First meeting of ECSC Parliamentary Assembly (78 members). Paul-Henri Spaak elected President.

March 10, 1953 Draft treaty embodying Statute of the European Political Community, adopted by the Ad Hoc Assembly in Strasbourg (but not adopted by Council of Ministers).

August 30, 1954 EDC proposal defeated in French National Assembly.

October 23, 1954 West Germany and Italy join the Western European Union.

June 1, 1955 The ECSC countries decide in Messina to create a common market.

March 25, 1957 The Treaty of Rome establishes the European Economic Community (EEC) and the European Atomic Energy Community (EURATOM), the Parliamentary Assembly and the Council of Ministers being common to both and also to the ECSC.

January 1, 1958 Treaty of Rome enters into force.

March 19, 1958 The Parliamentary Assembly (142 members) common to the three Communities elects Robert Schuman as President and gives itself the name of European Parliament (in German and Dutch).

May 12, 1960 Decision to speed up realisation of Treaty of Rome objectives.

May 17, 1960 The European Parliament adopts the first draft Direct Elections Convention, proposing a directly elected membership of 426.

February 11, 1961 Heads of state and government agree to promote increased European political cooperation.

July 9, 1961 EEC/Greece Association Agreement signed in Athens.

January 14, 1962 End of the first EEC agricultural prices marathon: agreement on the first regulations and on faster progress towards a customs union.

January 29, 1963 European Community accession negotiations with Denmark, Ireland, Norway and the United Kingdom are suspended.

July 20, 1963 Yaoundé Convention links Community with 17 African states and Madagascar and establishes Parliamentary Conference of the European Parliament and the Association of African States and Madagascar (AASM) on a basis of parity.

September 12, 1963 EEC-Turkey Association Agreement signed.

January 29, 1966 Luxembourg 'Compromise' virtually abolishes majority decision-making in the EEC Council of Ministers.

July 1, 1967 'Merger' Treaty creating single combined EEC-ECSC-Euratom Council of Ministers and European Commission takes effect.

July 1, 1968 Abolition of all customs duties between member states and full application of the common external tariff.

July 29, 1969 Second Yaoundé Convention between six EEC member states of the Community and 17 African States and Madagascar.

December 1, 1969 The Hague Conference agrees, *inter alia*, to an increase in Parliament's budgetary powers and to the launching of programme for economic and monetary union by 1980.

April 22, 1970 Signature of convention laying down new system of financing expenditure by the Community's 'own resources' and extending Parliament's budgetary powers.

June 30, 1970 Opening of new accession negotiations with candidate states.

October 27, 1970 Davignon Report on political cooperation approved by member states.

March 22, 1971 Adoption by EEC Council of Ministers of Werner Plan to strengthen the coordination of economic policies.

January 22, 1972 Treaties of Accession signed between the European Community and Denmark, Ireland, Norway and United Kingdom.

May 10, 1972 Irish referendum approves membership of Community.

October 2, 1972 Danish referendum approves Community membership (63.5% in favour). Norwegian referendum however rejects membership (53% against).

October 21, 1972 Paris summit meeting defines new fields of Community action – regional policy, environmental policy and energy policy – and defines objective of European Union.

January 1, 1973 Enlarged Community of nine member states comes into being.

December 10, 1974 Paris summit agrees allocation of resources to European Regional Development Fund. European Council established. Direct elections to the European Parliament decided in principle.

February 28, 1975 Lomé Convention signed between Community and 46 African, Caribbean and Pacific (ACP) states.

March 4, 1975 Joint Declaration by the Parliament, Council and Commission initiating 'conciliation procedure' in which Parliament plays an active part in the process of preparing and adopting decisions which give rise to significant revenue or expenditure for the Community.

June 5, 1975 United Kingdom referendum approves membership of the Community (67.2%).

June 6, 1975 Greece applies for EEC membership.

July 22, 1975 Signature of the second budgetary treaty establishing the European Court of Auditors and further strengthening the budgetary powers of the European Parliament.

December 1, 1975 The European Council decides upon 1978 (later postponed until 1979) as the date for the first direct elections of the European Parliament.

December 29, 1975 Presentation of Tindemans report on European Union.

September 20, 1976 Council adopts Treaty on Direct Election of European Parliament.

March 28, 1977 Portugal applies for EEC membership.

April 5, 1977 Joint declaration by Parliament, Council and Commission on the protection of human rights and fundamental freedoms.

July 28, 1977 Spain applies for EEC membership.

March 10, 1979 Creation of the European Monetary System (EMS) centred on the European Currency Unit (ECU).

May 28, 1979 Greek accession treaty signed in Athens.

June 7-10, 1979 Direct elections to the European Parliament (overall turnout: 61%).

July 17, 1979 First meeting of the directly elected Parliament (410 members) in the Palais de l'Europe, Strasbourg, elects Mrs Simone Veil as its first President.

October 31, 1979 Signature of 2nd Lomé Convention between Community and 58 ACP countries.

December 13, 1979 European Parliament rejects 1980 Community budget (288 votes for rejection, 64 against and one abstention).

May 30, 1980 Council mandates Commission to prepare proposals for improvement of Common Agricultural Policy (CAP) and for distribution of budgetary burden between member states (The 30th May Mandate).

January 1, 1981 Creation of an EEC of ten following the entry of Greece. 24 Members of the Greek Parliament are nominated to the European Parliament (434 members).

November 19, 1981 Foreign Ministers Genscher and Colombo present to European Parliament their plan for the creation of European Union.

February 23, 1982 A referendum on membership of the EEC results in Greenland leaving the Community on January 1, 1985.

May 18, 1982 The Council sets agricultural prices by a qualified majori-

ty in the absence of the British, Danish and Greek Ministers.

June 19, 1983 The European Council of Stuttgart signs the 'Solemn Declaration on European Union'.

February 14, 1984 The European Parliament adopts a draft Treaty on European union.

June 15-17, 1984 Second European Parliament elections.

June 25-26, 1984 The European Council of Fontainebleau gives the green light for the settling of the budget problem, the reform of the agricultural policy and entry of Spain and Portugal into the EEC.

December 8, 1984 Signing of Lomé III.

June 12, 1985 Signing of the Spanish and Portuguese Treaties of Accession in Madrid and Lisbon.

January 1, 1986 Entry of Spain and Portugal into the European Community.

February 18, 1986 Signature of the Single Act in Luxembourg. Denmark signed later after holding a referendum in which 56% of the Danish population voted in favour.

June 11, 1986 The Presidents of the European Parliament, the Council and the Commission adopt a Joint Declaration against Racism and Xenophobia.

January 20, 1987 The European Parliament elects Lord Plumb (European Democrat, UK) as its President with 241 votes against 236 for Enrique Baron Crespo (Socialist, Spain).

The Presidents

Presidents of the European Parliament

Paul-Henri Spaak	1952-1954
Alcide De Gasperi	1954
Giuseppe Pella	1954-1956
Hans Furler	1956-1958
Robert Schuman	1958-1960
Hans Furler	1960-1962
Gaetano Martino	1962-1964
Jean Duvieusart	1964-1965
Victor Leemans	1965-1966
Alain Poher	1966-1969
Mario Scelba	1969-1971
Walter Behrendt	1971-1973
Cornelis Berkhouwer	1973-1975
Georges Spenale	1975-1977
Emilio Colombo	1977-1979
Simone Veil	1979-1982
Piet Dankert	1982-1984
Pierre Pflimlin	1984-1987
Lord Plumb	1987-

Presidents of the European Executive

ECSC High Authority

Jean Monnet	1952-1955
René Mayer	1955-1958
Paul Finet	1958-1959
Piero Malvestiti	1959-1963
Dino Del Bo	1963-1967

EURATOM Commission

Louis Armand	1958-1959
Etienne Hirsch	1959-1962
Pierre Chatenet	1962-1967

EEC Commission

Walter Hallstein	1958-1967

European Commission

Jean Rey	1967-1970
Franco Maria Malfatti	1970-1972
Sicco Mansholt	1972-1973
François-Xavier Ortoli	1973-1977
Roy Jenkins	1977-1981
Gaston Thorn	1981-1985
Jacques Delors	1985-

General and technical supervision:
Ingrid SIJMONS, Annie VANDENHOUTEN
and Petrus VAN ROEMBURG

Picture research:
Elisabeth LAUWERS-DERVEAUX

Jacket design:
Jean VERSCHUERE

Phototypeset by:
PHOTOCOMPO CENTER, Brussels

Photogravure by:
TALLON, Brussels and
PRE PRESS COMPOSITIONS, Sint-Niklaas

Printed by:
ERASMUS, Wetteren

Bound by:
SPLICHAL, Turnhout

Library of Congress Cataloging-in-Publication Data

Europe: dream, adventure, reality.

Also published in French.
I. Europe.   I. Greenwood Press (Westport, Conn.)
D848.E87   1987   940   87-7489
ISBN 0-313-25954-2 (lib. bdg.: alk. paper)

ISBN: 0-313-25954-2

First published 1987

© 1987 by Elsevier Librico, Brussels, Belgium

Published in the United States and Canada by Greenwood Press, Inc., 88 Post Road West, Westport, Connecticut 06881

English language edition, except the United States and Canada, published by Uitgeverij Elsevier Librico

Sources of illustrations:
Our thanks are due to all the persons and institutions who have contributed to the realization of this project.
Photographies: American Cultural Centre, Brussels; Archiv Gerstenberg, Frankfurt; Archiv der sozialen Demokratie, Bonn-Bad Godesberg; Beeldbank- en Uitgeefprojekten, Amsterdam; Belga, Brussels; Bundesarchiv, Coblenz; Colothèque, Brussels; COPA, Brussels; Council of Europe, Strasbourg; Court of Justice, Luxembourg; D.P.A. Bild, Frankfurt; Elsevier, Amsterdam; Entraide et fraternité, Brussels; ESC, Brussels; Europa Television, Hilversum; European Commission, Brussels-Mr. Lambiotte; European Investment Bank, Luxembourg; European Movement, The Hague; European Parliament, Brussels-Mr. Debaize; Europ Flash, Strasbourg; Eurovision, Brussels; Giraudon, Paris; Goethe-Institut, Brussels; J. Guyaux, Brussels; Historisches Museum, Vienna; Isopress, Brussels; Landesbildstelle, Berlin; P. Levy, Brussels; Ministry of finances, Brussels; G. Naets, Sterrebeek; Photo News, Brussels; J. Pirlot, Brussels; Scala, Florence; Schöndube, Frankfurt; Sénépart, Brussels; Süddeutscher Verlag, München; Travel Pictures, Brussels; Ullstein Bilderdienst, Berlin; UNICE, Brussels; Library of the University, Groningen; Youth Forum, Brussels.
Colour plates: AKG, Berlin; Colothèque, Brussels; Council of Europe, Strasbourg; Court of Justice, Luxembourg; Elsevier, Amsterdam; Eureka Slide, Brussels; European Commission, Brussels-Mr. Lambiotte; European Investment Bank, Luxembourg; European Parliament, Brussels-Mr. Debaize; Germanisches National Museum, Nürnberg; Giraudon, Paris; Goethe-Institut, Brussels; J. Guyaux, Brussels; Historisches Museum der Stadt Frankfurt, Frankfurt; Mappa Mundi, Knokke; Musées Royaux des Beaux-Arts, Brussels; Museo Nazionale, Naples; Osterreichisches National Bibliothek, Vienna; Photo News, Brussels; Rijksmuseum, Amsterdam; Sénépart, Brussels; Sipa, Paris; Staatsbibliothek Preussischer Kulturbesitz, Berlin.